of HERBS & SPICES

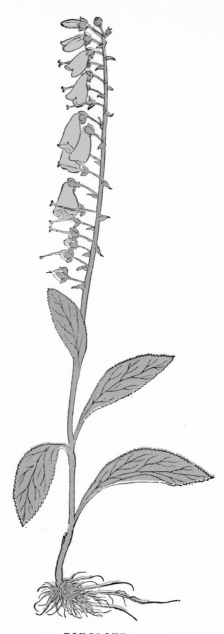

FOXGLOVE

of HERBS *&* SPICES

COLIN CLAIR

Abelard-Schuman
london new york toronto

© Colin Clair 1961
Library of Congress Catalogue Card Number 61:14872

london : Abelard-Schuman Limited 8 King Street wc2
new york : Abelard-Schuman Limited 6 West 57 Street New York 19
toronto : Abelard-Schuman Canada Limited 81 John Street 2B

SPICES

HERBS & HERBALS

ILLUSTRATIONS

*

The illustrations, taken from Fuchs' *De Historia Stirpium* (1542), were chosen for their artistic rather than their botanical merits

SPICES

LOOKING AT SOME OF THE OLD-FASHIONED SPICE BOXES IN our museums it is difficult for us to realise how precious their contents were to our ancestors. Yet from the earliest ages until comparatively recent times spices were a coveted luxury. Nothing in the coffer of the Venerable Bede contained anything so precious in the eyes of his brother monks as the pepper and incense which just before his death he distributed among them with affectionate love. Alaric the Goth demanded as tribute from the Romans not only gold and silver, but a vast amount of pepper, variously estimated at from two to three thousand pounds in weight. The very history of the world has been affected by the struggle for the lucrative trade in spices, and the voyages of the great navigators of the 15th century had as their primary object the discovery of a more direct route to those lands of the Orient whence came the drugs and spices which were then almost as valuable as gold and precious stones.

When on 21 May, 1498, the Portuguese fleet anchored off Calicut and one João Nunes went ashore, he was accosted by two "Moors" from Oran who asked him what the Portuguese sought in that part of the world. "Christians and Spices" was the reply. And need we presume it was in that order?

That spices were so expensive in those early days was largely due to the fact that until Vasco da Gama had opened up a new trade route by sea, spices and other Eastern commodities reached the Levantine ports only after a long overland journey by caravan routes beset with hazards during which the merchandise was forced to pay dues to a host of intermediaries on the way. Since at that time practically all the known spice plants of economic importance grew only in Asia, there was no way of avoiding this accretion of tolls.

The Eastern Mediterranean was for centuries a common market for the merchants of Europe, Africa and Asia, and these commercial relations probably go back to the time of the Phoenicians, that ancient sea-faring race whose vessels ranged the whole known world from Cornwall to the coast of India.

Tyre was their great commercial entrepôt, to which the caravans from the East brought produce which made of Tyre one of the wealthiest and most powerful cities of ancient times, as we are told in the book of Ezekiel.

The voyages of the Phoenicians, however, were limited to coastal traffic, for it was not until the 4th century AD that a knowledge of the monsoons enabled sailors to sail straight from Bab-el-Mandeb towards India. Most of the exotic produce of the East which poured into Tyre came overland by caravan, and of the three great routes which were the main arteries between Europe and Asia – the Caspian, the Red Sea and the Valley of the Euphrates – the last-named was the most direct. This was the channel along which flowed the gums, spices, ivory, silks and other exotic produce of the Orient. To Tyre they came, to be distributed by the Phoenicians along the Mediterranean shores.

When Tyre fell to Alexander in 332 BC, the Phoenicians disappeared from history, though for a time the colony they had founded at Carthage took the place of Tyre as a trading centre. When eventually the Romans made themselves masters of the Mediterranean, Alexandria became the great emporium of the Levant. With the expansion of the Roman Empire the demand for spices grew, and great warehouses were constructed at Alexandria for their storage. So great was Roman consumption of spices that the poet Aulus Persius Flaccus (AD 34–62) wrote:

> The greedy merchants, led by lucre, run
> To the parch'd Indies, and the rising sun;
> From thence hot pepper and rich drugs they bear,
> Bart'ring for spices their Italian ware.

Pliny complained that the Romans spent more than fifty million sesterces a year on exotic produce from India, and he also remarked that the merchandise brought back from there was sold at a hundred times its original cost.

Thus, although the early civilisations of Egypt and south-west Asia had originally absorbed all the produce of the Orient, when they declined the fabled "wealth of Ormus and of Ind" still found a ready market further west, and the laden caravans continued to ply with their produce either along the Euphrates Valley to the Mediterranean or along the coasts of Persia and Arabia, across to Ethiopia, and northwards through Nubia to Thebes and Alexandria, thence to be distributed to the marts of Greece and Rome. For centuries the trade flourished between East and West, though as yet no Western eye had beheld that fabulous land of Ophir "rich in golden mountains and sweet spicery".

The fall of Rome and the break-up of the Empire was followed in Western Europe by the period known as the Dark Ages, when the machine of commerce ran down as a result of four centuries of industrial and political chaos. The spice trade stagnated, for Europe, its industry and agriculture decaying as a result of the Barbarian invasions, had nothing to offer in exchange for the products of Asia.

When, at length, trade revived, new kingdoms had arisen, and once these had consolidated their position, trade with the East was resumed. But Alexandria found herself faced with a rival as the entrepôt for the spice trade, for the old Roman Empire, or what was left of it, was now divided into two parts, the Eastern and the Western, with Constantinople as the capital of the former. And since during the 6th, 7th and 8th centuries there was only one Roman Emperor, who reigned at Constantinople, that city became the chief mart for the Eastern trade. The Red Sea route declined in importance, its place again being taken by the ancient traffic-way along the Persian Gulf and the valleys of the Euphrates and Tigris. With the rise of Islam in the 7th century, Arab conquest and Arab commerce spread far and wide until by the middle of the 8th century the Arabian Empire stretched from Spain to the borders of China. In course of time many Arabs, as well as Greeks, Albanians and other Levantines settled along the west coast of India and became merchants, or factors for Oriental produce.

Spices 13

It was under Omar, the brother-in-law of Mohammed, that the chief conquests of the Moslems took place, and before he died in 643 Syria, the whole of the Euphrates Valley, Persia and Egypt had been conquered. Omar it was who, in 635, founded at the confluence of the Tigris and Euphrates, at the head of the Persian Gulf, the city of Balsara, Bassorah, or Basra, on whose waterfront walked Sindbad the Sailor; that flourishing port "serving as a Magazine for all the commodities of Arabia, India, Turkey and Persia, and as a thoroughfare for all Merchants travelling from one of these Countreys to another, but especially for such as here take shipping to the Isle of Ormus, India, Arabia, etc." So much we learn from *The Merchants Map of Commerce*, published in the 17th century.

During the five centuries which followed the death of Mohammed, his followers developed a civilisation greatly superior to anything which existed in Europe at that time. Bagdad, the seat of one of the three Caliphates which ruled the Moslem Empire in the 10th century, became a flourishing city, its great fair, like those at Bokhara and Samarkand, being visited by merchants from far-off lands. Not only did the Mohammedans show themselves skilful in trade and commerce, but they were remarkable scientists, and from the 8th until the 12th century they developed the study of medicine and pharmacy to a high standard of excellence owing to the thorough manner in which they studied the many valuable drugs which the regions under their sway produced, and which soon acquired a ready market in Europe.

But this fine civilisation perished as had many others before it. The great Moslem Empire split up into a number of separate states, and the Seljuk Turks made themselves masters in Asia Minor. Fanatical, and hostile to science, which they considered harmful to religion, they destroyed the fine flower of Arabic culture, occupied Bagdad in 1055 and profited by the decadence of the Bagdad Caliphate to make the reigning Caliph their puppet. In 1077 the Turks defeated in Armenia a great Byzantine army and captured the Emperor, and so great was the spread of their power that the Western World, as a counter-measure, began in 1096 the series of religious wars known as the Crusades.

Although certain spices had reached London in small quantities in Anglo-Saxon times, through the agency of Norsemen and Germans, it was without doubt the returning Crusaders who introduced into their respective nations the use of a number of Oriental spices, and a growing taste for these aromatic luxuries led to an extensive and lucrative commerce from the 12th century onwards. Mediaeval cooks made use of what we would now consider an immoderate amount of seasoning, and spices were used in almost every dish set upon the baron's table. They were, for a long time to come, far too costly for use at humbler tables, which had to rest content with home-grown flavourings, such as garlic, onions and saffron.

In the great houses, however, cinnamon and grains of paradise were handed round on salvers of gold and silver, and spice plates came into fashion. These were often richly embellished; Edward II had a spice-plate "enamelled with baboons", and Henry VI possessed a most resplendent one of gold with a cover, at the top of which was an eagle with a gem pendant in its mouth, and encrusted all around with precious stones.

There is little doubt that the Crusades, which lasted until the end of the 13th century, stimulated a large demand in the West for all kinds of Eastern produce, and many of the Mediterranean cities, notably the Italian cities of Genoa, Pisa and Venice, benefited enormously from the trade which followed in the wake of the Crusaders.

To the inhabitants of Western Europe, in those days of slow travel, when there was still little conception of geography, the origin of spices was still wrapped in mystery and in the popular imagination they were deemed to come directly from Paradise, and it was thought that the river which flowed out of Paradise was the Nile. The spices, they declared, grew on the banks of the Nile, fell from the trees into the river, the currents of which floated them to certain regions well known to the Egyptians, who took them from the water in nets. This tradition was given credence by the Sieur de Joinville in his *History of St Louis* (Louis IX), although he considered it most unfair that the Egyptians should sell so dearly to Europeans what they had only to fish out of the water. The legend subsisted for a long time, especially among pilgrims, even at a time when merchants knew quite well where and how the spices arrived in Egypt. It was, of course, to the interest of the wily Arab trader to conceal the true provenance of his spices, and invent such tales of monsters to be encountered on the way that even the most daring of Western merchants felt no desire to penetrate into the mysterious lands of the East.

As we have already stated, Alexandria at one time was faced with considerable competition from Constantinople as a trade mart, but after the fall of that city in 1204 it remained throughout the Middle Ages one of the major markets of the spice trade. Benjamin of Tudela, a noted traveller of the 12th century, was impressed by the enormous quantity of spices that the Nile boats transported to Alexandria and the nearby town of Damietta.

At this time these Egyptian ports were much frequented by European merchants because although they could obtain spices from Aleppo and other places in Syria, the long overland route thither made them extremely expensive, whereas they could be taken by sea and river to the Nile Delta at far less expense, and even though customs dues were much higher in Egypt than in Syria, on the whole the ruling prices on the Alexandria market were less. Also, there was the advantage, as far as Western traders were concerned, that they could supply Egypt in return with two basic commodities which she lacked – wood and iron.

Despite the religious hatred which existed between Moslems and Christians during the period of the Crusades, then as always the motto "business is business" prevailed, and trade with Egypt was sanctioned during the whole of the Middle Ages, even though on one occasion Pope Innocent III threatened with excommunication all who traded with the Saracens. But when Venice pointed out the blow to her commercial prosperity such a step must inevitably entail, the Pope relented sufficiently to confine his prohibition to materials of war.

Far from having dealt a crippling blow to trade with the Levant the Crusades stimulated it,* and whereas before that time Alexandria had been the resort chiefly of merchants from Genoa, Pisa, Amalfi and Venice, by the end of the 13th century many other nations were represented on the market there. Benjamin of Tudela names twenty-eight countries and towns whose merchants he saw there; among them Russia, Germany, France, Denmark and Flanders.

All the same, the Scandinavian countries were mainly concerned with the Baltic trade in wool, fish, metal and lumber. The lucrative trade in Oriental products along the Mediterranean was mainly in the hands of three merchant cities of Italy, to whose growth and prosperity it largely contributed. They were Venice, Genoa and Pisa, between whom there was bitter rivalry. After a long period of struggle Genoa finally vanquished Pisa in 1284 by the decisive naval battle of Meloria. A hundred years later she was, in turn, defeated by Venice off Chioggia in 1380, and although she remained for long a prosperous commercial city with large markets in France and beyond the Alps, the rich trade of the Orient was for a further one hundred and thirty years centered in Venice, which became the greatest trading emporium in the Western World.

* The Fourth Crusade, in particular, gave Venice considerable possessions in Greece and the Ægean.

Until 1317 the merchandise collected by the Venetian galleys at the eastern end of the Mediterranean was sold in Italian and French ports and then carried over the Alpine passes, or up the Rhône, to be distributed in Central Europe, France and Flanders, whence some of it would reach England by way of Bruges. At this time Venice had a commercial fleet of some three thousand merchant vessels which sailed in convoy protected by warships. At whatever Near Eastern port the caravans from the East arrived there would be a Venetian convoy to meet it: an Armenian fleet, which sailed to Aros in the gulf of Alexandretta; a Black Sea fleet which visited the ports of the Crimea and the Pontic coast; and an Egyptian fleet which called at Alexandria and Damietta. When in the course of the 14th century there came disagreements between Venice and France, the first of the Flanders fleets sailed out through the Western Mediterranean into the Atlantic and northwards to England and Flanders.

These galleys were often away from their home port for a considerable time, since it took them many months to reach their destination and they often remained for a month or more in a foreign port. There are many interesting references to these Flanders galleys in the Calendars of State Papers from the early part of the 14th century onwards. Although the arrival of a vessel freighted with spices was an event of considerable importance in England during the Middle Ages, the arrival of foreign sailors in an English port did on occasion lead to friction. Thus we find recorded on 10 April, 1323, a proclamation from the mayor and corporation of Southampton narrating an affray between the patrons, merchants, masters and mariners of five Venetian galleys on the one side and the inhabitants of Southampton on the other which was accompanied by loss of life and property.

Sailors are much the same the world over, and it is not surprising to read on another occasion, in 1408, that " as the oarsmen of the galleys, when in London and Bruges, pledge themselves in taverns beyond the amount of pay received by them in those ports, so that the masters are forced to go round the taverns and redeem the men at very great trouble and expense . . . the money so paid out is to be placed to the men's debit, and a fine of 50 per cent levied on each man on a sum exceeding four ducats." At times, too, the visiting Venetians tried to smuggle in goods without paying duty, and when the English Customs seized the merchandise, the Venetian Senate regretted that the Customs should have been defrauded and declared that Venetian subjects must pay in full what was due.

It was the custom for the English kings to grant letters of safe conduct to the Venetian galleys. On 17 September, 1399, Richard II not only gave the customary letter of safe conduct, but also granted permission for the passengers to sell their small wares (Venetian glass and earthenware plates) duty free on the decks of the galleys. Within a few days, on 29 September, Richard II was deposed; nevertheless, no sooner had Henry IV acceded to the throne than on 4 October, 1399, he writes to Doge Antonio Venier: "As by right of birth and by the unanimous consent of the Lords and Commons we possess the royal sceptre, your citizens and subjects need not fear to come to our realms, for we intend to treat them like our own lieges." The speed with which the new king sent this assurance to the Venetian Senate seems to show the importance attached to the arrival of these galleys.

Usually from three to five galleys made the London and Flanders voyage, some of them staying at Southampton, the others proceeding to Sluys or Antwerp where merchants of the Hanseatic League and of the Fugger organisation took charge of the distribution of the merchandise. The Flanders galleys remained there for a period of forty days and then went to Armuyden to await suitable weather. They then crossed to Sandwich or Southampton where they remained for sixty days, at the end of which time the period of demurrage was considered at an end. On the return journey they called at Cadiz,

Majorca, Palermo and Messina, remaining in each port a few days. From time to time this schedule might be altered slightly by decree of the Venetian Senate, but generally speaking the movements of the Flanders galleys during the 14th century were as outlined above. Galleys which went direct to Southampton remained there until rejoined by those from Flanders, for we find that by a decree of the Senate dated 3 March, 1453, the master was forbidden to remain in London for more than 110 days.

These galleys were large vessels, rowed by nearly two hundred oarsmen, and protected by a company of archers. The post of captain of the Flanders galleys was usually given to some Venetian nobleman, two doctors were carried in each vessel, and there were frequently musicians and entertainers on board to help pass the long journey agreeably. In 1518, when the Venetian galleys called at English ports after an absence of nine years, Henry VIII himself went down to Southampton to visit the flag-galley, and on this occasion, when some three hundred persons were feasted on board, these entertainers performed, for the edification of their English guests, fantastic feats on slack-ropes suspended between the masts.

Spices, drugs and wines formed a considerable part of the cargo carried on these galleys, together with sugar – for sugar was beginning to replace honey as a universal sweetener and Venice was then the chief centre of the sugar trade, based on the Sicilian sugar cane, which had been introduced into that island and Cyprus by the Moors. There were, of course, those in England who deplored the vogue of foreign medicines and spices, notably the author of a poem called *Libelle of Englyshe Polycye*, written during the 15th century, who declares:

> The grete galees of Venees and Florence
> Be wel ladene wyth thynges of complacence,
> All spicerye and other grocers ware,
> With swete wynes, all manere of chaffare,
> Apes and japes and marmusettes taylede,

Nifles, trifles, that litell have availed,
And thynges wyth whiche they fetely blere oure eye,
With thynges not endurynge that we bye;
For moche of this chaffare that is wastable
Mighte be forborne for dere and dyssevable.

And he goes on to assert that there are commodities enough in England without the need of assistance from other lands. Medicines just as efficacious as rhubarb and senna, he says, grow in England, so that "a man may voyde infirmytee wythoute drugges fet from beyonde the see".

Nevertheless, during the whole of the Middle Ages, and even in Tudor times, there was a great demand in Northern and Western Europe for spices and condiments. Until the latter part of the 17th century, when a few farmers at the instigation of Charles, Viscount ("Turnip") Townshend began to experiment with clover and turnips, introduced from Holland, English farmers had so little winter keep for their stock that most of the cattle was killed around Martinmas and salted down or pickled. There was little rich pasture, and no pedigree cattle, in those days, and the salt beef was a hard diet. With no refrigeration, the fish eaten during Lent and on the Church's fast days, had also to be salted. There were no potatoes, for although this root was introduced into England in the reign of Elizabeth I, nearly two centuries elapsed before it became a field crop, and far fewer vegetables were grown than we have today. The only source of fresh meat during the winter was the pigeon-loft, that once prominent feature of the English countryside, or birds and animals which could be hunted or snared by country dwellers.

It is not surprising therefore that to add flavour to (or to mask the odour of) the insipid and often tainted winter meat strong seasonings were popular. The beverages which we nowadays take for granted – tea, coffee and cocoa – were unknown, and spices were widely used to add pungency and aroma to the weak beer and sour wine and home-made possets of the common people. Also the shelves of the apothecary were filled with drugs and spices whose rich aroma gave promise to the untutored mind of powerful therapeutic virtues. For these reasons, among others, there was a constant demand, in spite of high prices, for the aromatic products of the Asiatic lands.

Pepper was the first of the eastern spices to be introduced into England (see page 68), and is mentioned as early as the 10th century. Rogers* says: "The general prevalence of pepper rents (the term has survived, but in the altered meaning of a nominal payment) indicates how great was the desire on the part of the wealthier classes to secure the favourite condiment. An obligation laid at that time upon the tenant to supply his lord with a certain quantity of pepper would never have been imposed, one would think, except the demand was very great and the market not always certain." The price of this condiment, however, put it beyond the reach of the poorer classes, who had perforce to find the seasoning for their dishes in what they could grow, notably the onion family. A favourite condiment was Garlic Mustard (*Alliaria officinalis*), popularly known as "Sauce-Alone" or "Jack-by-the-Hedge". So costly were spices in those days that those possessed by collegiate or monastic houses were entered on a separate account and kept in the custody of the sacristan or cellarman.

The importance of the trade in spices is shown by the antiquity of the laws passed in connection with them. One of the oldest of the trade guilds of the City of London was that of the Pepperers, an organisation dating from the 11th century. In 1312 representatives of the Pepperers and other trades appointed the weigher of the King's Beam, a highly responsible officer entrusted with the maintenance of standard weights. The King's, or Great Beam – the *peso grosso* – was used only for goods sold by avoirdupois (*averium ponderis*) as distinct from the scale used for weighing wool, which was called the *Tron*.

* *History of Agriculture and Prices in England.*

In 1328 the Pepperers were registered as *grossarii*, from which our term "grocer" is derived, and in 1373 we find them referred to as the *Compaygnie des Grossers*. The term "Spicers", commonly encountered at this period, seems to have been the general name for anyone connected with the spice trade, for it was applied both to pepperers and apothecaries, whose respective trades were not, at that time, clearly differentiated. John Grantham, a well-known member of the Pepperers, was sometimes referred to in documents as *ipothecarius*.

In 1386 the Grocer's Company (which was legally incorporated in 1428) took control of the entire spice trade in England, and all who dealt in spices and drugs came under its rule. Although the pepperers traded mainly in spices and condiments for domestic use and the apothecaries in drugs for medical use, there was in fact considerable overlapping, for many things which we now buy at the grocer's, such as sugar and ginger, were classed as drugs, and rice and almonds came under the heading of spices. During the greater part of the Middle Ages the apothecaries' shops contained an assortment of products suggestive of a general store, for only the simplest medicaments were available, such as medicated treacle imported from Italy, and cough mixtures whose main ingredients were honey and ginger. As an instance of what might be bought in a grocer's shop at that time, Miss Edith Rickert in *Chaucer's World* gives an extract from a grocer's bill of 1380, when one Robert Passelewe was summoned by a London grocer, Edmund Fraunceys, for money owing for purchases which included pepper, saffron, ginger, cloves, dates, almonds, rice, saunders*, powder of ginger, powder of cinnamon, raisins and myrrh.

The price of pepper between 1250 and 1400 seems to have remained fairly steady at between 1s and 1s 2d per lb, except for the decade which followed the pestilence of 1348 known as

* Sandal-wood.

the Black Death, when the price soared to 2s 6d per lb. When we consider that the wages of an ordinary labourer in the 15th century was on an average 4d a day, and that a skilled workman such as a carpenter earned only 6d a day, it is clear that pepper must have been used very sparingly, if at all, by the common people. Cloves, and even the home-grown saffron, were very much dearer, and Rogers (*op. cit.*) tells us that the price of cloves fluctuated between £1 1s 4d a lb at Oxford market in 1329 and 3s 4d at Bicester seventy years later.

One of the abuses with which the Grocers' Company had to contend during the Middle Ages was the inclusion in the bales of spices reaching them from abroad of a great deal of rubbish with which unscrupulous traders sought to increase their profits. In their own interests the grocers had to undertake the cleansing, or "garbelling"*, of imported spices and drugs. In 1393 they petitioned the Lord Mayor of London that no spices should be re-sold to the public until they had first been cleansed by an officer duly chosen by themselves for that purpose. The petition was granted, and a "garbeller" was appointed whose seal was necessary before any bales of spices or drugs could be weighed by the keeper of the King's Beam.

At first this garbelling was confined to the port of London, but in 1439 a petition was presented to the Commons requesting that in all ports where spices were landed they should be cleansed "in gode manere and trewe fourme as hit is used in the Porte and Citee of London". As a result a Patent Roll of 26 Henry VI (1447) granted to the Company of Grocers the right of garbelling in Southampton, Sandwich and other places throughout the kingdom where necessary, for it was found that owing to the stricter conditions prevailing in London the foreign merchants were sending a great deal of their merchandise to the southern ports.

Until 1442 the Grocers had kept to themselves the right of appointing the City Garbeller, but in that year the king took the

* From Arabic *Karbala*, through Italian *garbellare*, to sift, select.

office as his own prerogative and sold it to Richard Hackdye, Clerk of the Chandlery, and William Aunsell, the King's Serjeant, as an appointment in survivorship, to hold the office themselves or by deputy. In 1448 the officers appointed to garble spices and other merchandise in Southampton, Sandwich and other places (the City of London excepted) were William Wetnale, Richard Hackdye and Thomas Gibbs, "wardens of the mistery of grocer of London".

"Garbelling", writes Lewis Roberts in *The Merchants Map of Commerce*, "is a cleansing, severing, sorting and dividing of the good from the bad, being a habit of working according to right reason and mechanical or handy-craft; the full knowledge thereof was partly gotten and attained by use at that time by Richard Hackdye and William Aunsell, Citizens, and partly by instruction and reason taught and showed by the Merchants and Grocers. Also it is the duty of the Garbler or his servants to tare all such Cask, Hogsheads, Barrels, Bags, Serens, etc., wherein such Spices, Drugs and Merchandises are brought in, truly, justly and indifferently betwixt buyer and seller." He adds, however: "In the beginning faults were but few and easily supressed, but in time grew like Hydra's head. The greediness of gain did infect some of this Fraternity with the practice of deceit."

Some of the abuses are dealt with at length in a book published in 1592, called *A Profitable and necessary Discourse, for the Meeting with the bad Garbelling of Spices*. The author, probably the London merchant Thomas Man, or Mun, tells us that "the workmen take libertie to packe the commoditie uppe verie corruptlie, and will give such secret marks, either by a knot in the bagge made up, or by a spot of inke, that being confederate with another of their friends who shall come to buy the same of the marchant, may thereby know how much or how deepe the best sort doo lie under the second, or worst sort, the which is laied up on purpose upon the top of the bagge."

The office of garbeller continued for about two hundred years, and is frequently mentioned in the State Papers. By letters patent of 37 Henry VI it was granted to William Godfrey, a Groom of the Chamber, and Thomas Babham, Groom of the Robes, for their lives. What happened to them is uncertain; perhaps both died, for two years later the office was granted to William Eliott, Clerk of the Spicery, for life. In 1525, Henry VIII granted it on lease to Robert Cowper, a goldsmith of London, for a hundred years; in 1567 Queen Elizabeth granted it for 58 years to Anthony White, a London grocer. Although issued under Letters Patent of the Crown, the grant of the Office of Garbeller of Spices remained in the hands of the Mayor and Corporation of the City of London. Thus we find Lord Burghley writing in 1581 to the Lord Mayor stating that he understood the office had become vacant by the death of one Blaise Saunders, and requesting the Lord Mayor and Aldermen to stay proceeding in the matter until he communicated with them further, as he meant to be a suitor to them for the office for a friend of his.

Gradually, however, the office of garbeller fell into desuetude, coming to an end with the Revolution of 1688. The last holder was, significantly enough, a Mr Stuart!

*

An important factor which stimulated merchants and explorers to seek a new route to Cathay was the increasing difficulty in trading with the Far East by the old caravan routes. The irruption of the Mongol hordes into the valley of the Euphrates, followed later by the great expansion of Turkish conquests in Asia Minor, caused a severance of normal trade routes and was slowly throttling the Eastern land trade. The Turkish invasions closed the route from Bagdad to Antioch and that from the Persian Gulf to Trebizond by way of the highlands of Asia Minor and Armenia, completely disrupting Venetian commerce in the Black Sea. After the fall of Constantinople in 1453 its importance as a market dwindled away, and with the Turkish conquest of Egypt by Selim I around 1517 the route by way of the Nile was also blocked.

With the old routes rendered unsafe by the spread of the Ottoman Empire it became necessary to find a new way to the East by sea, and this led to a great improvement during the middle part of the 15th century in ships, maps and navigational instruments, which culminated in two great geographical discoveries: the existence of the New World in the west, and the opening up of the sea-route to India in the east.

The first steps towards the discovery of the new sea route to the Spice Islands were taken in 1418, when Prince Henry of Portugal, son of John I of Portugal and his wife Philippa, daughter of John of Gaunt, Duke of Lancaster, built a ship-yard and a school for navigators at the south-western extremity of Portugal facing the vast Atlantic.

He became known as Henry the Navigator, yet he never navigated. But although he found no new lands himself he may aptly be called the Discoverer, for having gathered around him in the bay of Lagos artisans and scientists, instruments and charts, mariners and pilots, he began to launch his caravels on all the seas of the known and unknown world. And these caravels were in their day the fastest sailing craft afloat. The Portuguese were a hardy folk, with great practical skill in seamanship, though hitherto lacking the profounder mysteries of the art of navigation. Under the tuition of Henry the Navigator they grew to a stature commensurate with their destiny.

When the time came, he sent out expeditions to journey down the coast of Africa farther than man had been before, and year after year his ships sailed farther and farther south, until finally Gil Eanes doubled Cape Bojador and disproved the old legend that beyond that point was no water, no tree, nor any green herb.

In 1463 Prince Henry died without having achieved his

heart's desire of sailing right round that mysterious Africa whose configuration was then unknown, but which somehow he divined would lead to the lands of the Saracen, the enemies of his faith, and also to that realm of Prester John, alliance with whom would break the power of the Muslims and secure the triumph of the Cross. For Henry, Grand Master of the Order of Christ, was animated mainly by religious motives, and for him any commercial advantage which might accrue would be merely a side issue. His device, four French words which were inscribed over the portals of his castle at Sagres, he ordered his captains to engrave upon the stones or cut in the bark of the trees of whatsoever land they might discover. They were *Talent de bien faire*, the first word being understood in its primitive sense of *volonté*.

Henry had provided the initial impulse. Those who followed him continued his work. In the year 1486 Bartholomew Diaz reached the southern point of Africa which he named the Cape of Tempests, but which his royal master renamed the Cape of Good Hope.

Wars with Castile and the death of King John II delayed further expeditions for another eleven years. Then, on 8 July, 1497, began one of the most momentous voyages in history, when Vasco da Gama sailed from the Tagus on the expedition which was to reach the goal at last. In the interval that had elapsed since Diaz reached the Cape of Good Hope everything possible had been done to ensure the success of the new venture. Not only were the latest navigational aids then available procured for Gama's fleet, but two ships were built to a new design, better suited to a long voyage in rough weather than the caravel, though less speedy. One of these, the *São Gabriel*, was the Captain's flagship.

On 21 May, 1498, Vasco da Gama brought his small fleet to anchor off Calicut. It was a day that meant ruin for the Venetians, for thenceforward the sailing ship replaced the camel. The voyage thus auspiciously ended led to commercial disaster for the great port of the Adriatic and to the foundation of a vast colonial empire for Portugal.

Calicut was at that time the greatest commercial port on the west coast of India – a free port ruled over by a Hindu known as the Samuri. After a few initial misunderstandings the Portuguese managed to establish satisfactory if not altogether cordial relations with the ruler, who was anxious not to antagonise the rich Mopla merchants (descendants of Arab fathers and native women or of forcibly converted Hindus) who brought considerable trade to the city. After a stay of three months Vasco da Gama began his return journey, bearing with him a letter from the Samuri to King Manoel of Portugal stating that he was willing to trade cinnamon, cloves, ginger, pepper and precious stones in exchange for gold, silver, corals and scarlet cloth. After an absence of two years Vasco da Gama returned in triumph to Lisbon, the quest for spices accomplished.

The news of the Portuguese discovery of the sea route to the East broke upon Venice like a bombshell. Being able to buy at first hand gave the Portuguese an enormous advantage. They had only to embark the goods and set sail, with no vexatious tolls to pay on the homeward journey. Some Venetians hoped that the toll of shipwreck might offset any benefits and that the Portuguese would in the end be obliged to renounce the trade; others counted on the Turks doing all in their power to keep the Indian trade in their hands. But an intelligent minority was at once aware of the extreme gravity of the situation. When Pedro Alvares Cabral followed in the wake of Gama in 1500 (discovering and claiming for Portugal the rich empire of Brazil on the way) and loaded his ships with pepper at Chochin and Cananor, a dearth of that commodity was at once felt on the markets of Egypt and Syria.

In 1502 the Beyrut galleys returned to Venice with only four bales of pepper and the Alexandria fleet fared little better. Pepper became too scarce and too dear for the Venetian market and her customers transferred their allegiance to other markets, where they could get Portuguese pepper cheaper. Although the Venetian Senate sent a special embassy to the Sultan of Egypt, pointing out what a disaster it would be for that country if the Portuguese were to take away their trade, the Sultan could do nothing.

Clearly the Venetians could not compete with Portugal on the same footing, for there was then no Suez Canal, and the voyage, already a long one for the Portuguese, would have been far too long for the Venetians, whose ships, moreover, were not built for Atlantic storms. When Vasco da Gama returned to Lisbon from his second voyage on 1 September, 1503, the Venetians heard with consternation that his vessels had brought back between thirty and thirty-five quintals of Oriental produce, including cinnamon, ginger, pepper, nutmegs and precious stones. The merchants of Lisbon were by now convinced that Portugal was in a position to supply Western Europe with all the spices it needed.

And thus the wealth that had been enjoyed almost exclusively by the merchants of Venice passed swiftly into other hands. From 1509 no Venetian galleys visited England as had been their custom, and when in 1518 one solitary galley arrived at Southampton it was so poorly freighted that Cardinal Wolsey complained to the Venetian ambassador in London stating that he intended to forbid the Venetian merchants to load merchandise of a greater value than their own effects. In former days, he declared, the galleys used to come so richly freighted that a small addition to the value of their imports was sufficient to defray the cost of their export, but this time the whole of their imports would not equal the value of one-sixth part of the homeward cargo. In 1531, in reply to a complaint from England that the Venetian galleys no longer brought spices, "but glass and other things of no value", the Venetian Senate made reply that this was not the fault of the Signory, but of the change in the times; that the spices which used to come to Venice now went to Portugal.

Soon the Portuguese became known in every port along the Malabar coast and a regular trade was established between Portugal and India. The crusading ideals of Henry the Navigator soon took second place to the policy of securing complete monopoly for the King of Portugal in the products of India and East Africa. But the Mohammedans, who had previously enjoyed possession of the coastal trade between India and Egypt, were not going to surrender it without a struggle. In 1508 a great sea battle took place between Egyptian and Portuguese fleets to decide which country should be master in the Indian Ocean, and it was only after great carnage that the Portuguese commander, Dom Francisco de Almeida, who had been appointed Viceroy of the Portuguese possessions in India, succeeded in gaining a decisive victory which firmly established Portuguese power in India.

Two years later Almeida's successor, Alfonso de Albuquerque, gained possession of Goa, which became the centre of the Portuguese empire in India. The island of Ceylon they had already seized, and as this was the island where grew the great cinnamon forests they were soon able to establish a monopoly in that commodity. Malacca and Ormus fell into their grasp. With Malacca as his base Albuquerque was able to send his ships still farther east until they came across the almost legendary Spice Islands, the knowledge of whose whereabouts the Arabs had tried for centuries to conceal from Europeans. Among those who took part in this expedition to the Moluccas, or Spice Islands, was the famous Magellan (Fernão Magalhães) who, after his return to Europe, entered the service of Spain and made the remarkable westward passage to these same islands by way of the Strait which now bears his name, though he himself did not live to enjoy the rewards he had so richly earned, for he was killed by natives of the Philippines before he reached his goal.

A good deal is known about both of these early expeditions to the Spice Islands, for from survivors of Albuquerque's mission a Portuguese official named Duarte Barbosa obtained a great deal of information which he afterwards published, while the westward voyage of Magellan is related in the journal kept by a young man of Vicenza named Pigafetta. To these two writers we owe the first detailed accounts of the Spice Islands and the methods of cultivation of the clove and nutmeg trees.

What remained of Magellan's expedition returned to San Lucar in September, 1522, under the command of the Biscayan pilot Sebastian del Cano, who sailed back in the *Victoria* with twenty-six tons of cloves aboard, together with large quantities of cinnamon, mace, nutmegs and sandal-wood. In addition to receiving a handsome pension, the pilot was granted armorial bearings, the arms being appropriately enough two sticks of cinnamon, three nutmegs and twelve cloves. The supporters were two native kings, crowned, holding in the exterior hand a branch of a spice tree, the crest a globe, and the motto: *Primus circumdedisti me.*

But this voyage only exacerbated the rival claims of Portugal and Spain with regard to the Moluccas. Following the discovery of America by Columbus, the unexplored world had been divided by the Pope between those two countries; Spain to have all the territories discovered, or to be discovered, in the Western seas, and by the Treaty of Tordesillas in 1494 a boundary line was agreed upon which should separate Spanish and Portuguese hemispheres of influence. But the treaty remained little more than a matter of form and neither party respected the convention save when it suited his purpose. And so, after the Moluccas had been discovered by Magellan on a westward course, the Spaniards laid claim to them – a claim that was naturally contested by King Manoel of Portugal, who had by now assumed the magniloquent title of "King, by the Grace of God, of Portugal and of the Algarves, both on this side of the sea and beyond it, in Africa, Lord of Guinea and of the Conquest, Navigation, and Commerce of Ethiopia, Arabia, Persia and India".

In 1529 a compromise was reached by which Charles V ceded whatever rights he might possess in the Moluccas to the Portuguese in return for a loan, for an indefinite period, of 350,000 ducats. In 1564 the ruler of the Moluccas ceded to the King of Portugal and his successors the rights, dominion and seigneurage of the islands. In 1580 Portugal was conquered by Spain and the two nations were united under a common crown. Nevertheless it was stipulated that her possessions in Asia and Africa should still belong to Portugal.

But the eastern colonial empire of Portugal, though rapidly acquired, lasted no more than a century. The avarice and oppressions of the Portuguese viceroys and officials, and the cruelty with which the natives were treated, sowed the seeds of destruction. The spirit of monopoly which excluded other countries from any share in the spice trade led to the hostility of other nations. Neglect of proper defences with which to retain her possessions in the Far East hastened the ruin of Portuguese colonial power in that area.

In 1592 a native of Haarlem, Jan Huygen van Linschoten, began writing a book, the *Itinerario*, which embodied the information he had acquired during five years residence as a merchant in Goa. Linschoten pointed out to his compatriots the great importance of trade with Java, and the eventual choice of this island as their headquarters in the Malay archipelago was a contributory cause of the rapid rise of Dutch power in the East Indies. Linschoten, whose book had considerable influence in Holland, pointed out that the colonial empire of the Portuguese was rotten and that an energetic rival would have every chance of supplanting them.

In 1595 a fleet of four ships under Cornelius van Houtman sailed for the Spice Islands. After various skirmishes with the Portuguese he visited Java, Madura and other islands, returning to Holland after two years with a rich cargo of spices. His account of his voyage with its emphasis on the vast resources of the islands he had visited made a great impression on the merchants of Amsterdam, and this first expedition was speedily followed by others. Many Dutch companies fitted out ships, and in 1602 these various enterprises were merged into the Dutch "United East India Company".

Meanwhile the English were beginning to show some interest in the spice trade. During the early period when navigators were extending the boundaries of the known world, England lagged somewhat behind in the race for new territories. Apart from the voyages of the Cabots to Labrador, England could show little to compare with the overseas achievements of Spain and Portugal; but at the time policy forbade any encroachment on the regions claimed by these two powers, and those adventurous spirits to whom such a policy was galling had to act at their own risk. Moreover, it was not until the end of the Wars of the Roses and the advent to power of the Tudors that England emerged from a position of comparative backwardness compared with her continental neighbours.

By the middle of the 16th century English commerce had grown to a point where new markets were badly needed. With the defeat of the Spanish Armada in 1588 English confidence grew and, after the renunciation of Papal authority at the time of the Reformation, Englishmen no longer felt themselves bound to accept the Pope's division of the unexplored world between Spain and Portugal.

But there was much leeway to be overhauled, for although Drake had sailed round the world in 1578–80, it was not until 1582 that the first English sailor, Captain Stephens, set out with the intention of sailing direct to India by the Cape route. By 1599 Dutch enterprise was paying such rich dividends that English merchants turned their attention to the Far East. The Dutch voyages proved a great factor in the establishment of the East India Company, which was incorporated in 1600 under the style of "The Governor and Company of Merchants of London Trading unto the East Indies".

Between 1595 and 1601, when the first English expedition set out, at least ten Dutch expeditions had sailed to the East – a total of forty-three ships. On 20 April, 1601, the East India Company's first fleet, consisting of four ships and a small victualler, set sail from Torbay under the command of James Lancaster, whose flagship was a 600-ton privateer of 36 guns, the *Red Dragon*, which under its original name of the *Scourge of Malice* had seen action against the Spaniards off the Azores and the Caribbean islands. The cargo taken out consisted mainly of cloths, kersies, lead, iron and tin; while for barter with the natives of Africa the usual supply of knives and glass trinkets was carried.

On the way to the Cape a Portuguese vessel was taken without a fight and the cargo distributed among the English vessels. At the Cape Lancaster remained for seven weeks to enable his crews to regain their strength, for he had already lost 107 men, mostly through the ravages of scurvy. At Madagascar the fleet spent another two months and it was not until June, 1602, that Lancaster arrived at Achin, in Sumatra. The ceremonious presentation of a letter from Queen Elizabeth, which was carried to the palace of Sultan Alauddin in a gold basin placed on the crimson-covered howdah of a state elephant, pleased the aged monarch hardly less than the presents which accompanied it.

But although a commercial treaty was signed and Lancaster was permitted to trade, he could get little pepper, for his competitors had already bought up most of the crop, which was a small one that year. Lancaster, debating "how to lade his shippes to save his owne credit, the merchants' estimation that set him aworke, and the reputation of his countrey", determined to capture a cargo from his rivals and was fortunate enough to take a Portuguese carrack some seventy miles from Malacca. In November, Lancaster sent two of his ships back to England with cargoes of spices and himself went on to Bantam, in Java, about a thousand miles from Achin, where he delivered a similar letter to the young king. Trading privileges were granted and Lancaster was permitted to establish a factory where he left some of his men.

The market at Bantam was much better, and within a few weeks enough commodities had been purchased to load the remaining ships, which returned to England in July, 1603. The total cargo brought back on this first expedition included 210,000 lb of pepper. It so happened that the fleet got back at a rather unfortunate time, for the Plague was raging in London, business was at a standstill, and the market was already glutted with pepper. Large consignments had recently arrived from the Low Countries, and according to the Calendar of State Papers the queen's contractors for pepper were unable to dispose of it because they insisted on an integral cash payment instead of allowing any credit. The result of an overloaded market was that the Company's shareholders, instead of a dividend in cash, had to accept 5,339 lb of pepper for each £250 share held and dispose of it as best they could. However, a start had been made with the East India trade.

Nevertheless, compared with the Dutch the English were slow off the mark. In the six years which followed the founding of the East India Company only two small fleets were sent out – the second under the command of Henry Middleton – and only one factory, that at Bantam, had been established. By this time the Dutch company's ships were to be found all over the Indian Ocean and the Dutch were showing every intention of replacing the monopoly of the Portuguese by one even more stringent. Although there was no general hostility between Dutch and English in the Far East until 1609, the commercial opposition which the English faced, both from Dutch and Portuguese, was so great that for a good many years the amount of trade done by the English company was comparatively small.

In 1609, when Pieter Both was appointed first Governor-General of the Dutch East Indies his instructions were to see that the commerce of the Moluccas, Amboina and Banda should remain in the hands of the Dutch "and that no other nation in the world should have the least part." One result of the enforcement of the Dutch monopoly was that cloves, which sold between 3s and 4s a lb in England up till 1602, were now fetching 7s a lb. Jan Pieterszoon Coen, Governor-General from 1618, was even more determined to make his country predominant in the Far East, and although in 1619 an agreement was concluded by which the two rival companies were to share the Eastern trade in fixed proportions, and jointly to bear the cost of defending the islands, this "Treaty of Defence" as it was termed pleased neither party, and was short-lived.

Matters came to a head in 1623 with the so-called "Massacre of Amboina", when the Dutch arrested a number of the English factors on a charge of conspiring to seize the Dutch fort, and ten of them were tortured and put to death after an irregular trial. This tragic event put an end for a long time to English trade in the Moluccas and poisoned Anglo-Dutch relations for more than half a century.

One way in which the Dutch tried to ensure a complete monopoly of the spice trade was by persuading the kings of Ternate and Timor, the chief of the Molucca Islands, to uproot all the clove and nutmeg trees in their dominions in return for a pension from the Dutch. The cultivation of the nutmeg was thenceforward confined to Banda, and that of the clove to Amboina. Every year expeditions were sent out to destroy all clove and nutmeg trees found growing elsewhere. In addition no one was allowed to trade in the four fine kinds of spices unless they bought them in the first place from the Company. By 1681 the Dutch monopoly was virtually complete.

During the 17th century the English were expelled from Bantam and Jakarta, and in the course of fierce wars with the Portuguese the Dutch gradually ousted them from their eastern possessions, driving them out of Malacca in 1651 and from Ceylon in 1658. In 1660 they conquered Celebes, one of the last remaining possessions of the Portuguese in that area. But whereas it was the fate of the Portuguese to succumb to Dutch power, England managed to retain her footing in the East, where her power gradually grew to the detriment of the Dutch. Obliged to quit Bantam in 1682, the English established their factories at Bencoolen.

Taking a long-term view, although the East India Company lost most of the spice trade by reason of their expulsion from the Moluccas, this very rebuff forced them to concentrate on India, where they developed their trade to such an extent that by 1670 some forty large vessels were engaged in general commerce with India. In various countries bordering on the Malabar Coast pepper was extensively cultivated, and as that commodity became increasingly difficult to obtain from Sumatra and Java at a reasonable price, owing to the Dutch hold on those islands, the English established themselves in India, where in the long run the trade in calicoes, silks, indigo, saltpetre, coffee and pepper was to prove more remunerative than that in cloves and nutmegs.

Yet at the beginning of the 17th century the profits made in the spice trade must have been very considerable, even allowing for all expenses. So much may be inferred from the table given in a book by a London merchant, Gerard de Malynes, called *Center of the Circle of Commerce*, and published in 1623. Pepper cost 2½d per lb in India and was sold in England at 1s 8d per lb; Cloves costing 9d per lb were sold at 5s per lb; Nutmegs bought for 4d per lb were sold on the London market at 3s per lb; and Mace, costing 8d per lb sold at 6s per lb. At this date there is no quotation for Cinnamon, since the Portuguese still held the monopoly and the spice was obtainable only from Lisbon.

Although the Dutch had acquired the monopoly of the trade in cloves and nutmegs, its maintenance was, quite naturally, strongly resented by other nations. A Frenchman from Lyons named Pierre Poivre, who had travelled extensively in Asia, and had discovered that there were some fifty or more islands, apart from Amboina and Banda, which produced clove and nutmeg trees, decided to send an expedition to some of these islands, which were sparsely inhabited, to secure seeds and plants. As *Intendant*, or Administrator of the Ile de France (which later was to become the British island of Mauritius) and a botanist by training, he was convinced that the spices could equally well be grown in the French tropical possessions.

In June, 1770, there arrived at Ile de France more than 400 nutmeg and 70 clove trees, as well as 10,000 nutmegs ready to germinate and a chest of cloves, some of which had sprouted. Two years later an even greater quantity was imported, and some of the plants were then distributed among other French islands – Seychelles, Bourbon and Cayenne. In Cayenne the clove flourished and was thence transported to Dominica and Martinique, and later to other West Indian Islands. But in the Ile de France the cultivation of spices gave way at the beginning of the 19th century to that of sugar, which still remains one of the standard products of Mauritius.

Although the quality of the spices grown in the French islands never reached that of the produce of Amboina and Banda, the success of M Poivre's experiment proved that clove trees could be cultivated elsewhere than in the East Indies and this led to their introduction into Zanzibar, which was destined in due course to become the world's chief supplier of cloves and clove oil.

ALLSPICE   *Pimenta officinalis* (Lindley)   Myrtaceae
Jamaica Pepper
Pimento
FR *Toute-épice*; *Poivre de la Jamaïque*
GER *Nelkenpfeffer*; *Piment*

When the Spaniards arrived in the Caribbean they found large
areas of the island of Jamaica covered with strange trees
bearing aromatic berries which, when dried, appeared to com-
bine the flavours of nutmeg, cinnamon and clove, for which
reason we term the ground berries Allspice. But the Spaniards
left some confusion of nomenclature in their wake. They
called this spice *pimienta*, or pepper, and the name, corrupted
into *pimento*, has remained. Nor did it make matters any better
when botanists bestowed upon the tree the name of *Pimenta
officinalis*, for it is no relation to the peppers, but is a bay, and
a member of the Myrtle family.

Allspice is the dried, unripe full-grown berry of this evergreen tree, indigenous to the West Indies and cultivated
especially in Jamaica, which has almost a monopoly in the
production of Allspice, since the climate and soil of that island
seem particularly favourable for its growth. In fact it hardly
needs cultivation and is found in groves scattered over the
savannas and limestone hills of the south-western portion of
the island.

The trees, which grow slowly, range from 20 to 40 feet in
height, and the glossy green leaves resemble those of the common bay tree. The round, brownish-black berries, which are
attached to the tree by a barely perceptible peduncle, are about
the size of a pea, and contain the seed, which is itself aromatic,
but less so than the pericarp.

The fruit clusters are picked off the tree before they are
fully ripe, for in ripening the fruit loses a good deal of its
aroma. The twigs are spread on sacking and flailed until the
berries are all removed, and then these are dried in the sun for

several days, or in a fruit evaporator. The yearly average yield of a mature tree is in the region of 75 lb of the dried fruit.

Allspice is marketed as berries or in powder, the latter being prone to adulteration with pea-flour, starches and other substances. For culinary use it is not nowadays as much employed as formerly, but it was once in enormous demand, and in the year 1804–05 the total quantity shipped from the British West Indies was 2,257,000 lb.

The leaves harbour an essential oil, containing eugenol, which is used in medicine as a stimulant and aromatic, and is also largely employed as a flavouring. In France Allspice is not greatly used for culinary purposes, but it forms an ingredient of the composite spice known as *quatre épices*.

A near relative is the "melegueta", *Pimenta acris*, from the leaves of which bay oil and bay rum, used as hair lotion, are obtained.

| CAPSICUM | *C. frutescens* | Solanaceae |
| | *C. annuum* | |

The genus Capsicum comprises a wide range of forms, particularly as to the shape and pungency of the fruit. At one time or another many of these variations have been described as species. . . . Irish, in his monograph on the capsicums, reduced the number to two species, *C. annuum* and *C. frutescens*. Bailey reduced these two species to a single form, i.e. *C. frutescens*. A study of the garden varieties presents material evidence in support of this point of view. A. T. ERWIN

Capsicums, Sweet Peppers or Pimentos, and Chillies are fruits of various plants belonging to the genus *Capsicum*. Known generally as Capsicum Peppers to distinguish them from the true peppers, they are America's main contribution to the world's condiments, for they are all native to that continent.

Capsicum 41

When the Spaniards arrived in the New World they found no pepper such as had been found in the Orient; but they found something equally pungent in the plants bearing pods of various shapes and sizes that had for centuries preceding their arrival been cultivated by the native Indians, in the tropical regions of that land. Some of the names by which they were known to the Indians have survived – the *Chilli* in Mexico and the *Aji* in Peru.

Some of these indigenous fruits, especially the larger varieties, were not unduly pungent, and could be used as vegetables; whereas others, like the Bird Peppers, or Devil Peppers, as they were sometimes called, were fiery in the extreme. But since they were all more or less pungent the Spaniards called them by the Spanish name for pepper, *pimienta*, and to distinguish them from the pepper which came from India they added the Mexican name of *chilli*. Later, botanists gave them the generic name of *Capsicum*, because the hot seeds were contained in a case or capsule.* Today we call the milder varieties Pimentos (a corruption of *pimienta*), or Sweet Peppers, or Bell Peppers.

The earliest mention of the Capsicum is in a letter written in 1494 by a physician named Dr Chanca, who accompanied Columbus on his second voyage. He gives it the local name of *Aji*. At about the same time Peter Martyr wrote that Columbus had brought to Spain "pepper more pungent than that from the Caucasus". And it was not long before the larger varieties of Capsicum, the Sweet Peppers, began to be cultivated in those parts of Europe where soil and climate were suitable, notably in Spain itself, so that Clusius, the celebrated botanist, was able to note, in his translation of Monardes's account of medical plants lately brought to Europe from America: "This Capsicum, or Pepper of the Indies (or America rather), is now cultivated with great diligence throughout the land of Castile;

---

* The name *Kapsikon* was first used by a Greek doctor, Actuarius, in the 11th century, but cannot have signified this plant.

not only by gardeners but also by women in pots which they place on their balconies. For they use it all the year round, both fresh and dried, in sauces and to replace pepper."

All that series of plants constituting the genus *Capsicum* seem to be indigenous to tropical America, for neither Marco Polo, who travelled throughout Asia, nor Garcia da Orta, who resided for some years in India, mention them. But once they had been planted in the East Indies by the Portuguese they soon became well established throughout the eastern tropics. In his *Exoticorum* (1605), Clusius observes that the American Capsicum, which both he and Dodoens call "Brazilian Pepper", was brought from the Spanish West Indies and carried to India by the Portuguese, who cultivated it under the name of Pernambuco Pepper. Already, in the 1618 edition of Dodoens's *Cruydtboeck*, there are woodcuts of twelve different kinds of Capsicum. Gerard tells us that in his day they were "verie well knowne in the shoppes at Billingsgate by the name of Ginnie pepper" (Guinea pepper).

The Sweet Peppers, gathered when ripe, partly ripe, or green, are an excellent culinary vegetable, capable of being used in many ways – raw or grilled in salads, stuffed with a variety of fillings and cooked, or pickled. They are an excellent source of vitamin C.

Chilli is the Mexican name for most varieties of Capsicum, but the term is more usually employed for the small and very pungent peppers, cultivated not only in Central America, but also in Africa and Japan.

Japanese chillies are of medium size, deep red in colour, and less pungent than the African varieties, which can be very hot indeed. These are cultivated mainly in Sierra Leone, Nigeria, Nyasaland, Mombasa and Zanzibar. Cayenne pepper is the ground product of several of the small-fruited species of Capsicum, including *C. minimum*, or Bird Pepper, the fruits of which are seldom more than half an inch long. Chillies are also grown in India and Indonesia.

The pungency of Cayenne Pepper depends both on the variety of Capsicum employed and also on the removal or otherwise of the seeds. Some cayenne peppers produced in the West Indies are made by adding flour to the ground pods, leavening with yeast and baking until hard. The product is then finely ground and sifted. Tiny peppers of Central America, known from their fiery nature as Devil Peppers, are used in the making of Tabasco sauce, which is named after a river in Mexico on the banks of which it is cultivated. Tabasco chillies are also grown in other regions bordering on the Gulf of Mexico.

Certain of these very hot peppers are official and used in medicine as stimulants, counter-irritants and stomachics under the name of Capsicum. They are used, also, in the preparation of medicated cotton wool, which is made by mixing a liquid extract of Capsicum with alcohol and saturating cotton wool with this solution. The pharmaceutical Capsicum, to be official, should be the dried ripe fruit of *C. frutescens* grown in Africa, and in practice the variety grown in Sierra Leone is mainly employed.

Nepal Pepper, light golden brown in colour, is prepared from *C. annuum* var. *acuminatum*, grown in that country. It is pungent without being fiery and has a very pleasant odour. It is highly esteemed as a condiment, and possibly owing to the soil and local conditions it cannot be grown anywhere else without losing its special character.

Paprika is a mild pepper made by grinding the dried ripe pods of certain varieties of *C. annuum*, cultivated extensively in Hungary, Bulgaria and, to a lesser extent, in Portugal. The finest quality paprika, Rose Paprika, is made in Hungary from selected pods, of which only the fleshy pericarp and the seeds are ground. A second grade, known as King's Paprika, is made from unselected pods, and often includes the stems. As with Cayenne Pepper, the colour, aroma and pungency of paprika varies considerably according to the variety of *C. annuum* employed and the method of processing.

Peppers are used throughout India and Pakistan, both as an ingredient in curries and for medical purposes. In addition to Nepal Chillies and Bird Pepper, other varieties, such as *C. annuum* var. *cerasiforme* (Cherry Pepper) and var. *longum* (Black Nubian, etc.), are also cultivated.

CARDAMOMS   *Elettaria cardamomum*   Zingiberacea
FR *Cardamome*
GER *Kardamonen*

Cardamoms are the fully-ripe fruit of a large perennial plant, a native of Ceylon and India, which is extensively cultivated in many parts of south-east Asia and grows wild on the mountain sides of southern India. The rhizome of the plant sends out fibrous roots from which are thrown up leafy stems growing to a height of around 10 feet. The fruit, in the form of a capsule, is of a grey-green colour, and the capsule itself is ovoid and three-celled, each cell containing a quantity of small, dark brown seeds which are highly aromatic.

Until comparatively recently it was the seeds of the wild plant which were exported, but nowadays increasing demand is supplied by the cultivated plant. The seeds form an ingredient of curry powder and are much used in India as a flavouring. Cardamoms are employed in Germany for imparting an aromatic taste to ginger-bread, in certain kinds of sausages, and in Russia and Scandinavia for flavouring cakes. The seeds are also used in making pickles, and in the preparation of aromatic drugs.

Various varieties of Cardamoms are used as spices, but for medicinal use, as a carminative and stimulant, the British Pharmacopoeia recognizes only *E. cardamomum*. The most important galenical made from Cardamoms is the compound tincture prescribed for the relief of dyspepsia. The volatile oil contains terpenes and an ester, terpinyl acetate, together with cineole and limonene. It is cineole, the main constituent of eucalyptus oil, which gives the seed its camphor-like taste and smell. Cardamom oil enters into the preparation of certain perfumes and is also an ingredient of the liqueur known as Dantziger Goldwasser.

In the time of the celebrated botanist Clusius, who mentions it in his *Exoticorum* (1610), the Cardamom was a rarity and by the end of the 18th century it had almost disappeared from commerce; but it returned about a century ago, and is now in considerable demand.

In common with most other spices Cardamoms had a reputation as an aphrodisiac, and it is said that young men used to chew the seeds before hastening to a gallant rendezvous.

So that they may retain their aromatic properties, it is best for the seeds to be kept in their pericarps and only separated when required. For this reason considerable importance is attached commercially to the appearance of the seed-capsules, which are bleached in the sun or by sulphuring until they lose their greyish-green colour and become creamy, almost white. This creamy appearance and the papery texture of the capsule is often enhanced by a light coating of starch. The fruits are harvested before they have obtained full ripeness, since at maturity the capsules split open and eject the seed.

The world's supply of true Cardamoms comes mainly from Malabar, Mangalore, Mysore and Ceylon, and commercially they are supplied bleached, semi-bleached, decorticated and ground. The whole fruit are supplied commercially graded, according to size, as "shorts", "short longs" and "long longs".

When using Cardamoms moderation is needed, otherwise the camphor-like flavour becomes unpleasantly strong.

CASSIA   *Cinnamomum Cassia* (Blume)   Laurineae
FR *Cannelle de Chine*; *Casse ligneuse*
GER *Sinesischer Zimt*; *Zimtcassie*

Cassia is the dried aromatic bark of *Cinnamomum Cassia*, an evergreen tree cultivated extensively in South China, especially in the province of Kwangsi, and also in Indonesia. Marsden, in his *History of Sumatra* (1783), says of Cassia: "This is a coarse species of cinnamon . . . mostly procured in those districts which lie inland of Tappanooly. The leaves are about four inches long, narrower than the bay (to which tribe it belongs) and more pointed; deep green, smooth surface and plain edge. The young leaves are mostly of reddish hue. Trees grow from fifty to sixty feet high."

There is often confusion between Cassia and Cinnamon, though in fact the bark of Cassia is much thicker than that of true Cinnamon while the taste is more pungent, the flavour less delicate and rather sweeter. When ground as a spice Cassia is hard to distinguish from Cinnamon by appearance alone and is sometimes substituted for it by the unscrupulous trader, though the expert knows that Cassia spice is darker and ruddier than Cinnamon.

The chief uses of Cassia bark and the oil (*Oleum Cassiae*) are as flavourings for liqueurs and chocolate, and for cooking generally; that is to say they are similar to those for which Cinnamon is used, Cassia being a cheaper substitute. It is frequently preferred to Cinnamon by chocolate manufacturers owing to its stronger flavour.

Bark is stripped from branches of the trees as soon as they have reached maturity – in from six to ten years – by making two longitudinal slits diametrically opposed and then loosening and stripping off the bark. After exposure to the sun for about twenty-four hours the epidermis is shaved off with a plane or knife, and the pieces of bark, which curls up as it dries, are tied into bundles.

Cassia varies in quality, colour, thickness and flavour since the bark is obtained from different species of *Cinnamomum* grown in widely separated regions of the Far East.

CINNAMON   *Cinnamonum zeylanicum*   Laurineae
                     (Breyn)

FR *Cannelle*
GER *Ceylonzimt*

> Cinnamon was so highly valued by princes, that Cleopatra
> carried it into her sepulchre with her jewels.
>
> SIR THOMAS BROWNE *Miscellany Tracts*

True Cinnamon is the dried inner bark of *C. zeylanicum*, a
small and bushy evergreen tree* with leathery, bright-green
aromatic leaves, native to Ceylon; or, more accurately, the
inner bark from the truncated stocks, for the trees are pollarded
to form stools from which a few shoots are allowed to grow.
When these shoots have grown to a certain length and thickness they are cut off and the bark is then slit lengthwise and
detached with a special kind of knife, like a bill-hook.

After a short period of fermentation followed by scraping
and drying, the pieces of detached bark are inserted one
within another by skilled peelers, until the compound
pieces become an almost solid rod, about three-eighths of an
inch in diameter and from 36 to 42 inches long. These are the
"quills" of commerce, which are then graded according to
colour, quality, size and thickness of bark. Damaged and
broken pieces are termed "quillings", whilst "featherings"
are short shavings and tiny pieces of left-over bark. The best
Cinnamon comes from Ceylon, but a certain amount, of
inferior quality, is obtained from southern India, Indonesia,
Brazil and the West Indies.

The bark, which is thin and brittle, is a pale, yellowish
brown on the outer surface and darker brown within. The
odour is fragrant and the taste aromatic, due to the volatile oil,
which consists largely of cinnamic aldehyde. This Oil of Cinnamon is distilled from the bark, and Tincture of Cinnamon is

---

* The tree in a wild state grows up to 40 feet in height, but as cultivated,
it does not exceed about 8 feet.

48 *Cinnamon*

highly valued as a stomachic and carminative. Cinnamon is also used in medicine as an intestinal astringent in the treatment of diarrhoea, for which a compound powder is frequently used consisting of equal parts of Cinnamon, Cardamom seeds, and Ginger. Cinnamon leaf oil and root oil differ in composition from *Oleum Cinnamomi* and are not so valuable.

The Cinnamon tree is grown extensively in the western part of Ceylon, around Colombo, and when well sited it will be ready for commercial production in about five years; though, in less favoured positions the time may be doubled. Commercially the bark is of little use after about eighteen years.

In former times Cinnamon trees flourished all along the Malabar coast, where a thriving trade was done in the bark and its essential oil. But the Dutch in their attempts to gain a monopoly of the spice trade, bought from the king of Cochin the right to destroy all the Malabar plantations in order to enhance the value of those which they possessed in Ceylon.*

Westwards the Cinnamon was discovered by the Conquistadores, and the Spanish physician and botanist Nicolas Monardes in his book translated by John Frampton under the title *Joyfull Newes out of the Newe Founde Worlde* (1577) tells how

In the yere of 1540 Francis Pissarro did provide to make to his brother Gonsalo Pissarro governour of the Province of Quito, and the Spaniards went thither with a good will, and they went also unto the countrie that was called the Synamon, which was another Province beyond Quito, and the Sinamon was muche spoken of amongest the Spaniards, for it was understood of the Indians that it was a thing of great riches. . . . It hath the same pleasauntness of taste as the same Sinamon hath, which they bring from the India of Portingale.

The pomanders once carried as a preservative against infection usually contained cinnamon bark amongst other

* See J. B. Tavernier's *Travels in India*, Book II, Chap. 12.

aromatic substances, and Cinnamon was also used for spicing wines and as an ingredient of cordials. Today it is used as a flavouring, mainly in the bakery trade, but more so abroad than in England, where even the cinnamon cakes so popular in Victorian days seem to have disappeared.

From the various allusions to Cinnamon and Cassia in ancient books it is evident that from early times there was a great deal of confusion between the two spices.

CLOVES *Caryophyllus aromaticus* L. Myrtaceae
FR *Clou de girofle*
GER *Gewürznelke*

The cloves of commerce are the unopened flower-buds of the Clove tree, indigenous to a small number of islands in the Moluccas, but later introduced into other tropical countries. The buds are gathered before the corolla has become detached and when the petals, still compact and unopened, form a round head above the calyx. When the buds are dried their resemblance to a nail has given them their name in many languages – *clove, clou de girofle, kruidnagel, clavo, chiodo,* etc. The French word for the clove tree, *girofle,* is a derivation from *caryophyllon.*

The clove tree grows to a height of from 12 to 20 feet, and its aromatic leaves bear minute oil glands, the scent of which can be detected from a great distance in the hot, still nights of the tropics. The climatic needs of the tree has restricted its cultivation to comparatively few localities in the world, and these are fairly close to the sea. A moist but warm and equable climate is needed for the successful cultivation of the clove tree, with a moderate but not excessive rainfall. The German, G. E. Rumpf, who lived and died in Amboina, in his time (1626–1693) the seat of the growth and trade of cloves, wrote in his *Herbarium Ambionense* that the clove tree was "the most

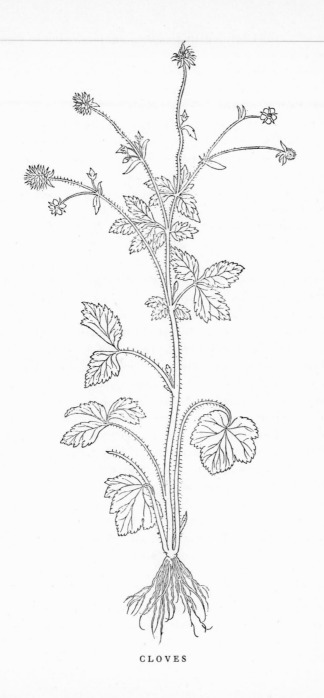

CLOVES

beautiful, the most elegant, and the most precious of all known trees".

Crawford, in his *Descriptive Dictionary of the Indian Islands*, says "it is very difficult to understand how the clove could have come first to be used as a condiment by foreign nations, considering the well-ascertained fact that it has never been used as such, and indeed hardly in any other way, by the inhabitants of the countries which produce it". The Chinese seem to have been the first to use the Clove as a spice, but from about the 8th century onwards it was regularly imported into Europe, though at a price which placed it beyond the reach of all but the richest. In 1265 the price of cloves in England was around 12s per lb, at a time when a labourer earned about a 2d a day!

There is no mention of cloves in the Scriptures, and most authorities consider it doubtful whether the *garyophyllum* of Pliny refers to the clove. Indeed, the time when cloves were first brought to Europe, by way of India, is a matter of inference rather than of certainty; on the whole it seems likely that cloves were known in Europe by the end of the 2nd century.

Comparatively few cloves reached England before the discovery of the Cape of Good Hope passage, and those consignments which did reach our shores were sold at fantastic prices, amounting to nearly four hundred times their first cost. Crawford says that "our ancestors must have ascribed curative virtues to the clove which it does not possess, or they never could have been tempted to give the enormous prices quoted for a mere condiment".

The Portuguese made their first appearance in the parent country of cloves in 1512 and had the principal share of the clove trade for nearly a century before they were expelled by the Dutch in 1605. When the Dutch gained possession of the Spice Islands they endeavoured to maintain a monopoly (see page 37) but were unable to keep the trade entirely in their own hands, for in 1609 the British East India Company's ship *Consent* reached England with a cargo of 1,000 cwt of cloves, on which duty amounting to £1,400 and an import tax of as much again was paid. The cloves were sold at from 5s 6d to 6s per lb, a price we can multiply by twenty to bring it up to the monetary value of our day.

During the 18th century the clove tree was introduced into Mauritius and the West Indies, while the clove industry of Zanzibar is a striking example of the way in which a plant not native to the country may become the staple economic product of its land of adoption.

Towards the close of the 18th century, soon after the British East India Company had founded a settlement on the island of Penang, they introduced there clove trees brought from the Moluccas, and the spice gardens of Penang proved a capital investment, for the soil and climate was particularly suitable and the Penang cloves soon became among the most highly valued.

The flower buds of the clove tree appear about January or February and are ready for picking about July. In a good year picking may continue for six or seven months, with a partial cessation in October and November; for a new crop of buds begins to appear around August and is ready for picking towards the end of the season.

Great care is necessary when harvesting the cloves, for the buds, which are plucked by hand, must be gathered at a particular stage in their development; if picked too soon the bud has not grown sufficiently, with consequent loss of weight: if left too long on the tree, the aromatic qualities of the bud are attenuated and the buds themselves are more liable to crumble. Below the trees a covering is laid on the ground to catch any buds which fall, so that they shall not be wasted.

When gathered, the buds are spread out to dry in the sun whenever possible. Otherwise, as they must be dried rapidly, they are plunged into boiling water and afterwards exposed to smoke and heat until they take on a brownish colour. Those that are dried rapidly and completely in the sun are of better quality, and the best cloves are those which are plump, not unduly wrinkled, and of a purple-brown colour.

Young trees begin to bear about the fifth year, but it is not until the eighth year that a sizeable crop is obtained, after which the tree may go on bearing for another fifty years or more.

Immature cloves, either picked before they are ripe or beaten to the ground by wind and rain, are known as *khoker*. *Mother of Cloves* is the one-seeded drupe developed after fertilisation of the flower. The stalks which are pulled off when the fruit is dry are exported as "clove stems" and are used as a mordant for dyeing silks.

The essential Oil of Cloves, obtained by distillation, is colourless or pale yellow when fresh, darkening on exposure to the air. This oil, *Oleum Caryophylli*, is official in the British Pharmacopoeia and used in medicine as a carminative and antispasmodic. It is also used in the perfumery and cosmetics industry, and because of its high antiseptic value is sometimes used for flavouring toothpastes.

In former times it was customary to stick an orange all over with cloves, so as to make a pomander, which was supposed to be a preservative against infection. Parkinson notes: "Garcias * saith that the Portugall women distill the Cloves while they are fresh, which make a most sweet and delicate water, no lesse usefull for sent then profitable for all the passions of the heart."

CORIANDER *Coriandrum sativum* L. Umbelliferae
FR *Coriandre*; *Punaise mâle*
GER *Koriander*

Unlike most of the aromatic spices, Coriander, *Coriandrum sativum*, is sufficiently hardy to be grown easily in this country, where indeed it was once extensively cultivated, particularly in Essex, but most of our supplies now come from Holland and

* Garcia da Orta, author of a Portuguese herbal.

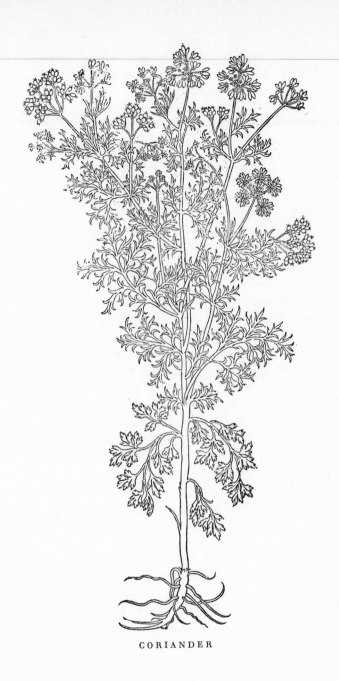

CORIANDER

the Mediterranean countries, though during the Second World War it was again planted as a commercial crop in East Anglia under Government contract.

Indigenous to the Mediterranean area and the Caucasus, Coriander is also extensively cultivated in Northern India, and it is repeatedly referred to in the old Egyptian and Sanskrit writings. The Romans are said to have introduced it into Britain.

All the plant, both leaves and seed, has a fetid and unpleasant smell when green; a smell which the ancients compared with that of bugs, hence the name, which derives from the Greek *koris*, a bug. But when dried, the thin outside layer of the pericarp drops off, and the seed, which is round, has an agreeable odour, becoming more pronounced when it is crushed, releasing the volatile oil coriandrol.

Gerard says that "the first or common kind of coriander is a very stinking herbe, smelling like the stinking worme called in Latin *cimex*". But the "well savoring seede", he adds, "easeth the squinancie". Albertus Magnus, in his work *De Virtutibus Herbarum*, includes Coriander among the ingredients of a love potion, and its use as an aphrodisiac is also referred to in the *Thousand and One Nights*. Also, in conjunction with fennel and other herbs, it was used by the magicians of old to make a kind of incense which, if burned, would, we are told, conjure up a legion of devils!

Christopher Wirzung, in his *Praxis Medicinae*, informs us that coriander "dryeth up the ascending vapors of the stomack it strengtheneth and drieth the braynes, it is good against all swimming of the head, and against the Palsie".

In the Orient Coriander is used as an ingredient of curries. In the West it is a component of mixed spices, employed for flavouring confectionery and also to mask the unpleasant taste of some medicines. In the British Pharmacopoeia *Oleum Coriandri*, which possesses stimulant and stomachic properties, is used in preparing Syrup of Senna. In France it enters into the composition of certain liqueurs and is used in the preparation of *Eau de mélisse*. In the 17th and 18th centuries Coriander was highly esteemed for the making of cordials and as a toilet water; it was also a constituent of the famous *Eau de Carmes*, invented in the pharmacy of the Carmelites in Paris in 1611.

The Coriander plant is an annual, growing to a height of between 1 and 3 feet, with pinnate leaves and small umbels of white or pale mauve flowers. The seed is round, brownish-yellow, and about one-fifth of an inch in diameter. It is easily grown on a medium soil in a warm and sunny position and should be harvested in August or September as soon as the seed is ripe. Young leaves for salads or soup flavourings can, however, be gathered as required.

Coriander was at one time endowed with remarkable properties, as this passage from *Lemnies Touchstone*, published in 1581, testifies:

The better to represse fumes and propulse vapours from the Brain, it shal be excellent good after Supper to chaw with the teeth (the mouth being shut) a few graines of Coriander first stieped in veneiger wherein Majoram hath been decocted and then thinly crusted or covered over with Sugar. It is scarce credible what a special commoditye this bringeth to ye memory.

CUBEBS   *Piper cubeba* L.   Piperaceae
Tailed Pepper
Java Pepper
FR *Cubèbes* ; *Poivre à queue*
GER *Kubeben*

Cubebs are the dried full-grown but still unripe fruits of *Piper Cubeba*, a climbing perennial pepper indigenous to Indonesia. The fruits are gathered while still green and dried in the sun until they become almost black in colour.

As met with in commerce Cubebs resemble black pepper-corns, but at the base of each fruit is a firmly attached stalk, from which they get the name of Tailed Pepper. The odour of the fruit is spicy and the taste aromatic though somewhat acrid, with a slight flavour of turpentine. It has none of the pungency of black Pepper. Fruits of similar appearance are occasionally substituted for Cubebs, but if the genuine fruit is crushed and some of the powder sprinkled on sulphuric acid it will impart to it a crimson colour.

During the Middle Ages the fruits seem to have been used in Europe as a spice or condiment, but nowadays Cubebs are used mainly as a drug, for use as a stimulant to the bronchial mucous membrane in chest ailments, and occasionally for the treatment of affections of the urinary tract.

Oleum Cubebae, British Pharmacopoeia, the oil distilled from the fruit is pale yellowish-green and consists of a mixture of terpenes. The tincture is one part in five of alcohol. Oil of Cubebs is often a constituent of cough lozenges.

FENUGREEK   *Trigonella Foenum-*   Papilionaceae
graecum L.

Greek Hayseed
FR *Fénugrec*; *Sénégrain*; *Trigonelle*
GER *Bockshornklee*; *Griechisches Heu*

Fenugreek seed is really a pulse, but is employed as a spice on account of its aroma. This spice is the seed of a plant of the peaflower tribe, an erect annual herb about 2 feet high, which grows around the Mediterranean basin and is extensively cultivated in North Africa, India and Pakistan. The pods containing the seeds are harvested when ripe, and after threshing the separated seeds are dried and packed.

One of the characteristic features of the plant, noted by Turner and other early herbalists, is the conspicuous horn-like pod containing the seed, very large for the size of the plant, which gave the plant its Greek name of *Keratitis*. Lyte, after Dodoens, says: "Fenugreeke hath tender stalkes, round, blackish, hollow, and full of branches; the leaves are divided

FENUGREEK

into three parts, like the leaves of Trefoyle, or three leaved grass: the floures be pale, whitish, and smaller than the floures of Lupines. After the fading of those floures there come up long cods or huskes, crooked and sharpe poynted, wherein is a yellow seede." These seeds, rhomboidal in shape, are small (some 2,500 of them to an ounce) and are marked with a deep furrow. Though they have a pleasant odour, reminiscent of celery or lovage, the taste is disagreeable when uncooked.

Soaked in water until they form a thick paste, these seeds are used in Egypt as a febrifuge, for which purpose they are said to be as good as quinine. More generally, the seeds, which are marketed either whole or ground, are used in the preparation of hot mango pickle and green mango chutney, and in the United States they are employed to make an artificial maple flavouring, used by confectioners.

At one time Fenugreek was commonly prescribed by veterinary surgeons for horses, and it is still used in some veterinary medicinal preparations as an appetiser and stomachic. The seeds contain a great deal of mucilage in their outer coating and at one time were used for emollient purposes and for poultices.

In regions bordering on the Mediterranean, Fenugreek is used as fodder, particularly for bovines, but since it imparts a rather unpleasant taste to their flesh, it is not fed to them for several weeks before slaughter.

GINGER   *Zingiber officinale* (Roscoe)   Scitamineae
FR *Gingembre*
GER *Ingwer*

> *Ruano*: Let us talk of ginger, which gives us a flavour on
> fish days.   GARCIA DA ORTA *Colloquies*

Ginger is the rhizome or underground stem of a herbaceous perennial plant, probably a native of the Pacific Islands, but now widely distributed in tropical countries. Although known in medicine as a stimulant and carminative it is used principally as a condiment. Ginger was one of the earliest Oriental spices known to Europeans, and it was certainly known to the Greeks and Romans, for Pliny quotes its price in the Roman market at 6 denarii per lb; but according to Ridley no one seems ever to have met with it in a wild state anywhere.

The Roman army doctor Dioscorides tells us (in Goodyer's edition) that "ginger is a private plant growing plentifully in Troglodyticall Arabia", the roots of which "have a warming concocting power, mollifying of the belly gently and good for the stomack". Marco Polo witnessed the cultivation of ginger during his travels in India and China between 1271 and 1292, but the first to give a description of the plant was John of Montecorvino, a missionary friar who visited India at the end of the 13th century.

Dioscorides also mentioned the fact that the preserved root of the plant was transported from the East to Italy "in earthen vessels fitt for meate", and we know from documentary evidence that three kinds of Ginger were classified by Italian merchants in the middle of the 14th century as *Baladi*, an Arabic name for common ginger; *Colombino*, referring to Columbum or Kolam, a port in Travancore; and *Micchino*, denoting that the spice had been brought by way of Mecca.

In England, Ginger seems to have been well known before the Conquest, for it is mentioned in the books of Anglo-Saxon leechdoms, and English recipes in which it figures are to be found in manuscripts of the 13th and 14th centuries. It appears to have been introduced into the New World by Francisco de Mendoza, who took it from the East Indies to New Spain, and to this day some of the finest Ginger is grown in the Caribbean area.

The Portuguese botanist Garcia da Orta, who lived in India for some years, wrote in his herbal,* published in 1563, "the green ginger is eaten in salad mixed with other herbs, oil,

* *Coloquios dos Simples e Drogas da India.*

vinegar and salt, and in pasties of fresh fish". In France it was already being extensively used during the 15th and 16th centuries for culinary purposes, for Pomet reports that "Ginger is very little used in Physick, but instead of that, great quantities of it are used by the hawkers and chandlers in the country, who mix it with Pepper; they reduce it to a powder, and then call it *White Spice*, which in France serves for several uses".

Gerard tried to grow Ginger in his garden at Holborn from plants brought to him from the West Indies, Barbary and other places, but without success, for, as he put it: "Ginger is most impatient of the coldnesse of these our Northerne regions". However, he claimed to reproduce in his herbal the first correct drawing of the plant, for, he wrote: "the true forme or picture hath not before this time been set forth by any that hath written, but the world hath beene deceived by a counterfeit figure."

Ginger is propagated by dividing the rhizomes into "fingers", each of which contains a bud from which a new plant develops. After the flowering is over, the rhizomes are dug up, washed, and then scraped to remove the bark-like outer layer, after which they are again washed and dried in the sun. The pieces are known commercially as "races" or "hands", the former being a very old term, "razes of ginger" being mentioned both in *A Winter's Tale* and *Henry IV, Part I*. This process, in which the epidermis is removed, gives the "uncoated" or "scraped" Ginger of commerce. When the wrinkled epidermis is left on, the ginger is termed "coated". Table or stem ginger, used as a dessert preserve, is made from the young runners of the rootstock preserved in syrup.

There are a great number of species of Ginger, those from Jamaica and Trinidad being considered the finest for flavour and aroma. Cochin Ginger is smaller and less aromatic, and African Ginger has still less aroma though it makes up for this in pungency. Jamaica and East India Ginger, uncoated, are for that reason sometimes called White Ginger. African and Cochin Ginger are coated and known as Black Ginger.

Ginger contains an aromatic, but non-pungent, volatile oil, together with resin and an extremely pungent liquid known as gingerol. Jamaican Ginger contains more of the aromatic principle but less of the pungent viscid liquid than most other gingers. Some gingers of inferior quality are bleached either by subjecting them to the fumes of burning sulphur or by a short immersion in a solution of chlorinated lime. In Jamaica it is the practice to classify ginger as yellow or blue according to the tint of the rootstock, the yellow being generally preferred. In China a mountain variety of ginger is used in making the succulent preserved ginger.

GINSENG   *Panax quinquefolius* L.   Araliaciae
                 Aralia quinquefolia

FR *Ginseng*; *Ninzin*; *Nindsin*

GER *Ginseng*

John Hill, in his History of the *Materia Medica* (1751), writes:

Ginseng is a root lately brought into Europe and extolled with immoderate Praises, but its great Price has prevented its hitherto coming into general Use. Ginseng is of very agreeable and aromatic Smell, though not very strong: its Taste is acrid and aromatic, and has somewhat bitter in it. . . . Before it is bought, it will be prudent to cut every Root through; for the Chinese, of whom we have it, are such expert Cheats, that they frequently find a Way to introduce Pieces of Lead into it to encrease the Weight.

The Chinese and Tartars collect the Roots of this Plant with infinite Pains in Spring and Autumn. They are forbid to touch them with any iron Instrument, so that they can only clean them with wooden Knives. They wash them in a decoction of Millet seed and afterwards hang them over the Fumes of the same Liquor. . . . It is famous in the East for giving Strength and Spirits to Persons who have disabled themselves by too free a Use of Women.

The Ginseng plant grows about a foot high, and the fruits, borne in clusters, are bright red when ripe. The roots, when fully developed, are spindle-shaped and sometimes forked. Native to China and Korea, Ginseng is also found, both wild and cultivated, in many parts of North America, from Quebec and Manitoba in the north to Alabama, Louisiana and Arkansas in the south.

The root is from one and a half to three inches long and more yellow than Senega root, for which it is sometimes substituted. In the course of years it has been used as a remedy for almost everything, and the Chinese, who use most of that which is grown, employ it as an aphrodisiac, as they did in Dr Hill's time, and as a cardiac, though without any scientific justification.

Ginseng has been exported from America since the early part of the 18th century and total annual export of Ginseng root from the U.S.A. totals about 100,000 lb.

NUTMEG *Myristica fragrans* Myristicaceae
FR *Noix de Muscade*
GER *Muskatnüsse*

> Nutmegs cause a sweete breth, and amend those that do
> stinke.   JOHN GERARD

Many of the spices used in olden times to render palatable the coarse and unsavoury food have long since declined in favour among European nations, but nutmegs, like cloves, persist in their popularity. The nutmeg is the dried seed kernel of *Myristica fragrans* – *Myristica* being a genus of evergreen aromatic trees of which upwards of a hundred species are known. But despite the considerable number of wild nutmeg trees that exist, one only contains sufficient of the aromatic principle myristicin to warrant extensive cultivation.

The Nutmeg tree is native to those eastern islands of the Moluccas known as the Spice Islands, and especially to the group known as the Banda Islands. It is now cultivated in

Malaya, throughout Indonesia, in western New Guinea, and, since its introduction into Grenada in 1843, also in parts of the West Indies.

It is a tall and bushy tree, growing to heights of between 30 and 50 feet, with shiny, dark green foliage. The fruits, when ripe, are oval, pale orange-yellow, and smooth, with a groove running down one side, and measure between two and two-and-a-half inches in length. When fully mature the fruits split almost in half along the groove, the parted husk affording a glimpse of the seed, the nutmeg of commerce, the deep brown and shining seedcoat of which is enclosed by a reticulated crimson arillus, or sheath, which, when dried, is termed mace. This *Myristicae aryllus*, or mace, is the French *macis* and German *Muskatblüten*.

A nutmeg tree in full bearing should give from 1,500 to 2,000 nuts in a year, but it does not reach its highest bearing capacity until about twenty years old, though beginning to yield at about six or seven years. When the fruits ripen they are collected and the husks, or pericarp, removed. The mace is carefully separated, flattened and dried, after which it is stored in darkness for several months until its crimson hue fades to a pale orange or cream, and then it is packed in cases ready for sale.

The nuts themselves are first air-dried and then sun-dried, until the kernels are fully cured, when they can be heard to rattle in their shells. The shells are left on until the kernels are packed for shipment so as to preserve them from the attacks of insects, and after the shells have been carefully broken and the kernels extracted they are sometimes dusted over with slaked lime for the same reason. For export the nutmegs are usually graded as 64's, 80's, 100's, etc., the numbers indicating the count per lb.

These two articles, nutmeg and mace, constitute the spices which for centuries have been in great demand throughout Europe and Asia, although strangely enough, as Crawford has pointed out, never used as a condiment by the inhabitants of the countries that produce them.

Pomet's advice for choosing the nut still holds good. He writes: "As to the common Nutmegs, we ought to chuse such as are heavy, firm, hard, and of a full Plumpness, of a light grey, whose Outside is finely marbled, and the Inside reddish, being of a fat, oily Body, which are the Signs of their Newness."

The nutmeg yields an essential and a fixed oil, the former being obtained by distillation and the latter, termed "nutmeg butter", by expression from the powdered nuts, which are steamed and pressed while hot. The essential oil is used medicinally as a stimulant and stomachic, and for masking the taste of some of the more nauseating medicines. It is also largely used in perfumery.

The old herbalists credited the Nutmeg with virtues that appear somewhat exaggerated today. Thus Salmon, in his *Family Dictionary* (1696), says: "Nutmegs are somewhat Astringent and Stomachick, Cephalick and Uterine; help Concoction, discuss Wind, take away the offensive Fumes of a strong Breath, are good in the Palpitations of the Heart, and prevent Faintings, lessen the Spleen, and stop Looseness and Vomiting, provoke Urine, and quicken the Sight; are of great use in Fluxes, especially the Bloody-flux, having all the Virtues necessary for a Medicine fit for these diseases."

Of Mace, the very early compilation known as *Banckes' Herbal* has this to say: "To cleanse the brain of superfluous humours, take a quantity of maces and chew them well in thy mouth, and hold them there awhile, and that shall loose the fumosity of humours that rise up to the brain, and purge the superfluity of it." That popular error, I fancy, comes originally from Platearius.

> I speak severely to my boy,
> I beat him when he sneezes;
> For he can thoroughly enjoy
> The pepper when he pleases.
> *Alice in Wonderland*

True peppers belong to the genus *Piper* (N.O. Piperaceae). So-called Cayenne Pepper is made from fruit of the genus *Capsicum* (q.v.) and among other spices to which the name pepper is given are Jamaica Pepper (see Allspice) and Melegueta Pepper, or Guinea Pepper, otherwise known as Grains of Paradise (*Amomum melegueta*).

By far the most important member of the genus *Piper* is the black pepper (*P. nigrum*), the pepper of commerce, a perennial climbing plant native to the forests of Travancore and Malabar, and now extensively cultivated in the Philippines, Malaya, Thailand, Indonesia and the West Indies.

Pepper is a product of nature which exercised a profound effect upon the world of commerce for many centuries and formed one of the earliest articles of Indo-European trade of which it formed a staple commodity. It is frequently mentioned by the old Sanskrit medical writers, and in the 4th century BC by the botanist-philosopher Theophrastus, who mentions both black pepper and long pepper. White pepper is first mentioned by Dioscorides, in whose time and for long afterwards it was generally supposed that white and black pepper came from different plants.

It does not appear that the Greeks made much use of pepper as a condiment, but it was apparently common in ancient Rome. Pliny describes it minutely and it is often mentioned by Roman writers of the Augustan age. Horace, in one of his letters*, begs that he shall not be celebrated in ill-favoured verse and "be conveyed into the street where are sold frankincense, and spices, and pepper, and whatever is wrapped up in foolish writings". It is related that Alaric demanded from Rome as part of the city's ransom 3,000 lb of pepper, and after the conquest of Caesarea by the Genoese in 1101 AD each soldier was rewarded with 2 lb of pepper as part of his booty.

Possibly the earliest reference to the pepper trade in England is in the statutes of Ethelred (978–1016), wherein it was enacted that the Esterlings bringing their ships to Billingsgate should pay at Christmas and Easter, together with other tribute, 10 lb of pepper. Throughout the Middle Ages the payment of a pepper rent for land held in socage was exceedingly common and this obligation of a tenant to supply his lord with a fixed quantity of pepper (usually a pound) seems to indicate that the demand for this commodity was at all times great on the part of the wealthy classes. Although the term "a peppercorn rent" has survived to this day, it now has the meaning of a merely nominal payment, whereas at the prices prevailing for pepper in the Middle Ages it must have been a considerable imposition.

In England a Guild of Pepperers was in existence at a very early date, being mentioned in 1180 as one of the eighteen guilds fined for not having sought a royal licence. In 1345 the guild was entirely reorganised and a new fraternity formed by twenty-one pepperers of Sopers Lane, near the Guildhall. Pepper was, indeed, one of the most profitable articles of commerce during the Middle Ages, but its high price put it beyond the reach of the poorer classes.

The pepper fruits or berries are borne on long racemes in bunches and in the early days of the trade it seems as though pepper was often imported in bunches as it grew, for Walter Bailey, in *A Short Discourse of the three kindes of Peppers*,

* *Epistolarum Liber II. Epistola I. Ad Augustum.*

published in 1588, writes: "I have often seene at Poole, in Dorsetshire, and also in London, the whole clusters of pepper preserved in brine and in salt."

In former days pepper was much used for medicinal purposes, especially in the form of a decoction known to the physicians as *Diatrion Piperion,* the ingredients of which were White Pepper, Black Pepper, Long Pepper, Thyme, Ginger and Aniseed, pounded and boiled in a solution of sugar in Hyssop water. This remedy had great virtues according to *The Widdowes Treasure* (1595), which gives a recipe for making the best *Diatrion Piperion* and adds:

> This decoction is good to eate
> alwaies before and after meate.
> For it will make digestion good,
> and turne your meate to pure blood.
> Besides all this it doth excell
> all windines to expell;
> And all groce humors colde and rawe
> that are in belly, stomacke or mawe,
> It will dissolve without paine,
> and keep ill vapors from the braine.
> Besides all this it will restore
> your memory though lost before.
> Use it therefore when you please,
> for therein resteth mightie ease.

In the *Grete Herball* of 1529 we read of Pepper that "Powder thereof put in the nose causeth to snese and to clense the brayn of flewmatyke humours as snyvell and rewme".

Black pepper is an aromatic carminative, stimulant and mild febrifuge, but its use in the western world today is mainly as a condiment. It is employed most extensively in the sausage-making and meat-preserving industries, and from the commercial point of view its use in the household is of secondary importance.

Marco Polo was the first European traveller to describe India from actual experience and show how the cultivation of pepper was spread over several kingdoms along the coast, but until the Portuguese navigators had opened up the sea-route to India much legendary lore accumulated around the pepper tree, as exemplified in this extract from the famous 14th-century work by Friar Bartholomew, *De Proprietatibus Rerum*:

Pepper [he writes] is the seed or the fruit of a tree that groweth in the south side of the hill Caucasus, in the strong heat of the sun. And serpents keep the woods that peppers groweth in. And when the woods of pepper are ripe, men of that country set them on fire and chase away the serpents by violence of fire. And by such burning the grain of pepper that was white by kind, is made black and rively.

Pepper is the dried, unripe fruit of *Piper nigrum*. This plant is a climber, and needs support for its cord-like stems while it is growing. For this purpose, on the plantations other trees, such as betel nut, palm or mango, are used in preference to any form of artificial support.

Sir John Mandeville, not always a reliable authority, is correct in this when he tells us that "the Pepper groweth in manner as doth a wylde Vyne, that is planted faste by the Trees of that Wode, for to susteynen it by, as doth the Vyne". If left to trail along the ground the plant would root at every joint and produce very little fruit. The pepper tree begins to bear in its third year; the branches are then cut at a certain height and bent horizontally to concentrate their sap. The plant remains in full bearing until about the ninth or tenth year, after which it is worthless commercially.

The berries are borne in clusters on long racemes, and receive different treatment according to whether black or white pepper is wanted. For black pepper the berries are gathered when they are just turning red, before they are completely ripe. They are left in heaps for a few days to ferment and then spread out on mats to dry in the sun. The berries must be dried rapidly, to prevent formation of mould, and have to be constantly turned. As they dry the berries gradually turn black and the skin and part of the pulp adhere in the form of a black, reticulated covering to the seeds.

In the preparation of white pepper the berries are allowed to ripen more than for black pepper. When gathered, they are put in large sacks and left to soak for about a week, preferably in running water, until the pericarp and pulp have become soft and loose, and can be easily detached from the seed, which forms the white pepper of commerce.

Black pepper is stronger and more aromatic than white since part of the spice's pungency resides in the pericarp or skin. For many centuries the grinding of pepper was performed with pestle and mortar, but today, of course, ground pepper is mechanically milled, and it is usually a blend, for not all white pepper is produced in the manner just described. Sometimes a trader will select a particularly bold growth of black pepper and mill off the outer covering in a decorticating machine, a process which gives a white pepper of excellent colour. But since the grinding off of the husks results in considerable loss of weight, this white pepper is naturally rather more expensive.

The pungent taste of pepper is due to the active principles it contains – a volatile oil, piperine and resin. From the piperine is obtained heliotropin, used in perfumery.

There are many varieties of pepper, the best of which are perhaps the Balamcotta pepper from Tellichery, and Alleppey, both of which are produced on the Malabar coast of southern India, which in the early days of the pepper trade had almost a monopoly. Gradually, however, more and more pepper was cultivated in Malaya and what is now Indonesia and even further east, until India's former pre-eminence was overshadowed. Lampong is a generic name denoting the black pepper from the various parts of Indonesia, and from those islands, too, comes the imported white pepper known as White Muntock. Saigon pepper is also a general term for pepper which comes from Vietnam and the surrounding countries. Mangalore is a very bold Indian growth, deep black in colour, but demand exceeds supply. The flavour is excellent. The best pepper is not necessarily the strongest – strength should be allied to aroma.

LONG PEPPER (FR *Poivre long*. GER *Langer Pfeffer*)

Long pepper, extensively used for flavouring pickles, is the fruit spike of either *Piper longum*, native to India, or *P. officinarum*, indigenous to Indonesia. It is from the Hindustani name for the Long Pepper, *pipat*, that our word "pepper" comes. *P. officinarum* has larger leaves and greater pungency than *P. longum*.

Both varieties are related to the common pepper of commerce, but Long Pepper is a creeping as opposed to a climbing vine, and bears erect fruiting branches about an inch or so in length. The spikes are harvested when fully grown but while still unripe, for if left to mature, most of the pungency is lost. After gathering, the catkins of berries are sun-dried, or oven-dried, without delay to prevent formation of mould.

Long Pepper, used in the East in native medicines as well as in curries, was known in Europe many centuries ago, and Saladinus of Ascoli, a noted physician of the 14th century, lists *P. longum* among the drugs which should always be kept in stock by apothecaries.

TURMERIC   *Curcuma longa* L.   Scitamineae
FR *Curcuma*; *Souchet des Indes*
GER *Gelbwurzel*

Turmeric is an underground stem or root allied to the Ginger family. These rootstocks, thick, scaly, and ringed, are of a grey or yellowish colour outside and a deep orange, sometimes almost red, inside. It has but slight aroma and is of value chiefly on account of the abundance of its yellow colouring principle, which is used to colour mixed pickles and curry powder, and, in the Orient, sweetmeats. In China it is now employed more as a dye-stuff than as a spice.

India is one of the largest consumers of Turmeric and vast quantities go into the making of curries. The greater part of the Turmeric sold commercially comes from Madras and Bengal.

In the Middle Ages Turmeric was known as *Crocus Indicus*, or Indian Saffron, by which name the Portuguese botanist Garcia da Orta mentions it. When the root was first introduced into Europe it appears to have been used almost exclusively as a dye, for Pomet writes: "This root is chiefly used by the Dyers, Glovers and Perfumers. The Founders employ it to tinge their Metals, and the Button-makers to rub their Wood with, when they would make an imitation of Gold."

Medicinally Turmeric is said to be tonic, diuretic and anti-scorbutic. Marsden, in his *History of Sumatra*, informs us that the natives made use of a mixture of Turmeric and rice, powdered and made into a paste, which they applied externally in cases of colds and pains in the bones.

Propagation of the plant is carried out by division of the rhizomes, as in the case of Ginger, and after harvesting the roots are washed, heated in earthenware pots and then dried in the sun for a week or more. The rootstock alone is of commercial value, but the plant itself grows to a height of 2 or 3 feet, and bears long lanceolate leaves in tufts of from six to ten. Its white or yellowish flowers are borne in scaly, conical spikes.

The chief varieties of Turmeric met with in commerce are the Chinese, Javanese, and those of Madras, Bengal and Indo-China. Very similar to Turmeric is Zedoary, the rhizome of *Curcuma Zedoaria*, also of the Ginger family, which was once widely used as a spice but now used only by the Indonesians in curry powder. Its odour, taste and properties are rather similar to those of ginger.

VANILLA   *Vanilla planifolia*   Orchidaceae
FR *Vanille*
GER *Vanille*

Vanilla is the pod or siliqua of a climbing orchid. Two species of the plant provide the Vanilla of commerce: *V. planifolia*, the true Mexican Vanilla, and *V. pompona*, a West Indian Vanilla with shorter and thicker pods. The first named, indigenous to the *Tierra caliente* of eastern Mexico, and found in British Honduras, Costa Rica and Guatemala, is the most extensively cultivated species, and is now grown in all parts of the tropics including the Seychelles, Réunion, Mauritius, Java, Tahiti and the Fiji Islands.

The ripe pods are cylindrical, fleshy capsules, about six inches long and a quarter inch thick, and are quite odourless, for they do not develop their pleasant aroma until fermentation occurs during the curing process. The vanilla pods are gathered before complete maturity, or otherwise they will split open and allow the balsamic juice they contain to run out.

During the curing process the pods, in their natural state yellow, gradually change colour until they become a dark chocolate brown. At the same time the pod, as it dries, tends to split into two. The preparation of Vanilla is long and thorough, and different methods are employed in different countries. In Mexico the pods, after harvesting, are heaped up in drying sheds, where, after a few days, they begin to shrivel. They are then "sweated". First, they are spread on blankets in the sun for a full morning, and at midday the blankets are folded over the pods, which are left to sweat. At night the Vanilla pods are put into air-tight boxes to continue this sweating. This process is repeated until the pods are properly cured. In the absence of sun, oven-heating is resorted to.

In Guiana the pods are placed in hot ashes. In Peru they are put in baskets and dipped into boiling water for a few seconds, being afterwards hung out in the sun to dry. In Réunion the pods are heated in stoves at a moderate temperature and afterwards wrapped in oiled coverings to preserve and activate the production of the aroma.

When cured and perfectly dry, the pods are packed in tins lined with paraffin wax or prepared paper. Vanilla is classified according to the country of origin, and the product of each country is graded for size and quality. The finest quality Vanilla should have long, plump pods of a rich chocolate colour, well frosted with crystals of vanillin, the odorous principle of the bean. Mexican Vanilla is the most highly esteemed on account of its delicate perfume, followed by the so-called Bourbon Vanilla, the product of the French island of Réunion and of Madagascar. Seychelles Vanilla is very similar.

Vanilla was used by the Aztecs for flavouring chocolate long before the discovery of America by Europeans, and its use was soon adopted by the Spaniards. It was brought by them to Europe about the year 1510, and was first described, under the name of *Araco aromatico* by Hernandez in his *Rerum medicarum Novae Hispaniae Thesaurus*, published in 1651. In the time of Pomet, who published his history of drugs in 1694, Vanilla was imported into Europe by way of Spain, and was much used in France for flavouring chocolate and scenting tobacco.

The tree is a true orchid, and like many other species of orchid it is a climbing vine which puts out twining aerial roots ; by means of these it attaches itself to the bark of trees, from which it derives nourishment as well as from the soil. The large, greenish flowers have no scent. The fertilisation of the flowers, which is performed by birds and insects in the case of the wild Vanilla, is done by hand for the cultivated species, and only the best flowers are pollinated. After pollination the pods develop quickly, but require many months to ripen. A vanilla plant in full bearing may put out as many as two hundred racemes of flowers, but on commercial plantations a maximum of ten flowers out of fifteen to twenty on each raceme are pollinated.

Vanilla owes its delightful perfume to the vanillin found in a crystalline state inside and on the surface of the bean. Artificial vanillin can be made synthetically from eugenol, found in oil of cloves.

HERBS & HERBALS

THE WORD *HERB*, DERIVED FROM THE LATIN *HERBA*, GRASS
or herbage, was formerly used in a much wider sense than it is
now, and was applied to all green crops. By "herb" we mean
nowadays a plant of which some part or all is used either for
food, for medicinal purposes, for flavouring, or for its smell.
The smell may serve more than one purpose: it may be a sweet
fragrance to perfume the surrounding air or objects with
which the herb is placed in contact (i.e. Lavender); or it may
be an odour repellent to insect life, like that of Southernwood,
which is considered so efficacious in keeping away moths that
the French call it *Garde-robes*.

Man's earliest interest in plant life was almost certainly the
essentially practical one of finding food, and he must soon
have found out by trial and error, though probably not
without occasional tragic results, those plants which could be
eaten without harm; and at a very early stage he had already
found out that certain plants which are toxic in their natural
state can be made innocuous by cooking. Empirical research of
this nature, allied to intuition, soon taught him also that
various sicknesses and injuries could be cured by the consumption or application of certain plants. Those who were excep-
tionally observant in such matters became medicine-men and
magicians.

In that dawn of civilisation, man was not yet aware of the
manner in which certain plants afforded relief to pain or
healed wounds, and so to these were attributed supernatural
powers, a belief not yet entirely extinct. A natural presump-
tion of early man that everything in nature was intimately
connected by mysterious and magical laws led to a selection
and preparation of herbal remedies by a primitive system of
astrological botany which never entirely died out until the late
18th century.

The use of certain plants for relieving distress or illness is
probably much older than any civilisation of which we have
records. In India there seems to have been a very ancient

system of medicine, for in the Rig Veda of the Brahmans, compiled some thousands of years BC, there are references to the use of medicinal plants; and there are likewise many references in ancient Egyptian papyri. In China, too, there is a long tradition of medical knowledge, and some say that the earliest herbal was written by an ancient emperor named Chin Nong, who ruled about 2700 BC.

Of Egyptian medicine we know a good deal from the various papyri which have survived the many intervening centuries, and these show that of the many varieties of medicine prescribed, most were decoctions of herbs. The first doctor whose name has come down to us was Ymhetep the physician to Zoser, a king of the 3rd dynasty, who reigned about 2980 BC, and was himself called the Medicine King from his wide knowledge of that science; a knowledge he had most probably acquired from Ymhetep, who was also renowned as a magician and astrologer. In fact, as W. R. Dawson has pointed out,* the medical papyri of the ancient Egyptians are really magical documents and the true medical elements in them are later interpolations.

Although we have evidence of herbal knowledge extending far back into antiquity, it is not until we reach the times of classical Greece that we find the origins of a herbal tradition of which we are the legatees. First, though, we must thread our way carefully through the intricate maze of the Greek mythology, according to which Chiron, the centaur, son of Cronos and Philyra, was the originator of pharmacy. He was, says Pliny, "the first herborist and apothecarie, renowned for the knowledge of simples and composition of medicine".

When we leave this realm of legend, so fascinating yet so exasperating because the myths and realities are so interwoven as to defy separation, we meet Hippocrates, one of the great minds of all time, who is justly called the Father of Medicine, for it is from his time, and as a result of his observations and

* *Studies in Medical History.*

treatises, that the real history of medicine and of pharmacy may be said to have begun. There had been in Greece, long before Hippocrates was born on the island of Cos about 460 BC, a lengthy history of medical teaching and practice; ever since the establishment at Epidaurus and elsewhere of temples founded in honour of Asklepios (Æsculapius) the benefactor of mankind and Olympian God of Healing. But Hippocrates was among the first who attempted to dissociate medicine from the supernatural. "His recognition of disease as a natural phenomenon", writes La Wall, "and his practice of diagnosis and prognosis as we understand them now, entitle him to be recognised as the Father of Medicine." He knew the value of herbs, for in his writings he names about 400 simples for their medicinal value. Strangely enough they were never listed until comparatively recently and the first Greek herbal of which we have record, though unfortunately it has not survived, was compiled by an Athenian physician named Diocles of Carystus who practised during the first half of the 4th century BC.

Throughout this period there were two classes of people who followed a regular calling of gathering, preparing and selling drugs; they were called respectively rhizotomists (root gatherers) and pharmacopolists (drug sellers). The former gathered roots and herbs used for remedies, and the latter sold drugs* and other medicinal substances at their stalls in the market-place. These rhizotomists were for the most part ignorant and superstitious folk, though there were exceptions, as we know from Theophrastus, one of the first botanists, who singled out for praise one Thrasyas Mantinensis, and a certain Cleidemus, who investigated the diseases of plants.

The rhizotomists were so called because they gathered mainly roots, since it was believed that the curative properties of

---

* Our word "drug", though of uncertain etymology, may have come from the Anglo-Saxon *drygean*, dry, thus indicating the dried herb. It was certainly used for herbal simples long before the use of mineral and chemical substances in medicine.

perennial plants were concentrated during the winter months in their underground system. Being in the main superstitious and unlettered, they usually followed a complex ritual in the pursuit of their calling, gathering their roots only at certain favourable hours of the day or night, to the accompaniment of prayers and incantations. Root-gatherers continued to ply their calling for many centuries, and there are many references right up to the time of the Renaissance to those who made it their business to search the meadows and woodlands for roots and herbs which they sold to apothecaries.

Theophrastus of Eresus, in Lesbos, philosopher and friend of Aristotle, who lived between about 370 and 287 BC, wrote upon a variety of subjects, and among those of his writings which have come down to us are two treatises of the natural history of plants which give him an assured place in the history of botany. Out of some five hundred species and varieties of which he treats practically all are cultivated plants, and he tells us that in his day the wild plants of woods and mountains were for the most part unknown and unnamed. He was the first man to try to set down some real system of plants and the eminent botanist and scholar Albert Haller called him "the first of the real botanists".

In the 2nd century BC the Greek didactic poet Nikandros of Colophon (Nicander) wrote a treatise on poisons and their antidotes (mostly vegetable) which he entitled *Alexipharmaca*; although it was printed and had a measure of popularity during the Renaissance, as a scientific work it is almost valueless. Nicander was followed in the 1st century BC by Cratevas, a rhizotomist of more intelligence than most, who not only collected, but also drew plants; and as some copies of his drawings have come down to us, he may perhaps be regarded with some justification as the father of the herbal.

In assessing the contribution of Rome to the study of plants it is impossible to avoid mentioning the work of the elder Pliny, whose immense industry and curiosity expressed itself in a vast number of works, many since lost, on a wide variety of subjects. His greatest surviving achievement is the *Natural History* in 37 volumes, dedicated in AD 77 to the future Emperor Titus. Seven of these volumes are devoted to the medical properties of plants, but although they contain much information, expressive of the current views on the nature and uses of plants, their author was too gullible and too superficial for his work to have any great scientific value. Pliny was apt to put down every fact he came across without verification and with complete absence of critical insight. Nevertheless, so popular were the works of Pliny that for many centuries afterwards his *Natural History* was plundered mercilessly.

Dr Singer writes of him: "Read throughout the ages, copied and re-copied, a large part of Pliny's work has gradually passed into folk-keeping, so that through his agency the fortune-teller of today is still reciting garbled versions of the formulae that Pliny himself took from the works of Aristotle and Hippocrates written two-and-a-half millennia ago."*

Even more influential down the ages was the *Materia Medica* of the Greek physician Dioscorides, who served as a doctor with the Roman army and wrote his celebrated work during the reign of Nero. For more than sixteen centuries Dioscorides was regarded as one of the chief authorities on medical botany, and his treatise on some 600 plants and their medical uses formed the main source of the herbals written after his time. Latin translations of his work, often illustrated, were used in the early medical schools, and the first printed edition, in Greek, was published by Aldo Manuzio in Venice in 1499. Scores of Latin editions of his work were printed during the period of the Renaissance and he was soon translated into many European tongues. Yet strangely enough there was no printed edition in English until 1933, when the manuscript version made by the Petersfield botanist John

* *From Magic to Science.*

Goodyer about 1655 was edited and printed by Robert T. Gunther.

So popular was this *Materia Medica* of Dioscorides that the work was extensively copied in manuscript before the days of printing and a number of Latin versions were produced during the Middle Ages. Some followed the Greek text fairly closely; others were modified by additions and alterations. One of the most famous of these manuscript versions, now in Vienna, and known as the *Codex Aniciae Julianae*, is said to have been copied for the daughter of Anicius Olybrius, Emperor of the West, 512 AD.

From the time of Dioscorides until the invention of printing in the middle of the 15th century there were numerous manuscript herbals in circulation among the ancient medical schools, ranging from small volumes devoted to a few of the more familiar plants to enormous tomes like the *Pandectae* of Matthaeus Silvaticus (c. 1300).* Some again formed portions of encyclopaedias, as, for instance, the botanical section of Vincent de Beauvais' *Speculum Naturae*, which was written about the middle of the 13th century. Both these writers borrowed freely from other sources, in particular from the Arabian physician Avicenna, who died in 1037.

After Dioscorides, probably the earliest extant herbal containing plant illustrations is that of Apuleius, an author of whom nothing is known, and who has no connection, it would seem, with that famous Lucius Apuleius who wrote the *Golden Ass*. The great drawback of these manuscript herbals was that not only did the text become corrupted by errors in transmission as the book was copied by scribe after scribe, but also the figures of plants, when there were any, were often so crudely drawn that they could hardly have afforded any means of recognition. "The copying of figures from hand to hand," writes Dr Singer, "century after century, gave rise to traditions of plant illustration, and these soon became so heavily stylized that

* First printed Mantua, folio, 1474. 354 leaves in double columns.

although often remarkable technically, they cease to become recognizable as plants."

Our Anglo-Saxon ancestors made a great study of herbs, and seem to have had a remarkable knowledge of plants, for we are told that the surviving records indicate that they knew at least five hundred kinds. Dr J. F. Payne went so far as to say that the Anglo-Saxons had a much wider knowledge of herbs than the doctors of Salerno, the oldest school of medicine in Europe. But though the various Anglo-Saxon manuscripts which have survived are of great interest as being the first vernacular treatises of their kind, they failed to escape the paralysing tradition of Pliny and Dioscorides. The oldest Saxon manuscript is the *Leech Book of Bald*, written by the scribe Cild some time between the years 900 and 950 AD. Another interesting work, full of strange folk-lore, is the Lacnunga, a 10th-century manuscript containing an alliterative lay in Wessex dialect in praise of nine sacred herbs. From books such as these we find that ritual and magic still played as important a part with the herbalist as it had done in early Egypt, and the use of herbs as amulets to cure diseases was common practice among our Saxon ancestors – a practice, it must be confessed, which has not entirely disappeared in our own time.

With the arrival of the Norman conquerors the old Anglo-Saxon writings fell into disrepute, and probably a large number of Saxon manuscripts were destroyed. During the early part of the Middle Ages most of the herbal manuscripts in use were transcriptions of Macer's Herbal, the immense popularity of which, from the 10th century onwards, is testified by the numerous versions issued both in manuscript and in print. This work is a poem in Latin hexameters on the virtues of seventy-seven herbs, whose authorship cannot be traced with any certainty though it owes its name to one Æmilius Macer, whose herb lore is mentioned by Ovid. It has been attributed to Odo of Meung and to Hugo of Tours among others. The name of the first translator of Macer into English, in the 12th century, is lost to us; but there is an English translation of one of the many versions, by a schoolmaster of Hereford named John Lelamour in the British Museum, dated 1373 (Sloane MS No. 5).

During the Middle Ages the olitory, or herb garden, was an important part of horticulture. That herb gardens existed in Anglo-Saxon times is very probable, but no descriptions of them have come down to us. There was certainly nothing in England at the time comparable with the physic garden which existed at St Gall, in Switzerland, as early as the 9th century. This is clear from a plan still extant in the library of the Benedictine monastery at St Gall, and which was made by a monk of that Order between 820 and 830 AD. It shows that the monastery possessed both a Herbularius, or Physic Garden, planted with sixteen kinds of herbs useful for medical purposes, among which were cumin, lovage, fennel, tansy, sage, rue, penny-royal, fenugreek, peppermint and rosemary; and a Kitchen Garden comprising a number of long, narrow beds, each planted with a different species of pot-herb.

In fact, during the Middle Ages the monks were the chief horticulturists, their calling giving them security from interference in troubled times, and their intercourse with other Houses on the Continent increasing their knowledge of herbs, both culinary and medical. At times, and in some places, the monks would be the only persons with a knowledge of medicine and pharmacy, and the Farmery, as the infirmary was then called, received not only the ill and weak among the brethren of the Order, but the sick who could not be cared for in their homes. At Barnwell it was a standing rule that the *infirmarius*, or Master of the Farmery, should always have "ginger, cinnamon, penny and the like, ready in his cupboard, so as to be able to render prompt assistance to the sick if stricken by a sudden malady". Those among the monks who were apt studied the rudiments of medicine, and the Norman drawing of

86 *Herbs*

Christ Church, Canterbury, shews a *herbularius* in the garth of the infirmary cloister.

One of the most important writers on husbandry during the Middle Ages was Petrus de Crescentiis (Crescenzi), a native of Bologna, who wrote his *Opus Ruralium Commodorum* towards the end of the 13th century. The work, divided into twelve parts, is based on the works of ancient Roman agronomists such as Cato, Varro and Columella, supplemented by the author's own observations, and Meyer, in his *History of Botany*, categorically states that as a writer on agriculture there is not found anyone of equal merit several centuries before and after his time. In Part VI he deals with gardens and plants, describing some 120 plants of medicinal or culinary value. Of the herb garden he says: "it should be planted with fragrant herbs of all kinds, such as Rue, Sage, Basil, Marjoram, Mint and the like. . . . Behind the turf plot let there be a great diversity of medicinal and aromatic herbs, among which Rue should be mingled in many places for its beauty and greenness, and its bitterness will drive away poisonous animals from the garden."

One of the earliest English writers on gardens was Alexander Neckam (1157–1217), an Augustinian monk educated in the abbey of St Albans, who completed his studies at Paris and eventually became abbot of Cirencester. His book *De Naturis Rerum*, although mainly a compilation from ancient writers, does describe some of the herbs and flowers which were cultivated in the gardens of his day. Similar evidence of plants actually to be found in an English garden of the Middle Ages is given in a unique manuscript of *The Feate of Gardening*, c. 1440, (in Trinity College, Cambridge) in which the author, "Mayster Ion Gardener" gives practical instructions for the "sowing and settyng of Wurtys and of other maner Herbys".

A document of exceptional importance in the history of gardening is the celebrated *Capitulare de Villis*, thought until recently to have been drawn up by Charlemagne about the year 800, but now known to have been drafted by his son, Louis the Pious, probably in 795.* It gives detailed directions for the administration of the royal domains in Aquitaine and the south of France, and was probably transmitted to the king's agents.

From the many chapters into which this particular Capitulary is divided, Chapter 70 gives a number of rules to be observed in the care of orchards and enumerates the trees and plants to be cultivated – mostly fruit trees and medicinal herbs, together with a few ornamental plants. The section begins: *Volumus quod in horto omnes herbas habeant, id est . . .* (We require that all the following plants shall be planted in the garden, namely . . .)

In this list figure a great many medicinal herbs, and later on it was with the help of this list that many herbs were also planted by monks in their physic gardens or cloister garth. It should not be forgotten that at this time almost all knowledge – that of botany included – was, as a rule, in the possession of the clergy. From such monastery gardens in the course of time these herbs of healing made their way into secular gardens, where they served as home remedies for common ailments. Meanwhile the various herbals constituted a form of manual.

From the 8th until the 12th century a strong new influence made itself felt in the world of medicine. Following the era of Mohammedan conquests, the Caliphs founded a number of great universities from west to east of their new empire; from Cordoba, by way of Cairo, to Basra and Bagdad. For a considerable time the Arab world became pre-eminent in science and philosophy, and at a time when in Europe the practice of medicine was at a low ebb and quacks and charlatans abounded, the Arabs were developing a real science of medicine. Several

* Capitularies were a series of legislative or administrative acts emanating from the Merovingian and Carolingian kings. They were so called because they were divided into chapters (*capitula*). A list of the herbs included in this *Capitulare de Villis* is given in the Appendix, page 261.

Arab physicians became famous, among them Avicenna (Ibn Sina), born in 980 at Bokhara, in Turkestan, who was known as "The Prince of Doctors".

After the annexation of Sicily by the Moors there grew upon both sides of the Straits of Messina an organised society half Western and half Oriental which embodied the flower of civilisation at that time. A great school of medicine was established at Salerno, about thirty miles south of Naples, which became a meeting-place for both Italian and Saracen students where mingled the various currents of medical thought. The actual date of its foundation is not known, but it reached its apogee in the 13th century under the patronage of one of the cleverest men of his age, Frederick II, King of Sicily and Naples, and Salerno rapidly acquired the name of Civitas Hippocratica.

From this *Schola Salernitana* came several influential medical manuals, one of the most famous of which was the *Liber de simplici medicina*, a herbal compiled by Matthaeus Platearius,* a doctor of the Salerno school who flourished around the middle of the 12th century, and must not be confused with the earlier Johannes Platearius, the presumed author of a medical handbook *Practica brevis*. The book of Matthaeus, usually referred to as *Circa instans* from its opening words, was made up from old Latin sources with the addition of new material gathered from the Arabs, and had considerable influence during the Middle Ages. There are manuscript versions of this work in most of the great libraries, all of which present numerous variants as well as additions and interpolations. It was first printed at Ferrara in 1488, together with the *Practica* of Serapion. The second printed version was published, in French, at Besançon about 1490, and is excessively rare, for there is no copy in either the British Museum or the Bodleian Library, nor in America. This French version was called

---

* De Renzi (*Collectio Salernitana*) believes there were at least six doctors of the name of Platearius.

Arbolayre, the title being changed in subsequent editions to *Le Grant Herbier*. *Circa instans* is a treatise in 276 short chapters of materia medica, of therapeutics, and of the adulteration of drugs, in which one comes across a number of pharmaceutical formulae. In the main it deals with the uses of medicinal plants.

Another work which presumably had its origin at Salerno was the *Regimen Sanitatis Salerno*, one of the most popular medical works ever written, which was translated into almost every European and some Asian languages and was published in scores of editions. Its author is not known, but it is thought likely that most, if not all, of it was put together by the Catalan astrologo-physician Arnold of Villa Nova who was for a time at Salerno. The work was translated into very racy English by Sir John Harington, under the title of *The Englishman's Doctor, or the Schoole of Salerne*, and published in 1608. It abounds in doggerel recipes such as

> If your hound by hap should bite his maister,
> With Honey, Rew, and Onyons make a plaister.

"The pen of that poet whose name is legion", writes Dr Singer, "has been busy with the Salernitan verses, and these form the basis of much mediaeval folk-lore.

> Joy, Temperance and Repose
> Slam the door on the doctor's nose."

When we come to the work of Albertus Magnus (d. 1282), only a small part of whose voluminous writings were concerned with botany, we find evidence of a somewhat more scientific approach, based on first-hand observation of plants, in the morphology of which he was particularly interested. In his book he says that he lists the properties of plants to satisfy the curiosity of his students. He refused to accept blindly what Pliny and others had said, for, he writes, "those philosophers tell many lies". Yet even Albertus shared the credulity of mediaeval men, and although sceptical at times, at others he shows himself preposterously gullible.

In the following century Konrad von Megenberg (1309–74) wrote his famous *Book of Nature*, a complete work on natural history written, not in Latin, as had been the custom hitherto, but in German. It was first printed at Augsburg in 1475. This book contains a long section devoted to plants, based largely on the *Liber de natura rerum* of Thomas Cantimpratensis, itself a compilation from ancient sources.

With the invention of printing and the Revival of Learning the Aristotelian botany began to have less influence, and in 1530 Otto Brunfels (1464–1534), earliest of the German "Fathers of Botany", brought out a herbal, *Herbarum Vivae Icones*, which not only relied on direct observation but was accompanied by drawings of plants which were notably in advance of any previous botanical woodcuts, even if they did not compare with some of the best work in manuscript of, say, Jean de Bourdichon, whose style may have had an influence on Grinling Gibbons.

Where Brunfels came to grief was in attempting to identify his plants with those mentioned by Dioscorides, forgetful of the fact that the flora of the Mediterranean region, which Dioscorides had described, was dissimilar to that of the Rhineland, where Brunfels had done his botanising.

With the *Kreuterbuch* of Hieronymus Tragus (Bock), first published in 1539, plant description takes a great step forward. Green calls its author "the first father of phytography [i.e. plant description] after Theophrastus and the first forerunner of Linnaeus". His descriptions of the plants he studied were so exact that plates, which only appeared in later editions of his work, were rendered almost superfluous.

Meanwhile, in the year which preceded the appearance of the work of Tragus, there was published a little book called *Libellus de re Herbaria*, by an Englishman, William Turner, born at Morpeth in Northumberland c. 1510. Turner, who became well-known in the triple capacity of divine, physician and botanist, was educated at Marie Valence Hall, Cambridge (now Pembroke College). Botany was evidently a subject ignored by the university, for Turner wrote later that when at Cambridge he "could learne never one Greke nether Latin nor English name even amongst the Phisicions of any herb or tre, such was the ignorance in simples at that tyme".

Turner, a staunch Protestant, and a friend of Ridley, was in his early days imprisoned for preaching without a licence, and on his release he travelled abroad, studied botany at Bologna under Luca Ghini, and took his M.D. either there or at Ferrara. Later he went to Zürich, where he became acquainted with Conrad Gesner, and afterwards visited Basle and Cologne, botanising in the Rhineland and in Holland. On his return to England during the reign of Edward VI he became chaplain and physician to Lord Somerset, and had a garden where he grew herbs at Kew, his residence.

Turner was forced to leave England during the reign of Queen Mary and stayed in many German cities, returning again to England on the accession of Queen Elizabeth I. He was the first Englishman to study plants scientifically and his *New Herball*, the first part of which came out in 1551, marks the beginning of the science of botany in England. Turner would have no truck with the many superstitions which still surrounded plants and the heavy hand of tradition affected him but little.

They that have red the first part of my Herbal [he writes] and have compared my writinges of plantes with those thinges that Matthiolus, Fuchsius, Tragus and Dodoneus wrote in the firste editiones of their Herballes, maye easily perceyve that I taught the truthe of certeyne plantes, which these above named writers either knew not at al, or ellis erred in them greatlye . . . And because I would not be lyke unto a cryer thet cryeth a loste horse in the market, and telleth all the markes and tokens that he hath, and yet never sawe the horse, nether could knowe the horse if he sawe him: I wente into Italye and into diverse partes of Germany, to knowe and se the herbes my selfe.

Turner's descriptions of plants were often most vividly expressed, as when he describes the Camomile that "hath floures wonderfully shynynge yellow and resemblynge the appell of an eye". In 1548 he published also a little work *The Names of herbes in Greke, Latin, Englishe, Duche and Frenche wyth the commune names that Herbaries and Apotecaries use*, in order, as he said, "that Potecaries shoulde be excuselesse when as the ryghte herbes are required of them, I have showed in what places of Englande, Germany and Italy the herbes growe and maye be had for laboure and money".

By this time the apothecaries in England were numerous. The term apothecary means one who keeps an *apotheca* (from a Greek word meaning a store), or repository for various drugs and medicines. In Rome the name *apothecarius* was given to the keeper of the place where herbs were stored, and the term was later applied to one who prepared drugs and spices for medicinal purposes. A druggist merely sold drugs and simples, but did not prepare them, whereas the apothecary's duty was "to exercise or compose certain ingredients to a medicinal form and to adhibit them in a decent manner to salutiferous use, according to the precept of some skilful physician".

The first time an apothecary is mentioned in England by that term is in a Pipe Roll of Henry II, in 1180. Chaucer, in the "Physician's Tale", says: "Ful redye hadde he hise apothecaries to send him drogges." Originally the Pepperers, Spicers and Apothecaries seem to have been branches of the same guild, and it was not until the Tudor period that the status of the apothecary became more clearly defined. In fact in England the different branches of the medical profession were not separately distinguished until the reign of Henry VIII, who took a great interest in medicine and had himself some practical knowledge of compounding drugs and devising various remedies, as we know from a manuscript which once belonged to Sir Hans Sloane and is now in the British Museum.*

* Sloane MS 1047.

For a long period ecclesiastical medicine had been predominant, and attained its apogee about the 10th century, though there were a certain number of lay doctors, many of them Jews, and the so-called barber-surgeons, and to these barbers who undertook minor forms of surgery, such as blood-letting, the clerics left the manual work, since the Church abhorred the shedding of blood. * But monastic medicine began to be frowned upon when monks and priests began to devote too much time to their speciality. Various ecclesiastical edicts limited the medical activities of the clergy during the 12th and 13th centuries, and after the Lateran Council of 1215 the clergy could no longer function as doctors, and lay medicine began to replace that of the priests.

In 1511 Henry VIII signed an Act for the regulation of medical and surgical practice, the preamble to which shows how widespread was the practice of illegal medicine, owing perhaps to the fact that it was not until 1518 that the medical profession in England had its own centres of training. The Act begins:

Foreasmuch as the science and cunning of physick and surgery is daily within this realm exercised by a great multitude of ignorant persons, of whom the greater part have no manner of insight in the same, nor any other kind of learning; that common artificers as smiths, weavers and women boldly and accustomably take upon them great cures and things of great difficulty in which they partly use sorcery and witchcraft, partly apply such medicines unto the disease as to be noxious and nothing meet, therefore to the High displeasure of God, great infamy to the Faculty and the grievous hurt and damage and destruction of many of the King's liege people.

As a result of the king's interest, the London College of Physicians was founded in 1518. But although its charter conferred on it powers for the suppression of charlatans, in

* A reminder of the calling of the barber-surgeon remains in the striped barber's pole of which the black represents the staff which the patient gripped; red for the blood; and white for the bandage.

practice "mountebanks and runnagate quack-salvers" continued to flourish. It was sufficient to call a phial of flavoured water by a name such as *Elixir Vitae* or *Aqua Coelestis* to conjure the money from the pockets of the ignorant, and for centuries imposters of every kind infested London despite all warrants for the arrest of "reputed Empiricks and Quacks".*

In the country districts herbalists sold their wares in the market places and on the village greens, for by the 16th century the art of herbalism had become firmly established. In this branch of medicine, too, charlatans abounded. But by now the literature of herbalism, thanks to the invention of printing, had reached large proportions, and though the accretion of centuries of herbal lore had resulted in more chaff than grain, the more scientific spirit which was now manifesting itself was enabling herbalism to become an effective weapon in the fight against disease. Physic gardens, devoted exclusively to the growing of medicinal herbs, were becoming more common, and John Gerard, whose *Herball or General Historie of Plantes* was first published in 1597, had an extensive herb garden at Holborn, "the little plot of myne owne especiall care and husbandry" as he terms it.

Gerard's herbal was extremely popular and was enlarged and amended by Thomas Johnson 1633. It is not an original work, for it leans very heavily on Dodoen's final work *Stirpium Historiae Pemptades Sex*, which a certain Dr Priest had been commissioned by the publisher John Norton to translate into English. He, however, died before the work was finished, and Gerard simply adapted Priest's translation and rearranged it.

The wood blocks used by Tabernaemontanus in his *Eicones* (1590), together with some others, were procured from Frankfurt by the publisher, Norton ; but Gerard's superficial knowledge caused him to mix up many of the figures. This

* Braunschweig, in his *Homish Apothecarye* (1561) says : "I my selfe have seen a strange peddelapotecary minister to the commun people that two or thre dyed of it."

led to so much confusion in the early chapters of the *Herball* that Norton's attention was drawn to it by a London apothecary named James Garret. The famous botanist De l'Obel was invited to correct the work, in which, according to his own account, he made about a thousand corrections.

The book is a curious mixture of straightforward description and fantastic fables, such as that of the "Barnakle tree" or the "tree bearing geese", a story as fantastic as anything in Pliny, and its importance in the history of botany rests mainly on the very much improved edition brought out by the London apothecary, Thomas Johnson, which, in addition to correcting numerous errors, dealt with no fewer than 2,850 plants.

Herbs were not exclusively the province of the professional herbalist, for on country estates the wife's concern was to see that the medicine chest was well stocked and to look after the herb garden which provided for it. In fact a vast number of traditional herbal remedies were handed down from mother to daughter, and as old Tusser wrote:

> Good huswives provide, ere an' sickness do come,
> Of sundry good things, in her house to have some:
> Good *aqua composita*, and vinegar tart,
> Rose-water, and treacle, to comfort the heart.
> Cold herbs in her garden, for agues that burn,
> That over strong heat, to good temper may turn,
> White endive and succory, with spinage enough,
> All such, with good pot herbs, should follow the plough.
> Get water of fumitory, liver to cool,
> And others the like, or else go like a fool.
> Conserves of barberry, quinces and such,
> With sirops, that easeth the sickly so much.

The methods of the herbalists of this period were similar in many ways to those employed by pharmacists today, but unfortunately there was one doctrine, accepted like so much else from the ancient writers, which for many a long day bedevilled all herbal treatment. That was the so-called Doctrine of

Signatures, a concept common in the days of Pliny and revived again in Europe, and explained at great length by Paracelsus in his *Dispensatory and Chirurgery*. The theory was that every plant by some peculiarity of its outward shape or colouring gave an indication of the medicinal purpose for which it was destined by a beneficent Deity. The doctrine professed to find resemblances either between the plant and the cause of the affliction or between the plant and the part of the body affected. Many of our popular plant-names, such as Lungwort, Liverwort, Heartsease, still reflect this curious superstition.

Listen to Paracelsus on the virtues of St John's wort. He writes: "The porositie, or holes in the leaves, signifie to us that this herb helps both inward and outward holes or cuts in the skin and strengthens Nature in expelling that which should be evacuated through the pores of the skin." And again – "the flowers of St John's wort, when they are putrified they are like blood; which teacheth us that this herb is good for wounds, to close them and fill them up". In a similar manner plants with yellow flowers, or which yielded a yellow juice, were considered a cure for jaundice; whilst *Echium vulgare*, with the livid spots on its stem and disposition of its corolla providing some analogy with the head of a viper, was supposed to be a powerful antidote against the venom of serpents, and so acquired the name of Viper's Bugloss.

The physicians of London, as we have seen, were incorporated in 1518. In 1540 it was the turn of the barber-surgeons to receive their charter.* In April, 1606, James I incorporated the apothecaries as one of the city companies, uniting them with the Grocers' Company. The apothecaries, not much relishing this forced partnership with those they looked upon as mere shopkeepers, appealed to the king for a separate charter, which was granted to them in 1617, for, said James, "Grocers are but

---

* This was the amalgamation in one corporate body of the Barbers' Company, first mentioned in 1308, and a rival company, the Fellowship or Guild of Surgeons, first mentioned in 1369.

merchants; the business of the apothecary is a mystery: wherefore I think it fitting that they should be a corporation of themselves", despite the fact that there were only 114 of them, all told, in London. Another reason given for the granting of the charter was because "very many Empiricks and unskilful and ignorant men . . . do make and compound many unwholesome, hurtful, deceitful, corrupt, and dangerous medicines . . . to the great peril and daily hazard of the lives of our subjects." There is a decided echo, here, of the 1518 Act of Henry VIII. In 1674 the Apothecaries' Company acquired the lease of land in Chelsea which they converted into a Physic Garden for the instruction of apprentices and for the practical study of medicinal plants. Later the ground was conveyed to them in perpetuity by Sir Hans Sloane, and the garden still survives as one of the oldest Botanic Gardens in England. *

Throughout the 16th century many privately printed formularies were published, which indicated the need for some official and authoritative dispensatory. This was provided in 1546 by the *Pharmacorum Dispensatorium* of Valerius Cordus (1515–44) of Simmtshausen. Although he died at the early age of 29, this "splendid and all too transitory phenomenon" had acquired a great reputation both as pharmacist and botanist. His dispensatory was the forerunner of numerous official pharmacopoeias, although it was not until 1618 that the first English one (in Latin), the *Pharmacopoeia Londonensis*, appeared. This volume, sponsored by the London College of Physicians, contained 1028 simple drugs and 932 preparations, and mentioned therein were 271 herbs, 138 roots and 138 seeds.

By the 17th century botanical knowledge had made such strides that whereas Konrad von Megenberg's *Book of Nature* of 1475 mentioned eighty-nine herbs, the herbals of the 17th century contained almost every plant known to the naturalists of that time. John Parkinson's *Theatrum Botanicum* of 1640

*The University Botanic Garden at Oxford dates from 1621.

describes nearly 3,800 plants, and even a book of pharmaceutical recipes such as R. James's *New English Dispensatory* included 737 herbs, as well as roots and flowers.

Parkinson, like Gerard, had a garden in London, at Long Acre, "well stored with rarities" as he tells us. He was both apothecary and herbalist, being appointed Apothecary to James I and receiving from Charles I the title of "Botanicus Regius Primarius". His first published work appeared in 1629 under the punning title of *Paradisi in Sole*. The word "paradisus" in Latin signified a large park or pleasure garden, so that a literal translation of the title would be "Of Park-in-Sun".

Whereas Parkinson's first book is in the nature of a treatise on gardening, his *Theatrum Botanicum*, published in 1640, was, as the sub-title explains, "An Herball of a Large Extent". Originally planned as an account of "A Garden of Simples" the work grew into one of a more general nature, in which the virtues of herbs are dealt with in considerable detail. As a herbal it showed a considerable advance on Gerard, especially as it incorporated much of the work of Caspar Bauhin, the famous Swiss botanist, and it remained the most complete English treatise on the subject until the time of John Ray.[*]

With Parkinson plants are still grouped according to their medical qualities, but the time was now fast approaching when physician and botanist were to go their separate ways. However, Nicholas Culpeper (1616–54), like Parkinson, was an apothecary, but, in the delightful phrase of Alice Coats, he "had a bonnet as full of bees as a border of catmint on a bright sunny morning". He was an exponent of what is termed astrological botany, believing, as did Paracelsus, in the influence of the heavenly bodies on the plant world. This belief was, of course, no new one, and had been held by many ancient peoples, but in the 16th and 17th centuries astrological ideas had a great hold on the popular imagination, and astrologers such as Dr John Dee (1527–1608) and Dr William Lilly (1602–81)

[*]His *Synopsis Stirpium Britannicarum* (1670) was the first British Flora.

wielded considerable influence. In the herbal of Bartlolomaeus Carrichter (1575) plants were arranged according to the signs of the Zodiac, and Nicolaus Winckler's *Chronica Herbarum* (1571) is an astrological calendar in which there is much information as to the most appropriate times for gathering various herbs. Leonhardt Thurneisser also wrote a book of astrological botany, a History or Description of Plants in Latin, which was published in Berlin in 1578.

Culpeper set up as physician-cum-astrologer in Spitalfields about 1640 and soon fell foul of the more orthodox physicians when he published a quite unauthorised English translation of the official *Pharmacopoeia Londonensis* in which he had many rude things to say about the College of Physicians, which he described as "a company of proud, insulting, domineering Doctors, whose wits were born above five hundred years before themselves". An augmented version of this work, which he entitled *The English Physician Enlarged*, was described on the title-page as "An Astro-Physical Discourse of the Vulgar Herbs of this Nation". It proved extremely popular and many editions of it have been published right up to the present century.*

The following extract from Culpeper's *Physicall Directory* is a fair example of this kind of astrological pharmacology and therapeutics:

Verbascum, Thapsus Barbatus [Mullein or Hedge-taper] Being gathered when the Sun is in Virgo and the Moon in Aries, their mutual antiscions [opposites] helps such of the falling-sickness as do carry it about them: worn under the feet it helps such as are troubled with fits of the mother.

Note the very ancient amulet use of the remedy in the above citation.

William Coles, who wrote the *Art of Simpling* (1656) and *Adam in Eden, or Nature's Paradise* (1657), although he

* A tercentenary edition was printed privately for Imperial Chemicals (Pharmaceuticals) Ltd. in 1953.

carried the doctrine of signatures to a point where it became ludicrous, would have none of the astrological botanists and poured scorn on Culpeper, whom he described as "a man very ignorant in the forme of Simples", saying: "it is evident to those that knew him, or are able to judge of his writings, that he understood not those plants he trod upon".

Towards the end of the 17th century the herbal began to die out. Plant description henceforward became the province of the scientific botanist. On the medical side the various dispensatories took their place; and as the status of the profession of medicine rose there was no longer such a need of popular treatises on the medical virtues of herbs. After William Salmon's *Botanologia: The English Herbal* (1710) there were published no more herbals of importance and by the middle of the 18th century the era of scepticism had arrived during which many of the ancient and highly-esteemed remedies were abandoned without compunction. In fact the pendulum swung so far in the opposite direction that for a considerable time, owing to this sudden relegation to undeserved oblivion of a host of herbal remedies, medicine lacked a number of valuable therapeutic agents.

When Dr Bullein, in his *Book of Compounds* (1576), drew up a code of rules to be followed by all good apothecaries, one of these was that "his garden must be at hand, with plenty of herbs, seeds and roots", which he was to "sow, set, plant, gather, preserve and keep in due tyme". And indeed, in those days, before London had been given over entirely to density building, there were many such gardens in the heart of the City. Gerard had one behind his house in Holborn, and Parkinson in Long Acre. Thomas Fairchild's gardens at Hoxton "were greatly resorted to, as well for the delectable situation as for the curious plants therein contained". Mr Gray, apothecary, had a garden "under London Wall", and Hugh Morgan, Apothecary to Queen Elizabeth, and "a curious conserver of rare Simples", had both a garden adjoining his house near Coleman Street in the City and another at his country house at Battersea, then a rural retreat.

If you would know what an apothecary's shop looked like at the end of the reign of Queen Elizabeth I, Shakespeare's *Romeo and Juliet*, Act V, Scene I, will give you a verbal picture, and those who are resident in or visitors to London can see an actual replica of a druggist's shop of 1620 in the Wellcome Historical Medical Museum in the Euston Road.

Thanks to an apothecary's bill still preserved among the State Papers* we know a good deal about the various drugs supplied by King Henry VIII's apothecary, Thomas Alsopp, to the Court in the year 1547. The enumeration of materials supplied covers some five and a half pages of close print and makes interesting reading. Succade, or Succat (fruit preserved in sugar), was always provided for the eve of holy days, and cost 3s 4d. In addition to Electuaries (medicinal powders mixed with honey or syrup), gargarisms, lotions, fomentations, urinals and glysters (clysters, or enemas), there were liquorice sticks, at 8d; cinnamon cumfettes (sweetmeats); pots of Venice green ginger priced at 5s; *pills de rubarbo*; penettes (barley sugar); and juleps (medicated drinks).

Perfumes were supplied in great quantities for all the royal residences at Sheen, Oatlands, Westminster, Windsor, Non-such, Byfleet, Wimbledon and Guildford amongst others. To cure morphew (a kind of scurvy) Alsopp supplied glasses of *aqua lactis virginis* – "Water of Virgin's Milk" – and a very popular remedy, prescribed for almost any complaint, was a paste or powder known as *manus Christi* (hand of Christ). For the baths there were "bagges with herbis, sponges, muske, cyvet" to the value of 5s 8d, and frontalls (bandages for headaches) cost 20d. Nor were the animals forgotten, for there was "horehound water for the hawks" and "to My Lady Margaret Duglas, treacle for her monkey, 8d".

* *Letters and Papers of Henry VIII, 1546–47*, Pt. 2, p. 394 *et seq.*

Reading the old dispensatories today, what strikes us at once is the profusion of herbs, roots and seeds employed by the old herbalists and apothecaries. And since so many of them were acclaimed as panaceas we begin to wonder how it was that patients ever died. But when we examine the complexity of some of the prescriptions and remember that the active principles of some plants are poisonous when taken in excess we find it just as astonishing that any of the patients recovered.

One of the most celebrated nostrums of the Middle Ages and the Renaissance was the Theriac, originally an antidote to the bites of poisonous animals (*theria* = wild beast) and later supposed to be an antidote to all poisons. As it was also considered to be a specific against the plague the theriac was in much demand. The name theriac was after a time spelt theriacle, which soon became corrupted to treacle, though having nothing in common with that word as used today.* One of the most reputed of these compositions was the famed Venice Treacle which gradually acquired the supremacy over those made elsewhere. In many cities of Italy, such as Genoa, Florence and Bologna, and at Montpellier in France, the theriac was prepared in public in the presence of professors of the Faculties of Medicine and the leading civic authorities.

Venice Treacle contained sixty-one ingredients, but Matthiolus published a formula containing no fewer than 250 ingredients, which included, in addition to a vast quantity of herbs, vipers, pearls, red coral and emeralds! When, in the 16th century, the Venetian galleys no longer called at the English ports, the apothecaries in England began to make theriacs of their own, which they claimed were much better than the imported product, and in 1585 Hugh Morgan, the queen's apothecary, issued a warning against the "false and naughty kind of mithridatum and threacle in great barrelles" which came into the country daily from abroad. In 1612 the Grocers'

* In Chaucer we read: *By corpus bones! but I have triacle.* ("The Physician's Tale.")

Company, also, called attention to the fact that "a filthy and unwholesome baggage composition was being brought into this Realm as Tryacle of Genoa, made only of the rotten garble and refuse outcast of all kinds of spices and drugs, hand overhead with a little filthy molasses and tarre to work it up withal".

This resulted in the College of Physicians devising its own formula, the manufacture of which was entrusted to an apothecary in the Poultry named William Besse. As late as 1722 this preparation was publicly compounded by the Society of Apothecaries.

That the learned were no less credulous than the common folk concerning drugs is shown by a series of letters sent by a Parisian apothecary, Nicholas Cabry, to the Secretary of State Sir Francis Walsingham between the years 1582 and 1587. Here is an extract from one of them, dated August 10, 1582:

I send you the muscardines [musk lozenges], also thirty-five cakes of bole armoniac, a rarity from the Levant, which I have received from a friend of mine, a renegade in the seraglio of the Grand Turk, whose effects are signal in many maladies. I should have sent some Mithridate treacle and salt earth, but I thought you had enough. The bearer of them has brought other excellent things from Constantinople for resisting poison, and especially unicorn's stone, which may be tried before buying it, with good success on animals to whom arsenic has been given. He has also balm of Judaea, turpentine of Scio, and other rare drugs. He has also silver medals, idols of Isis, taken from mummies, etc. I expect soon some manna from Lebanon, which will be good for your complexion. . . .

Even the restorative waters were often made up of an incredible number of ingredients. The *Aqua Coelestis* of Matthiolus contained the following herbs and spices: cinnamon, ginger, sandalwood, cloves, gallanga, nutmeg, mace, cubebs, nigella seeds, zedoary, anise, sweet fennel, wild parsnips, basil; roots of angelica, valerian, avens, calamus, liquorice; leaves of clary, thyme, calamint, penny-royal, mints, mother of thyme, marjoram; and flowers of red roses, sage, rosemary, betony, stoechas, bugloss and borage. All these were to be infused for fifteen days in twelve pints of best spirits of wine and then distilled. To the distilled water, as a finishing touch, were added such things as musk and ambergris.

By the middle of the 18th century a more rational system of scientific investigation of the properties of drugs had developed, under the influence of which medicine began to throw off the fetters of superstition and to free itself from the incubus of the ancients. Chemistry was coming into its own as an exact science and the process of extracting the active principles from vegetable drugs proceeded with quickening pace throughout the 19th century.

Investigation under controlled laboratory conditions has made known the chemical structure of many complex plant principles, even though it has not always been found practicable to synthesise them. And thus it has become possible to distinguish the really beneficial plants from those, and they are many, whose efficacy as remedies was based on nothing more solid than fanciful speculation and the cumulative legacy of tradition.

Nevertheless our debt to the empirical discoveries of the old herbalists is considerable, and even today it seems improbable that synthetic medicine will entirely oust our dependence on the vegetable kingdom, for many chemists are of the opinion that the active principles of plants in their natural state may be more efficacious than when they are isolated. To quote one research chemist, Noel L. Allport,* "A medicine is none the less valuable because the reason for its action is not understood, and . . . there would seem to be no valid grounds for supposing that the use of vegetable drugs will ever be superseded."

Inexact, extravagant, superstitious and garrulous the old herbalists may have been; but as we turn the pages of their

* *Chemistry & Pharmacy of Vegetable Drugs.*

faded volumes with their quaint embellishments, we find, in the words of Florence Hine, that "there is a sweet compulsion surviving in these old-fashioned herbals by which men are still led to read them with the herb of grace in their minds and with some of the gaiety and freshness of spring in their hearts".

The following is taken from a 17th–century manuscript book in the British Museum (Sloane MS 782):

A GENERALL USE OF ALL MANNER OF HEARBS

It is a general rule from the Eight Kalends of the moneth of Aprill unto the moneth of July all manner of leaves of hearbes be best and from the Eight Kalends of July unto the Eight Kalends of October the stalkes have most virtue and from the Eight Kalends of October unto the Eight Kalends of Aprill all manner of Rootes of hearbes be in theire full strength.

WHAT HEARBES AND ROOTS ARE GOOD TO BE USED IN SALLETTS FOR ALL MONETHS OF THE YEARE

JANUARIE In the moneth of Januarie is good to use in Selletts the roots of Parsneps and Cariotts boyled, and in Italy they doe use Cabages cutt smale with a little Pepper, oyle, salt, vinegar, Our Authors say that Parsneps and Kariotts are very good for they which are troubled with the stone and Cabages at that time to purifie the mallancholly humors.

FEBRUARY In this moneth we doe use Succorie rootes boyled, the which though they are somewhat bitter they are good for the Liver and they doe keepe the body somewhat soluble; some doe use in this moneth Nettle Pottage the which is very good and Alexander budds.

MARCH In this moneth it is good to use greene fennell boyled and alsoe Pottage newly come up, both of them are very good to purifie the bloud and for the sight. Some doe use all this tyme in the yeare

Rampions, Spinage, crops of hopps, and water Cresses, which is very good for the stone. In Spaine at this tyme they doe use potato rootes and at no other tyme having an opinion quod est semen augeat et confirmet viros.

APRILL In this moneth many yonge hearbes are used but not gathered, as they doe use here, for violett leaves, Primerose leaves, bloudwort leaves, Spinage and such others are not good for they are hard of digestion, but young Lattice, young Endife, young Parsley, mints, roketts*, Tarragon and such like are good.

MAY In this moneth it is good to use Selletts of Burage flowers, which is a very good Cordiall, the tender stalkes of Lange de beefe,† being boyled, and succory boyled is a good sellett which taketh away the heate of the liver. Sparagus are good in this moneth and also Ladyes thissell, in the midst of May it springeth the tender budds of which are very good and pleasant being dressed like Sparagus; we doe use att this tyme in the yeare Sykett rootes dressed like Rampion rootes, all other yonge and tender hearbes which we did express in the moneth of Aprill are alsoe good in this moneth of May.

JUNE In this moneth the blew flowers of succory they are a comfortable sellett; these flowers doe continue good all this and the next moneth, especially the begininge. The young crops of sage, with a few mints they say it is good against the Palsey. It is a sallett rather medcineable then pleasant. Capers with a few currants sodden are used in this moneth and in the next; as for lettice, Endife and such like, when they doe give milke they are not to be used in Salletts.

JULY In this moneth we doe use younge Sytornes [citrons] with Pepper, in this tyme mallows doe sett forth their flowers which being gathered and made to a Sallett are very good against the heate of the backe and for the stone; it is much used in Naples and in Rome where they doe use alsoe the great Sytornes, that are somewhat greater than Leamons; they doe use them as sallett which doth comfort the hart and keepeth a man from contagious diseases; it is good at this tyme to use younge white beets soden.

AUGUST In this moneth Purslane is good for them which are troubled with spittinge of bloud. Capers very good also in this moneth and all such other Salletts which we have named in the moneth of June.

* Rocket, a plant of the Crucifer family; a term formerly applied to cresses.
† Langue de Boeuf, or Ox-tongue: a popular name for Bugloss.

SEPTEMBER In this moneth younge Lattice, younge Endife, margerum, mints, Tarragon an other hearbes called hearba stella, soden Sycory and sodden burage are very good to be used.

OCTOBER, NOVEMBER, DECEMBER As for these moneths because the strenght of the hearbes goeth downe into the rootes, the rootes are better to be used then the hearbes as Parsneps, kerretts, succory rootes and such as were named in the moneth of Januarie.

AGRIMONY   *Agrimonia Eupatoria* L.   Rosaceae
Liverwort

FR *Aigremoine*; *Herbe de Saint Guillaume*; *Thé des Bois*
GER *Odermennig*; *Ackermänchen*; *Steinwurzel*

> And herbes coude I telle eek many oon,
> As egremoine, valerian, and lunarie . . .
> CHAUCER *The Chanouns Yemannes Tale*

Agrimony has been a herb of much repute since the time of the Anglo-Saxons, who called it Garclive, and whose leechdoms prescribed it both for wounds and snake-bites. Gerard quotes Pliny as calling it a herb of "princely authoritie" and adds: "a decoction of the leaves is good for them that have naughty livers".

The ancient Greeks called it *argemon* in the belief that it cured cataract, and it was given its second, specific, name because the herb was said to have been first used by Mithridates Eupator, king of Pontus, whom Edith Wheelwright calls "the most celebrated pioneer of toxicology".

In France it is an ingredient of the aromatic mixture known as *Eau d'arquebusade* said to have been used, according to Philippe de Comines, at the battle of Morat in 1476, and in that country today the fresh plant is often ground up and made into cataplasms for sprains and bruises. It was at one time included in the London official pharmacopoeia, and for centuries it was considered a cure for jaundice and liver complaints. It is still highly considered by herbalists and today is used medicinally for digestive disorders and as a blood purifier. In country districts of England Agrimony tea is made by infusing one ounce of the dried herb in a pint of water. (*cf.* FR *Thé des Bois*.)

This herb grows in dry spots in meadows, in hedgerows and by the roadside throughout most of England, and its tall spikes of sulphur-coloured flowers, known to country folk as "church steeples", can be seen from June until the end of

August. Its fruit takes the form of a stiff, hairy burr which clings tenaciously to everything, which may be the reason why Gerard said it was called *philanthropus*.

The plants are gathered at the moment of flowering and dried in the shade in a warm room or shed, the leaves and flowers being powdered when dry.

ALKANET   *Anchusa officinalis* L.   Boraginaceae
Dyers' Bugloss
FR *Orcanette (Orcanète)* ; *Langue de bœuf*
GER *Alkannawurzel*; *Rote Ochsenzunge*

This biennial, about 2 feet high, whose bright blue flowers seem to have an irresistible attraction for bees, is somewhat rare in Britain, though fairly common in most of Europe except the extreme north. The generic name *anchusa* is derived from the Greek, meaning to paint, or dye, since the root gives a red dye for which the plant was cultivated at least as far back as the days of the Roman Empire, for Pliny mentions its use as a dye, and Galen tells us that it was used in his time as a cosmetic.

It seems, indeed, to be one of the most ancient of all the facial cosmetics, and Gerard, who calls it Wild Bugloss, writes that "the Gentlewomen of France do paint their faces with these roots, as it is said". Was this the reason, one wonders, why the herb was at one time considered the symbol of falsehood?

The English name *Alkanet* has a similar significance, for it is a diminutive of the Spanish *alcanna*, itself derived from the Arabic *al henna*, the henna plant, with the juice of which the Egyptian women were wont to redden their nails.

Alkanet is believed to have been introduced into this country from France about the 16th century, and Parkinson says that it is called "of some Orchanet, after the French".

In appearance Alkanet bears a strong resemblance to the

Small Bugloss, which is sometimes called Field Alkanet. As with many of the plants of the Borage family, its tops and flowers were often added to wine to impart flavour and add a touch of colour. Like Borage itself, Alkanet was supposed to have "cheering vertues", but Dr Thornton, rather an old sceptic, writes, "what surprises most is the vaunted accounts of its efficacy in the cure of melancholia and other hypochondriacal diseases. But then, it must be steeped in strong ale or wine."

ANISE   *Pimpinella anisum* L.   Umbelliferae
FR *Anis vert*; *Boucage*
GER *Anis*

> Chi terranno in mano una pianta d'aniso
> Non saran' molestati dal mal caduco.
>
> *Italian saying*

Anise is an annual herb, a native of Egypt and the Mediterranean, now found in many parts of the world. It has small, dainty leaves, and yellowish-white flowers in large compound umbels, and grows to between one and two feet. The fruit consists of two coherent mericarps or "seeds".

This plant has been used both in medicine and in the kitchen since very early times, and was a favourite ingredient of the Roman cuisine. The ancient Greeks knew it also, for Pythagoras, who was born about 580 BC, looked upon bread baked with aniseed in it as a great delicacy. To this day it is extensively used in Europe as an ingredient in bread and cakes, and in confectionery. The leaves of anise, finely chopped, make a pleasant addition to salads, and in France it is often strewn over young carrots.

Anise has for long been renowned as a carminative. Gerard recommends it as "good against belchings and upbradings of the stomacke", and Sacchi di Platina was emphatic that "those should use it for their benefit who belch freely". The aniseed of the pharmacist is the dried ripe fruit of *P. anisum*, of which

ANISE

there are three varieties in commerce, the largest and finest being that exported from Alicante in Spain; the others are German and Russian anise, the last-named being much smaller than the others.

The oil, *Oleum Anisi*, obtained by distilling the fruits, is little used in modern practice, its place having been taken by the volatile oil of star-anise, distilled from the dried ripe fruit of *Illicium anisatum*, a small evergreen indigenous to south and south-west China, but grown also in Japan. Both oils, which have a similar aromatic taste, contain as their main constituent anethol.

The Star-Anise (*Badiane* in French) has lanceolate leaves, resembling those of the laurel, and it gets its name from the fact that the fruit is composed of a number of capsules which radiate from a central axis in the form of a star. These reddish-brown capsules contain an oval seed having an oily kernel. The whole fruit has the smell and taste of anise as well as a sweet and fragrant savour of its own.

Among the Chinese the star-anise is highly appreciated, being used both as a seasoning and as a drink, prepared in the manner of tea. The essential oil is used for many purposes; it enters into the composition of the French liqueur known as *anisette* and the Italian cordial called *Ratafia da Bologna*. Also it is used for making the condiment Soya sauce.

BALM	*Melissa officinalis*	Labiatae

Honey Plant

FR *Mélisse*; *Herbe au citron* ; *Citronelle*

GER *Melisse*; *Zitronenmelisse*

> The several chairs of order look you scour
> With juice of balm and every precious flower.
>
> *Merry Wives of Windsor*, 5, v

The lemon-scented Balm, by reason of its fragrance, was one of the strewing herbs used in the days when sweet herbs and green rushes were spread on bare floors. This hardy outdoor plant has always been a favourite in cottage gardens, and was a treasured herb in the days of Ancient Greece. The name *melissa*, which is the Greek word for a bee, was given to it because of its importance as a bee plant, and there is a widely-held belief that bees will not leave a hive as long as there is plenty of this plant in the vicinity.

In this country Balm has been to a large extent replaced in the kitchen by Lemon Verbena, another labiate, but whereas the former is a hardy outdoor perennial, dying down in winter and springing up again early in the year, the latter will only grow out of doors where the climate is very mild.

In the collection of prescriptions called the London Dispensary, it was claimed that "an essence of Balm given in Canary wine every morning will renew youth, strengthen the brain, relieve languishing nature, and prevent baldness" – a rich catalogue of virtues. In confirmation of this claim to bring longevity, it is said that a Welsh prince, Llewelyn, who lived to the ripe age of 108, drank Balm tea regularly every morning and evening. Balm tea, drunk with lemon juice and sugar, is to this day used in country districts as a remedy for feverish colds.

The plant is endowed with still further virtues in the 1649 edition of the *London Dispensatory*, which states that "Bawm outwardly mixed with salt and applied to the neck helps the Kings Evil, bitings of mad dogs and venemous beasts, and such as cannot hold their necks as they should do; inwardly it is an excellent remedy for a cold and moist stomach, cheers the heart, refresheth the mind, and takes away grief, sorrow and care". And Gerard tells us that Avicenna:" in his booke written of the infirmities of the heart, teacheth that Bawme makes the heart merry and joyfull, and strengtheneth the vitall spirits".

A once popular "restorative cordial" called Carmelite Water, supposed to confer longevity, is still made in France under the name of *Eau de Mélisse des Carmes*, according to what is reputed to be the original formula of the ancient *Carmes déchaussés*. This is made by macerating in fortified white wine the fresh flowers and tops of Balm, together with lemon peel, cinnamon, cloves, nutmeg and coriander.

The leaves of Balm are excellent for flavouring soups and stews, and finely shredded, for salads. In the Netherlands and in Belgium the leaves are used in pickling herring and eels, and in Holland the plant is popularly called *palingkruid* (eel-herb).

The plant is indigenous to southern Europe, and the volatile oil is used in the making of perfumery and cosmetics, and also for medicinal purposes, as a carminative and stimulant.

Moldavian Balm (*Dracocephalum moldavicum* L.), native of Moldavia and Siberia, is a regional substitute for the official Balm, and is cultivated both as an ornamental plant and as a medicinal herb.

BASIL	*Ocimum basilicum*	Labiatae

Sweet Basil
FR *Basilic*; *Herbe royale*
GER *Basilienkraut*

> With Basil then I will begin
> Whose scent is wondrous pleasing.
>   DRAYTON *Polyolbion*

As a pot herb Basil is not used in this country to the same extent as on the Continent, though this may be due to a modern variation in taste, for the famous 17th-century delicacy," Fetter Lane sausages", owed their popularity largely to the basil used as seasoning. Basil is certainly one of the choicest and most aromatic of those herbs which are hardy enough to grow in our uncertain climate, and in addition to Sweet Basil, which may grow as high as 2 feet, there is the compact Bush Basil (*Ocimum minimum*), once a window-box favourite, which grows not more than six inches high.

The basils are exotic herbs, indigenous to India, where the plant is revered as sacred to Vishnu and Krishna, and is to be found in every Hindu house. Basil reached Europe from India many centuries ago, but being, as Culpeper remarks, "a very tender plant", it was not grown in England until we had learned, in the 16th century, to raise the tender annuals from seed.

When it was first introduced into this country Basil was used not as a pot herb, but mainly for the preparation of sweet waters, scent bags and nosegays. John Swan, in his *Speculum Mundi*, says: "we in England seldome or never eat it; yet we greatly esteem it because it smelleth sweet, and (as some think) comforteth the brain".

As an example of the fantastic legends and traditions associated with herbs in the Middle Ages, this is what we read about Basil in *The Countrie Farme*, the English version of Charles Estienne's *La Maison Rustique*, first published in 1600. "Some report a marvellous strange thing of basill, as namely that it groweth fairer and higher if it be sowen with curses and injuries offered unto it: and further that there is a deadly hatred betwixt amber and basill; for whereas amber or blacke jet is given to draw strawes unto it upon the touching of them, it driveth and putteth farre from it the leaves and stalkes of basill." The same author goes on to say that the smelling of Basil "begetteth paine and heavines of the head; yea, sometimes it engendreth in the head little small wormes, like unto scorpions".

This last item of information was indignantly refuted by Sir Thomas Browne in his *Pseudodoxia Epidemica*. "According to Oribasius, physician unto Julian," he writes, "the Africans, men best experienced in poisons, affirm whosoever hath eaten basil, although he be stung by a scorpion, shall feel no pain thereby; which is a very different effect and rather antidotally destroying, than seminally promoting its production."

Dodoens, the great Belgian herbalist, though living in a credulous age, showed a certain amount of scepticism over some of the claims made for this herb in his day, for he writes:

"A woman in labour, if she but hold in her hand a root of this herb together with the feather of a swallow shall be delivered without pain, as some believe, or would have us believe."

John Goodyer, in 1620, was one of the first to give a detailed description of Basil, and in his MS edited by R. T. Gunther we read: "It hath manie fower square hairie stalks proceedinge from the root, sometimes two foot longe or longer, parted into a fewe branches; the leaves growe on the joynts in wide distances by cooples, one opposite against another, in forme like those of wild Margerom but smaller, and are hairie, rough, lightlie snipt or indented about the edges. The flowers are purple and resemble those of Betonie, but of a lighter purple colour and growe forth of rough round whorles or crownetts close above the leaves, and one allwaies at the toppe of the stalk and branches, in forme like those of Horehound."

Basil is much used in France for flavouring soups, stews and sauces, and it is one of the traditional seasonings for turtle soup. When using Basil for such purposes, a small pinch of the dried herb is quite sufficient, for the flavour is very pervasive. Both Sweet and Bush Basil can be used, and fortunately they keep their flavour well when dried. The fresh leaves, finely chopped, and employed with discretion, add an aromatic tang to salads. Oil of Basil plays its part in the manufacture of perfumes.

And if, dear reader, you are interested in any other possible uses of Basil, we are informed that: "Mr Thomas Hill, in his *Art of Gardening*, testifieth that the seeds of Basil, put up into the nose, procureth sneezing; and being mixed with shoemakers black, do take away warts killing them to the very roots."

The generic name of the plant, by the way, comes from *oza*, a Greek word signifying "odour". But why the royal name *basilicum*? Perhaps on account of the plant's long association with the Hindu deities already mentioned. Or was it, as a magic herb, supposed to afford protection against that fabulous beast the basilisk, which

> From powerful eyes close venim did convey
> Into the looker's hart, and killed farre away.

BAY LAUREL   *Laurus nobilis* L.   Lauraceae
FR *Laurier noble*
GER *Lorbeer*

> Then in my lavender i'll lay,
> Muscado put among it,
> And here and there a leaf of bay,
> Which still shall run along it.
>
> *The Muses' Elysium*

Although one cannot strictly call the bay-tree a "herb", yet it could hardly be omitted from any book on herbs and spices since its leaves have for so long been used in the kitchen as a most delightful flavouring. The leaf of the Bay Laurel has indeed been put to many uses and has been endowed with many virtues, both natural and supernatural.

So well-known was the tree to the ancients, who appreciated its tall and noble beauty, that it passed into Greek mythology in the legend of the nymph Daphne, who, loved by Apollo, fled from his amorous pursuit and was changed into a bay-tree, which henceforward became sacred to that god; and since Apollo was the god of poetry it followed that the crown of bay-leaves later became the customary award in the universities to graduates in rhetoric and poetry. In 1487 the German poet Konrad Celtes received the laurel crown from the Emperor Frederick III.

Konrad von Megenberg, author of one of the earliest herbals, was of the opinion that the German word for the Bay tree, *lorbaum* was more properly *lob-baum*, and derived not from the Latin *laurea*, but from *laudea*, seeing that this tree of old was a symbol of victory and triumph, of honour and glory.

To the natural virtues of the Bay-tree Parkinson bears witness, for he writes: "It serveth to adorne the house of God, as well as of man; to procure warmth, comfort, and strength to the limmes of men and women by bathings and anoyntings out, and by drinks, etc., inward: to season the vessels wherein are preserved our meates, as well as our drinkes; to crown or encircle as with a garland the heads of the living, and to sticke and decke forth the bodies of the dead; so that from the cradle to the grave we have still use of, we have still need of it."

Laurus nobilis is a tree native to the Mediterranean shores, where it often attains a height of from 20 to 30 feet. The leaves, three to four inches long, and an inch or more broad, have a pleasantly aromatic odour, and are one of the ingredients of the *bouquet garni* used for flavouring, in a *court-bouillon* or a *marinade*. In England, where sweets are generally preferred to savouries, Bay leaves were at one time a constant stand-by for flavouring custards and milk puddings. That the leaves were also a traditional garnish in the olden times we are reminded by the couplet

> Then if you'd send up the Brawner's Head,
> Sweet Rosemary and Bays around it spread.

This close association of Rosemary and Bay is observable in many customs of our ancestors, for both were commonly carried both at funerals and weddings; and in a pamphlet of 1640, called *A Perfect Journall* . . . describing the opening of the Long Parliament, we read: "Nov. 28. That afternoon Master Prin and Master Burton came into London being met and accompanied with many thousands of horse and foot, and rode with rosemary and bayes in their hands and hats."

"Neyther falling sickness, neyther devyll, wyll infest or hurt one in that place where a bay-tree is," wrote Lupton in his *Book of Notable Things* (1575). But if the bay-tree should wither, then it was considered an ill omen and a portent of

death, as when in *Richard II* the Welsh captain takes leave
of the Earl of Salisbury with the words:

> 'Tis thought the king is dead: we will not stay.
> The bay-trees in our country are all wither'd
> And meteors fright the fixed stars of heaven.

The oil, *Oleum Lauri*, obtained by distillation of the leaves
or the pressing of the berries, is used in herbal medicine for
rheumatic complaints, but the Oil of Bay which is used for
making Florida Water and Bay Rum, employed as an ingredient of hair tonics, is distilled not from the sweet Bay, but from
the fresh leaves of a West Indian plant, *Myrcia acris*.

Care should be taken not to use in error the leaves of the
Cherry Laurel, a plant belonging to the Rose family, for these
are a source of the glucoside laurocerasin and produce prussic
acid.

BELLADONNA   *Atropa belladonna* L.   Solanaceae
Deadly Nightshade
FR *Belladone*; *Morelle furieuse*
GER *Tollkirsche*; *Teufelsbeere*; *Belladonna*

> And I ha' been plucking plants among
> Hemlock, Henbane, Adder's tongue,
> Nightshade, Moonwort, Libbard's-bane,
> And twice by the dogs was like to be ta'en.
>
> BEN JONSON *The Masque of Queens*

The narcotic qualities of Belladonna were known and feared
in ancient times, for it was supposed to have been grown in
Hecate's garden, and is one of the nineteen herbs mentioned
by Hesiod as having been cultivated by the protectress of
enchanters and witches. Gerard says: "If you will follow my
counsell, deale not with the same in any case, and banish it
from your gardens, and the use of it also, being a plant so
furious and deadly; for it bringeth such as have eaten thereof
into a dead sleepe, wherein many have died."

Early physicians were very wary of this plant and confined

themselves to applying the leaves to the head in cases of severe headache and insomnia. They avoided giving it internally, since, as they said, "it troubles the mind and causeth madness". It fell into disfavour in the 18th century and did not figure in the official pharmacopoeia again until 1832, after its active principle, atropine, had been isolated and studied scientifically. Today, both root and leaves of Belladonna are extensively employed in pharmacy, and the plant is cultivated for medicinal purposes in many regions of the United States, in Europe (particularly in Germany), and also in various parts of Britain, including Bedfordshire, Hertfordshire and Suffolk. Miss Wheelwright tells us that it is often found in the neighbourhood of the ancient abbeys, where it was once cultivated, such as Furness, where the neighbouring valley, Bekansgill, was called the Valley of the Nightshade.

A. belladonna is a member of the Potato Order, several of which have poisonous properties. It is a tall, branching perennial, with ovate, dullish green leaves, tapering to a point, the underside marked by a prominent midrib. Its purplish bell-shaped flowers are followed by attractive black berries. The generic name of *Atropa* is derived from the name of Atropos, that one of the Fates who cut short the thread of human life. The specific name is said to have originated from the habit of Italian women, in the olden days, of making use of the drug to enlarge the pupils of the eyes and thus enhance their beauty.

In addition to the popular name of Deadly Nightshade, Belladonna has many folk-names, and during the Middle Ages was frequently called Dwale, from the Scandinavian word for sleep – an allusion to its narcotic properties. Most of the folk-names, both in England and abroad, stress the fact that it was the Devil's plant: i.e. *Devil's Herb, Duivelskers, Teufelsbeere, Duivelskruid*, and in Provence *Erbo doou diablé*.

The most important constituents of the living plant are the alkaloids hyoscyamine, atropine, belladonnine and scopolamine. The principal uses are as a sedative, antiasthmatic, and –

in ophthalmic work – a mydriatic (causing dilation of the pupil of the eye). The leaves and flowering tops are harvested as soon as the plant blooms; the roots are gathered in the autumn, cleaned, cut longitudinally to facilitate drying, and dried either in the sun or by artificial heat.

BETONY　　　*Stachys officinalis* (Treviranus)　　　Labiatae
FR *Bétoine*
GER *Rote Betonie*

Betony, formerly often spelt Betayne or Beteyne, figures largely in medical treatises of the Middle Ages, when it was considered a sovereign remedy for many ills, though today it is no longer officinal, for truth to tell it contains no special medicinal qualities. It does, however, embody the fragrant aromatic principles found in many of the labiates.

It is a downy perennial plant, from 1 to 2 feet high, with light purple flowers in dense whorls arranged in a spike. It is found in woods and hedgerows all over England, but rarely in Scotland.

In a 15th-century MS (Sloane 706) dealing with "Good medicines for diverse infirmitees of mannes body" we read that we should "take ye wheygt of a bene of ye powder of beteyne and medle it wyt hony and put it in your mowth and that kepeth wele ye stomak and maketh good degestyon".

An English translation of the same period of the treatise by "the Cunnynge and sage Clerke Macer" informs us that "the first virtu, Betayne doth make a body well to pysse and putteth out the stoon". Macer also recommends a plaster of "Betayne leves well stamped" for a black eye, and tells us furthermore that "the juyce of Betayne medled with oyl of rosys" will heal a man of "many divers siknesse".

Far back in Anglo-Saxon days Betony was known and used, for the Leech Book of Bald recommends as a cure for lumbago the drinking of this herb infused in hot, sweet wine. Going back even further, an early *Herbarium* of Apuleius contains a crude drawing of *Betonica officinalis* which has been partly lost through decay, and declares the herb to be "good whether for a mans soul or for his body: it shields him against monstrous nocturnal visitors and against frightful visions and dreams". The section on this plant in the *Herbarium* is supposed to be taken from a treatise on the virtues of Betony written by Antonius Musa, physician to the Emperor Augustus.

In popular medicine today Betony tea, made by infusing an ounce of the dried herb in a pint of boiling water, is said to afford relief from nervous headache. In parts of Europe the dried leaves of Betony are used as a substitute for tobacco; and in England they are frequently blended with Coltsfoot and Eyebright to form herbal smoking mixtures.

BORAGE   *Borrago officinalis* L.   Boraginaceae
Beebread
FR *Bourrache*
GER *Borretsch* ; *Gurkenkraut*

> Here is sweet water, and borage for blending,
> Comfort and courage to drink to your fill.
>
> NORA HOPPER

"Borage for courage." So runs the old proverb; courage in the face of adversity being implied rather than the physical quality. "Pliny calls it Euphrosinum," writes Gerard, "because it maketh a man merry and joyful." Evelyn tells us that sprigs of Borage in wine "are of known Vertue to revive the Hypochondriac and chear the hard Student". That belief has been long-lived and beneath the engraved frontispiece of Burton's *Anatomy of Melancholy* we read:

> Borage and Hellebore fill two scenes,
> Sovereign plants to purge the veins
> Of melancholy, and cheer the heart
> Of those black fumes which make it smart.

According to Dioscorides, Borage was that famous Nepenthe of Homer which Polydamna, wife of Thonis, sent to Helen for a token "of such rare virtue that when taken steeped in wine, if wife and children, father and mother, brother and sister, and all thy dearest friends should die before thy face, thou could'st not grieve or shed a tear for them".

Yet Borage is quite an unassuming little plant, redeemed from the commonplace by its "gallant blew floures", which Parkinson tells us "have alwaies been enterposed among the flowers of women's needlework", and had it no other virtues it could well be grown for its flowers alone.

It is a good plant to have in the herb garden; it seeds freely and if allowed to take care of itself will come up year by year in the same place. Bees love it.

Formerly the young leaves were used in salads "to ingender good blood", and today the flowers and leaves are added to claret and other cups, to which they impart a refreshing flavour of cucumber. Our grandmothers used to candy Borage flowers by boiling them in a syrup of sugar and rosewater, afterwards strewing finely powdered sugar over them and allowing to dry.

According to Fernie the name Borage is a corruption of "cor-ago", meaning "I stimulate the heart", and the herbal of Apuleius calls the herb "corago".

BUGLE *Ajuga reptans* L. Labiatae
Middle Consound
FR *Bugle rampante*; *Petite consoude*
GER *Kriechender Günsel*

> As bryght as bugyl or ellys bolace.
> LYDGATE *Minor Poems*

Bugle is a perennial herb which spreads and creeps along the ground; hence the specific name *reptans* (crawling). It has whorls of six to ten bright blue flowers in a spike, with reddish or purplish bracts beneath each whorl. It can be found almost everywhere in meadows, pastures, and more especially in woods.

In bygone days Bugle was a noted vulnerary plant, being one of the Consounds, or wound herbs, known to the old herbalists as *Consolida media* or Middle Consound. It was, says Pechey, "one of the ingredients for the wound drink of the *London Dispensatory* commonly called the 'Traumatick Decoction' (though the formula also calls for calcined crabs and 'one pugil* of Perewincles'!)"

Culpeper advises those who, being addicted to drinking, are troubled by strange sights in the night to take two spoonfuls of the syrup of the herb after supper, before going to bed. Tournefort calls it "Comfrey of the Meadows" and describes it as vulnerary, healing, balsamick and agglutinating.

For sores and ulcers, and even for broken bones, it was once customary to keep a pot of ointment made up of the bruised leaves of Bugle, Scabious and Sanicle, boiled in hog's grease. "It is so singular good", remarks Culpeper, "for all sorts of hurts in the body that none that knows its usefulness will be without it."

Yellow Bugle or Ground Pine (*A. chamoepitys*) is a tufted, much-branched plant, in habit quite different from the common Bugle. It has yellow flowers, in axillary pairs, and in Britain is usually only found in the eastern and south-eastern counties. It is much commoner in central and southern Europe. The erect Bugle (*A. genevensis*) is found at higher altitudes than the common Bugle and, though not common in Britain, is sometimes found in the Scottish Highlands.

BUGLOSS, SMALL   *Lycopsis*   Boraginaceae
                        arvensis L.
Field Alkanet
FR *Lycopside*; *Grisette*; *Petite buglosse*
GER *Krumhals*; *Acker Ochsenzunge*

Bugloss is a name that has been applied to several boraginaceous plants, and the Bugloss of the old medical writers was

*Fistful

BUGLOSS

usually the Alkanet (*Anchusa officinalis*) (q.v.). Bugloss has many points of similarity with Borage; it has leaves of similar shape and its flowers in some degree resemble those of Borage. But it is a much smaller plant, growing to a height of from a foot to eighteen inches, and its bright blue flowers are seldom more than a quarter of an inch across. It grows by hedges and in cornfields, flowering from April to June.

The name Lycopsis is from a Greek word meaning "wolf's face", apparently from some fancied resemblance. Bugloss, however, comes from two Greek words signifying the tongue of an ox, descriptive, according to Dioscorides, of the shape and rough surface of the leaves (*cf* German *Acker Ochsenzunge*).

The virtues of Bugloss are much the same as those of Borage, though the old herbal known as *Circa instans* says that wine in which Bugloss has been allowed to steep will restore the memory.

BUGLOSS, VIPER'S   *Echium*   Boraginaceae
                    vulgare L.

FR *Vipérine*; *Buglosse sauvage*
GER *Natternkopf*; *Frauenkrieg*

This rather handsome biennial, growing from 1 to 2 feet high, is the plant which William Turner called "Langdebeef", though what the French call *Langue de bœuf* is the Alkanet or *Anchusa officinalis*. Parkinson notes a certain confusion, for he says that Viper's Bugloss is "Echium of most Authours, yet of some *Buglossum silvestre viperinum*, and Serpentaria, and some also took it for Anchusa."

The spotted stem of the plant together with the shape of the nut-like seeds, resembling a snake's head, gave the plant its name, both in English and in Latin, for the generic name Echium is derived from the Greek word for a viper, *echio*. The tubular flowers are borne in a series of short, curved sprays, and their colour is purplish-red before they are fully opened. Later this colour turns to a brilliant blue, though a variety with white flowers is known. The flowering period is from June to August.

BURDOCK   *Arctium lappa* L.   Compositae
FR *Bardane*; *Herbe aux teigneux*
GER *Grosse Klette*

> They are burrs, I can tell you; they'll stick where they are
> thrown.   *Troilus and Cressida*, 3, ii

Burdock grows freely in waste places and by the roadside over the whole of Europe except the extreme north, and has become naturalised over most of the eastern half of the United States, and also grows in Japan. It is a branching, erect biennial growing to between 3 and 5 feet, and its thick stems bear dull purple flowers which eventually give place to the fruit, or burrs, which with their hooked spines cling to anything they chance to encounter. The leaves, heart-shaped, are very large, often a foot in breadth, green above and with a white cottony down on the underside. It was under such a leaf that Hop-o'-my-Thumb, in the old nursery tale, took refuge during a storm and was swallowed, wrapped in the leaf, by a hungry cow.

The plant was once known as the Clot-bur, and Chaucer tells in the prologue of the "Canon's Yeoman's Tale" how

> A clote-leef he hadde under his hood
> For swoot*, and for to kepe his heed from hete.

The generic name of the plant comes from the fact that Dioscorides first called the plant *arkteion*, from the Greek *arktos* = "a bear", though any resemblance to that animal is

*Sweat.

128 *Burdock*

not immediately apparent. The specific name *lappa* is also from a Greek word meaning to seize, possibly because the burrs seize upon anything they happen to touch.

This clinging quality of the burrs has gained for them many quaint names. Country children love to stick them on one another's clothing like buttons, thus giving rise to the name *Beggars' buttons, Sweethearts, Sticky-balls, Amor folia, Cockle-buttons* and *Philantropium* are also among the many other appellations.

Though occasionally used as a popular remedy in the form of extracts and tinctures for boils and as a blood purifier, it is now more or less obsolete, though herbalists still use it for affections of the kidneys. Burdock roots and leaves were once official, being used for their diuretic and diaphoretic action, but are so no longer.

In the Middle Ages Burdock was regarded as a valuable remedy for the stone, and was called *Bardana* (*cf* the French name *bardane*). The plant occurs in the *Capitulare de Villis* where the name is written *bardanam.* As late as 1649 the *London Dispensatory* has an entry: "Bardana, Clot bur, or Burdock . . . is held to be a good remedy against shrinking of the sinews." Parkinson writes: "The juice of its leaves given to drink with old wine doth wonderfully help the biting of any serpents, as also of a mad dogge." John Wesley, in his *Primitive Physic* (24th edn., 1792) recommends an infusion of dried burdock as a remedy for the "King's Evil", or scrofula.

In Japan, and among Japanese communities anywhere, the roots of burdock are used as a vegetable, boiled in salted water and eaten either with butter or a sauce, like salsify. It is cultivated in market gardens in the South of France for a similar purpose.

The Lesser Burdock (*Arctium minus*) is similar in appearance to the Common Burdock, but is smaller, growing to a height of from 2 to 3 feet.

BURNET (SALAD) *Poterium sanguisorba* Rosaceae
FR *Petite Pimprenelle*; *Pimprenelle des jardins*
GER *Kleiner Wiesenknopf*

> L'insalata non è buon', ne bella
> Ove non è la pimpinella
> *Old Italian saying*

The Garden or Salad Burnet acquired its generic name from *poterion* – a drinking cup – because its leaves, in ancient times, were used in the preparation of numerous beverages. It has been put to similar use in more recent times, for Culpeper says "two or three of the stalks, with leaves, put into a cup of wine, especially claret, are known to quicken the spirits, refresh and cheer the heart, and drive away melancholy" (which seems to have been a mental affliction fairly widespread during the 16th and 17th centuries). He adds that it is good for "the choleric belchings and castings of the stomach".

Salad Burnet had a regular place in the old herb gardens and Sir Francis Bacon recommended the planting of whole alleys with burnet, wild thyme and water-mints "which perfume the air most delightfully, being trodden upon and crushed".

The dark purplish-red flowers grow on a stem from 1 to 2 feet high, and the ovoid serrated leaflets, with a scent and taste reminiscent of cucumber, are occasionally used in salads, for which purpose they should be cut when young, for otherwise they are apt to be tough.

The Great Burnet (*Sanguisorba officinalis*) was in the olden days known as Bloodwort and was used as a styptic for staunching wounds. Correvon* writes: "This perennial plant, with its composite leaves and dark brown flowers arranged in close, erect spikes, haunts the marshes and damp meadows of our colder regions. Its leaves are employed for their vulnerary properties; they are applied, fresh, to wounds – and, dried and ground, on ulcers. The Piedmontese use them in cases of

---

* *Le jardin de l'herboriste*, 1896.

haemorrhoids." Whereas the Great Burnet grows in moist places, the Salad Burnet prefers dry pasture-land, growing especially well on chalk and limestone.

Burnet Vinegar can be made by adding half an ounce of dried and pulverised Burnet seed to a quart of vinegar. This mixture should be well shaken once a day for about a fortnight, after which it should be strained and kept in a tightly corked bottle.

S. Officinalis is in Fr. *Pimprenelle officinale* and in Ger. *Bluts-kugel*.

CAPER   *Capparis spinosa* L.   Capparidaceae
FR *Câpre*
GER *Kaper*

> And the grasshopper shall be a burden and the caperberry
> shall fall.   *Ecclesiastes* (R.V.)

"I once saw growing in Italy", said an Irish traveller, "the finest anchovies I ever clapped eyes on!"

Offended when a listener doubted his veracity, the Irishman challenged him to a duel, in the course of which he shattered his opponent's knee-cap with a shot from his pistol. The wretched man staggered about in agony, whereupon the Irishman's second remarked to his principal that at all events he had made his adversary cut some pretty capers.

"Capers!" shouted the son of Erin. "Capers! Faith, that's it." And turning to his antagonist he magnanimously exclaimed: "'Tis right you were; 'twas not anchovies but capers I saw growing. I beg your honour's pardon; think no more of it!"

This little tale may serve to start the conversation going when you next pass round the caper sauce.

Capers are not berries, as some think, but the tiny pickled olive-green flower buds of *Capparis spinosa*, a small shrub indigenous to the countries bordering the Mediterranean, where it grows in sunny places among rocks and on walls. The flowers are quite attractive and the plant can be grown under glass in this country. The generic name comes from the Greek *kaptein*, meaning "to eat up", probably owing to the fact that capers are used as an appetiser.

In France, Spain and Italy, where the plant is cultivated for commerce, the flower buds are picked as soon as they attain the size of a pea, before they begin to open. After being kept in the dark for three or four hours they are put into vinegar; they need no further preparation. After macerating for a week they are transferred to fresh vinegar and left for a further week.

When pickled the capers are drained and graded by means of sieves. The most sought after are the young tender buds classed by the growers as *non pareilles*; these are the dearest; then come successively, increasing in size and diminishing in value, *surfines*, *capucines*, *fines* and *capotes*. The capers are despatched in barrels after having been carefully drained again and pressed. On arrival at their destination they are at once bottled in vinegar to conserve them. *Cornichons de caprier* are pickled flower-buds which have been allowed to develop.

The shrub flowers during the whole of the summer and the buds are picked as soon as they appear. In France the chief centres for the commercial production of capers are placed around Roquevaire, in the Bouches-du-Rhône.

CARAWAY   *Carum carvi* L.   Umbelliferae
FR *Carvi*; *Cumin des prés*
GER *Kümmel*

> We will eat a last year's Pippin of my own grafting, with a
> dish of Caraways.   *Henry IV, Part II, 5, iii*

Caraway seed is the dried ripe fruit of Caraway, an annual or biennial plant native to western Asia and a large portion of north and central Europe. The fruit contains two roughly oblong seeds, strongly ribbed and laterally compressed, about one-eighth of an inch long and brown in colour. Both the seeds and the oil distilled from them are used – as a carminative in medicine, or as a condiment and flavouring agent.

The plant is commercially cultivated on a large scale in Holland, where it has been grown for centuries. Turner (1562) says, "it groweth in great plentye in Freseland in the meadows there betweene Marienhoffe and Werden, hard by the sea banke". It was extensively grown in England at one time, particularly in Essex and Bedfordshire, but now Britain's supplies are imported from Europe, mainly from Holland, where it is a striking sight to see whole fields of Caraway in bloom in the Harlemmermeer.

Caraway is one of a number of aromatic umbelliferous plants possessing carminative properties, such as Cumin and Dill, and was well-known to the ancients, for records of its use were found in the Ebers papyrus, an Egyptian compilation of around 1500 BC.

That Caraway seed was popular in Shakespeare's day is evident from Squire Shallow's invitation to Falstaff quoted at the head of this entry, and as an example of the survival of English traditions the custom of serving roast apples accompanied by a saucer of Caraway seeds is still kept up at Trinity College, Cambridge.

At one time the root of the plant seems to have been eaten as a vegetable, for Parkinson says: "The rootes of Carawayes may be eaten as Carrots, and by reason of the spicie taste doth warme and comfort a cold weake stomacke." The same writer also states that "the powder of the seede put into a poultis taketh away blacke and blew spots of blowes or bruises".

In England Caraway seed is comparatively little used except in seed cakes, but the German housewife never fails to keep a store of the seed by her to add flavour to soups, to sauerkraut, and also to cheese. The seed also forms an ingredient of bread in many countries and is used both by Germans and Russians for making the liqueur known as Kümmel. In many central European countries Caraway seed is strewn on bread under the name of "Kumin", which has led to some confusion.

Our ancestors imagined that Caraway would induce constancy in love, and for this reason it formed an essential ingredient of love philtres.

Caraway water is used as a carminative for children, and three hundred years ago Culpeper was recommending "Carray comfits" as "a most admirable remedy for those that are troubled with wind". The volatile oil, containing carvone (found also in the oils of Dill and Cumin), is used to scent soaps and various cosmetics, such as the French *Huile de Vénus*.

And to conclude: a note for the gourmet culled from Mr Redgrove's excellent *Spices and Condiments*. He writes: "Mixed with a trace of sugar and lightly sprinkled on bread and butter, powdered caraway seed forms an admirable accompaniment to gorgonzola cheese, a combination which has only once to be tasted to be highly appreciated."

CENTAURY   *Erythraea centaurium*   Gentianaceae
Earth-gall   (Persoon)
FR *Petite centaurée*; *Herbe à mille florins*; *Gentianelle*
GER *Tausendgüldenkraut*; *Biberkraut*; *Erdgalle*

> There Centaury supplies the wholesome flame,
> That from Thessalian Chiron takes its name.
> > LUCAN *Pharsalia*

In the *Pharsalia* Lucan names Centaury as one of the plants which were burned with the object of driving away serpents. The generic adjective signifies "red", from the rose-red colour of the flowers, which grow in terminal corymbs, or small heads, and the specific name is said to be derived from Chiron, the Greek centaur who taught mankind the use of

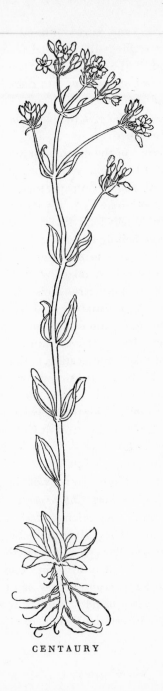

CENTAURY

medicinal herbs, and cured himself with Centaury of a wound he had accidentally received from an arrow poisoned with the blood of the hydra. The Germans, however, have resolved the word *centaurium* into *centum aureos,* and call it the "Thousand guilder herb", in which they have the backing of the French, who give the plant the popular name of the "Thousand florin herb".

This plant is one of the gentian family, and like its relatives it is valued as a tonic and stomachic. It is perhaps the most bitter of them all, and, as Culpeper says, "'Tis very wholesome, but not very toothsome". As a popular medicine it is used extensively as a remedy for dyspepsia in the form of an infusion made by pouring boiling water on the leaves in the proportion of one ounce of leaves to one pint of water. Herbalists also employ Centaury leaves, mixed with those of Barberry, in cases of jaundice and other renal disorders.

In the Middle Ages plants were closely associated with magic, but among the superstitious lore which found credence even in the minds of scholars, this account of Centaury by Albertus Magnus would take some beating. "Magicians assure us," he writes, "that this herb has a singular virtue, for if it is mixed with the blood of a female hoopoe and put in a lamp with the oil, all those present will see themselves upside down, with their feet in the air." He also says: "Put Centaury under someone's nose and he will run away as fast as his legs can carry him," and adds: "This recipe is infallible."

The Greater- or More-Centaury of the old herbals seems to have been the Yellow-wort (*Chlora perfoliata*) called *Chlorette* in France. In Linacre's translation of Macer we read: "More-Centory or Earthgall hath leves lyke to the Lesse Centory, but more whyter, and yelowe flowers, and flowreth not but in the top."

A 17th-century remedy for gout, known as the "Duke of Portland's Powder" because it was said to have cured him of that affliction, was a blend of gentian root, and the leaves of Germander, Birthwort and Centaury.

CHAMOMILE *Anthemis nobilis* L. Compositae

[COMMON OR ROMAN]

FR *Camomille noble*; *Anthémide*
GER *Römische Kamille*; *Edle Kamille*

The name Chamomile is loosely applied to a number of plants but the two most safely called by that name are the Anthemis and the Matricary. *Anthemis nobilis* was first named "Roman" by the 16th-century German humanist Joachim Camerarius, who in his travels found it growing near Rome.

William Turner, in his *New Herball* (1551), says : "it hath floures wonderfully shynynge yellow . . . the herb may be called in English, golden floure . . . In England it is so plenteous that it groweth not only in gardynes but also vii mile above London it groweth in the wylde felde, in Rychmonde grene, in Brantfurde grene. . . ." But although so plentiful in Turner's day, the Common Chamomile is not, despite its name, found everywhere in England but is confined mainly to the South, growing wild and profusely in Cornwall and cultivated in Hampshire, Surrey and other districts for medicinal use. It is commercially grown in France, Belgium, Hungary and parts of Germany.

The specific name *nobilis* was applied to this herb on account of its healing virtues, for which it has been renowned for centuries. The Anglo-Saxon leechdoms extol the virtues of *Maythen*, though as Miss Wheelwright has pointed out, "as to the Maythen of our ancestors we do not know for certain whether or not it was the true chamomile. It may have been *Pyrethrum inodorum*, called feverfew from its use as a febrifuge, or *Matricaria chamomilla* L., a similar plant of waste lands, formerly largely cultivated in Belgium".

This creeping branched perennial is often grown in gardens to form a compact carpet which seems to suffer no ill effects from being trodden upon and under pressure gives off a fragrant scent.

Chamomile 137

The flowers of the Common Chamomile are small, with white florets and golden yellow centres; the extract from the dried expanded flower-heads and the distilled *Oleum Anthemidis* are official in the British Pharmacopoeia and used as a stomachic and tonic.

An infusion of Chamomile is a mild sedative, very popular in France. Charles Estienne, in his *Maison Rustique*, remarks, in Richard Surflet's translation, "Cammomill is singular good to mollifie, resolve, rarify and loosen, and in this respect there is no remedie better for lassitudes or wearisomnes without just outward causes than bathes made with the leaves and flowers thereof". It is an ingredient in various formulae for Vermouth.

Commercially the double-flowered variety is grown, since this is preferred for medicinal use, but in private gardens it is more usual to find the single-flowered kind. The best time to harvest the flowers is when the white ligulate ray florets begin to reflex, but before the central yellow disc florets lose their colour.

CHAMOMILE   *Matricaria chamomilla* L.   Compositae
[GERMAN]

FR *Camomille commune*; *Œil de soleil*; *Amerelle*
GER *Echte Kamille*; *Blütenthee*

The generic name gives us a clue to the use of the herb in past centuries, when it was prescribed for a number of women's diseases, for the therapeutic value of this plant was already known in the time of Dioscorides.

The Matricary closely resembles Anthemis in habit, foliage and general appearance, but the receptacle, or *torus*, is without the scales found in the latter. There are three varieties of this plant found in Western Europe: *Matricaria chamomilla*, or Wild Chamomile, which closely resembles *Anthemis cotula*,

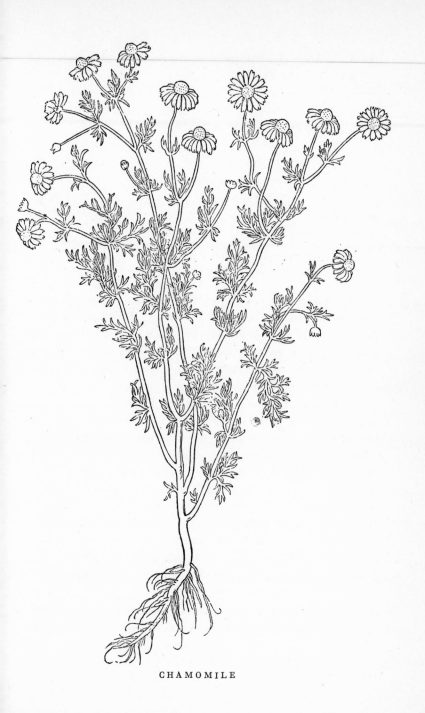

CHAMOMILE

the Stink Mayweed; *M. inodora*, the Scentless Matricary; and *M. discoidea*, the Disc Chamomile.

M. chamomilla grows wild in enormous quantities in Hungary, in the region of Debrecsen. There it is harvested for use as an ingredient of hair rinses.

CHERVIL   *Anthriscus cerefolium*   Umbelliferae
(Hoffman)

FR *Cerfeuil*
GER *Gartenkerbel*

> Chibolles and Chervelles and ripe chiries manye.
> *Piers Plowman*

Though commonly grown in kitchen gardens abroad, Chervil is but rarely seen in England. This is a pity, for it has a pleasant flavour, reminiscent of caraway, and is no trouble to grow. It is an attractive annual, with stems growing to a height of between a foot and eighteen inches, bright-green lace-like leaves, and tiny white flowers borne in umbels.

As a garnish it is just as decorative as Parsley, and the leaves can be used for seasoning, and in soups and salads. It is an ingredient of the French "fines herbes". Gerard writes: "Chervill is used very much among the Dutch people in a kinde of Loblolly or Hotchpot which they do eat, called Warmus." ("Warmoes" is the Dutch word for the general produce of the market garden.) Chervil soup is considered a delicacy in Holland, made as follows: take half a litre of salted water, 45–60 grams of chervil flowers, 50–70 grams of butter, 3 tablespoons of finely chopped Chervil, and one, or two, eggs. Heat the butter with the flowers in it, stirring continuously, till almost boiling; then add the liquid in small quantities, still stirring, and let this simmer for about ten minutes. Then mix in the finely chopped Chervil and pour on to the eggs, which have been beaten up in a soup tureen.

The name of Giant Sweet Chervil is given to Sweet Cicely (q.v.)

CHIVES   *Allium schoenoprasum*   Liliaceae
Rushleek
FR *Ciboulette*; *Petit porreau*
GER *Schnittlauch*

Chives were at one time extensively grown in England, and when Peter Kalm, the Finnish naturalist, visited England in 1748 he noticed that chives were amongst the vegetables most grown in the market gardens around London, for they were "esteemed milder than onions" and of a "quick rellish". But although the finest in flavour, as well as the smallest, of the onion tribe, Chives are today much more commonly used for culinary purposes in France than in England.

The local name of "rushleek" given to this plant in some parts of the country is a literal translation of the specific title *schoenoprasum*. In Holland and Belgium it is called *bieslook*, which has the same meaning.

Chives will grow in almost any soil, and can be raised from seed, though usually the plant is propagated by division of clumps in the spring or autumn. Each tiny bulb (which should not be eaten) makes a separate plant, and a fine bed can be easily grown, which makes it all the more surprising that this herb should have gone out of fashion.

The green, hollow spikes begin to appear in early spring, and this "grass" can be cut several times in the season. Finely chopped, these leaves, with their delicate suggestion of an onion flavour, are excellent both for flavouring omelettes and as an ingredient in salads. Where the climate is mild the "grass" can be gathered almost all the year round.

In the kitchen garden the plant should not be allowed to flower, since it is not possible to get both "grass" and seed

Chives 141

from the one set of plants, but in a herb garden it may be grown as an attractive edging, when the pinkish flowers on stems about a foot or less high are altogether attractive.

CLARY *Salvia sclarea* L. Labiatae
FR *Sauge sclarée*; *Orvale*; *Toute-bonne*
GER *Muskateller Salbei*

> Percely, clarey and eke sage,
> And all other herbage.
>   JOHN GARDENER *Feate of Gardening*

This charmingly decorative plant, with its pink pointed bracts and blue-purple flower, was used in the Middle Ages for clearing the vision, and for this reason it received its popular name of Clary, or Clear-eye. Gerard wrote that the purple Clary was a stranger in England, but adds "it groweth in my garden"; it was probably first introduced from southern Europe into England during the 16th century.

It seems to have been a familiar potherb in the Middle Ages, and appears among the ingredients for herb omelette in *Le Ménagier de Paris*, but nowadays it is not used as a culinary herb except locally in some parts of France.

According to Ettmüller the herb was once used as an adulterant by German wine merchants who made an infusion of Clary and Elder flowers, and then added the resultant liquid to Rhine wine. This was said to "convert it into the likeness of Muscatel". Hence the German name for the plant. Lyte, in his version of Dodoens' Herbal, writes: "It maketh men drunke, and causeth headache, and therefore some Brewers do boyle it with their Beere, in steed of hops." Clary wine was known for its narcotic properties.

Today Clary is cultivated commercially for its oil, which is used in the cosmetics industry as a perfume fixer. It is a highly aromatic oil, with a scent resembling ambergris.

Wild Clary (*Salvia verbenaca*) is a smaller plant than the

Garden Clary, growing from a foot to eighteen inches high, and is a native of Britain. It is sometimes called Vervain Sage, and its medical properties are somewhat more powerful than those of the garden variety. This is the plant which was known to the monks as *Oculus Christi* from its power of clearing the vision, and Lawson says of it : "one of these seeds put into the eye, within three or foure houres will gather a thick skin, cleere the eye, and bolt it selfe forth without hurt to the eye".

Gerard writes of the Wild Clary that it "groweth wilde in divers barren places, almost in every country, especially in the fields of Holborne neere unto Grayes Inne, in the high way by the end of a brickewall: at the end of Chelsey next to London, in the high way as you go from the Queenes pallace of Richmond to the waters side, and in divers other places". Lyte recommends the seed of the Wild Clary, drunk with wine, as an aphrodisiac.

Among the varieties of cultivated Clary, by far the handsomest is the so-called Vatican Sage, which often grows to a height of 5 feet, and is said to have been grown originally in the gardens of the Vatican.

Clary is grown commercially in Provence to be used as a *parfum de support* in the French scent industry. For the herbalist's shop the inflorescence is gathered when the plant is in full bloom ; for perfumery, when flowering is over.

COLCHICUM   *Colchicum autumnale* L.   Liliaceae
Autumn Crocus
Meadow Saffron
FR *Colchique d'automne*; *Tue chien*; *Dame nue*
GER *Herbstzeitlose*; *Nackte Jungfer*

> Or tempered every baleful juice
> Which poisonous Colchian glebes produce.
> HORACE

The popular names of this beautiful plant are misleading. It is not a crocus, nor has it anything to do with saffron, which is the commercial product of *C. sativus*, the true Crocus. It is a poisonous plant, of which both corm and seeds are used in medicine, though on no account should they ever be used as a home remedy. Once common in Gloucestershire and Herefordshire, it has been gradually eliminated by farmers because of its poisonous character, and is now mainly imported from Southern Europe where it is cultivated to supply drug houses.

The corm is short, fleshy and bulbous and is harvested in summer. The dried corm is prepared for the market by removing the outer and inner membraneous skins which enclose it, slicing the corm, and then drying it at not too high a temperature. The alkaloid, colchicine, present in the corm and seeds of the Colchicum, is used as a specific remedy for gouty affections. Colchicine, an amorphous, highly toxic alkaloid of a pale yellow colour, relieves the pain and inflammation occurring in gouty arthritis, but great care must be exercised in its administration, and continual use may lead to derangement of the central nervous system.

Old herbalists knew of the medicinal value of Colchicum, though the alkaloid was not isolated until 1819, and even now its action is not entirely understood. Gerard warned anyone who ate Colchicum by accident to "drinke the milke of a cow, or else death presently ensueth". Dioscorides (in Goodyer's translation) tells us that "being eaten it killeth by choking like to ye mushrumps", and Theophrastus called the plant *Ephemeron*, probably meaning that the unfortunate consumer would not live more than a day.

Although mentioned in the *London Dispensatory* of 1618 Colchicum was little used medicinally, being considered "corrupt and venemous", until it was popularised about 1763 by Baron Storck of Vienna, who recommended it as a treatment for the then all too prevalent gout. It was also an ingredient of the celebrated gout nostrum called *Eau Médicinale de Husson*, popular in the reign of Louis XV.

The flowers of Colchicum are usually of a lilac colour, but there are several varieties with various coloured flowers. It can be distinguished from the true Autumn Crocus, *Crocus nudiflorus*, because it has six instead of three stamens. The name *Colchicum* is derived from Colchis, in Asia Minor, where it has thrived for centuries, and because at the time of flowering there are no leaves, the plant has received in various countries the popular name of "Naked Lady" (*cf* French "Dame nue" and German "Nackte Jungfer").

Although, because poisonous to animals, it is often eradicated from meadows by farmers, it is still cultivated to some extent in England on herb farms, the corms being gathered soon after the fruits ripen in June and July. Utilisation of the corms is, however, becoming rarer, for the chemical industry now prefers the seed as raw material for the extraction of the alkaloid.

COLTSFOOT   *Tussilago farfara* L.   Compositae
FR *Tussilage*; *Pas d'âne*; *Pied de cheval*
GER *Huflattich*; *Hustwurtz*; *Eselshuf*

"*Tussilago* or Fole-foot", writes Gerard, "hath many white and long creeping roots, somewhat fat; from which rise up naked stalkes (in the beginning of March and Aprill) about a spanne long, bearing at the top yellow floures, which change into downe and are caried away with the winde: when the stalke and seed is perished, there appeare springing out of the earth many broad leaves, greene above, and next the ground of a white hoarie or grayish colour, fashioned like an Horse foot; for which cause it was called Fole-foot and Horse-hoofe: seldom or never shall you find leaves and floures at once, but the flours are past before the leaves come out of the ground."

On account of this idiosyncrasy the herb was called by old writers *Filius ante patrem*, or *Son-before-father*. In some parts of the Netherlands it is still known as *Zoon-vóór-de-vader*. The

10   *Coltsfoot* 145

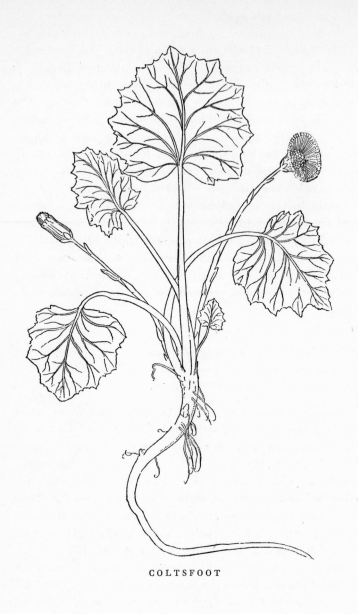

COLTSFOOT

generic name of the plant is from *tussis*, the Latin word for a cough, and for hundreds of years Coltsfoot has been an ingredient of cough cures. The dried leaves are often used in herbal tobaccos prescribed for sufferers from asthma.

The herb was used by Dioscorides as an inhalation; Gerard advocated the taking of "the fume of the dried leaves through a funnell or tunnell, burned upon coles"; and Linnaeus, in his day, wrote that: "the Swiss people cure their coughs with Coltsfoot used as tobacco".

Farfara, the specific name of this herb, derives from the Latin *far* = grain, owing to the appearance of the underside of the leaves, which seem to be covered with meal – in reality a cottony down.

A decoction of the herb, often in conjunction with other herbs noted for their pectoral and demulcent qualities, such as Marshmallow and Horehound, is a well-established remedy for coughs, and Dodoens remarks that "the greene leaves of Folefoot pound with hony doe cure and heale the hote inflammation called St. Anthonies fire".

But the *Essence of Coltsfoot* so popular in early Victorian days for the treatment of colds was a base deception for it contained no trace of Coltsfoot but was composed of equal parts of Balsam of Tolu and Friar's Balsam mixed with spirit of wine. According to Fernie, Dr Paris said of it: "If a patient with a catarrh should recover whilst using such a remedy, I should call it a lucky escape rather than a skilful cure."

A creeping perennial, with flowering stems about six inches high, and large, broad heart-shaped leaves, Coltsfoot grows wild over most parts of Europe, and its bright yellow flowers begin to appear as early as March, though the leaves do not, as a rule, show themselves until May.

COMFREY   *Symphytum officinale* L.   Boraginaceae
Consound
FR *Consoude*; *Oreille d'âne*
GER *Wallwurz*; *Beinwell*

> This, the Consound,
> Whereby the lungs are eased of their grief.
>
> TENNYSON

Comfrey is one of the old physic herbs whose name is derived
from a corruption of *con firmare*, since in the Middle Ages it
was used to help the knitting together of broken bones. Says
Pliny: "the roots be so glutinative that they will solder or
glew together meat that is chopt in pieces, seething in a pot, and
make it into one lump: the same bruysed and layd in the manner of a plaister, doth heale all fresh and green wounds."

The generic name is derived from a Greek word which
means "to unite", and this belief in the herb's efficacy as
a salve for fractures gave to it the old country names of Knit-
Bone and Knit-Back. In the *Speculum Mundi* we learn that
Comfrey "is highly commended of the learned for the curing
of wounds, especially of the intrals and inward parts, and for
burstings and ruptures; insomuch that they affirm the slimie
substance of the root made in a posset of ale, and given to be
drunk, cureth the pain the back gotten by any violent motion
as wrastling and the like; to which some add the overmuch
use of Venus".

Comfrey is allied to Borage, and like other members of the
Borage family it has rough hairy stalks and long rough leaves,
rather similar to the leaves of the common Bugloss. "The
floures bee round and hollow like little bells" was Lyte's
description, and the drooping clusters of these cream or pink
bugles appear early in the moist soil of low-lying fields or at
the edges of ponds. *S. tuberosum* is a much smaller plant than
the Common Comfrey, seldom growing more than a foot
high.

Though not official nowadays, Comfrey is still cultivated in some parts for its medicinal properties, both leaves and root being used. An infusion of the dried leaves (one ounce to a pint of boiling water) is widely used for chest ailments, whilst a poultice prepared with the fresh leaves is employed to reduce swellings and sprains. From the slimy root is prepared an ointment, the mucilage (the most important constituent) containing tannin.

The leaves of Comfrey, when crushed, emit a pleasant fragrance, and when young form a pleasant addition to salads. The old leaves should be avoided, as they are much too tough and coarse in flavour. The plant is a perennial which will grow profusely in any soil and likes the shade. It is easily, perhaps too easily, increased by root division. In fact it is easier to grow than to eradicate once it has been established in the garden.

CUMIN *Cuminum cyminum* L. Umbelliferae
FR *Cumin*; *Faux anis*
GER *Pfeffer-Kümmel*

> Rank smelling rue, and cumin good for eyes.
> SPENSER *Muiopotmos*

Cumin is the dried ripe fruit of *Cuminum cyminum*, an annual herbaceous plant native to the Mediterranean regions and north Africa, but now widely cultivated, though in England it is less grown today than formerly, and indeed is now rarely to be seen in herb gardens, probably because the seed is far less used in this country than it is elsewhere. Cumin is quite a small plant, rarely exceeding a foot in height, with white or rose-coloured flowers. The fruit is about a quarter inch long, formed of two carpels which remain united. In colour the fruit of Cumin is greyish-brown, containing a white and oily seed.

Cumin seed is used as a spice for flavouring foods of various kinds, bread, cheeses, sausages, in curry powder, and together with fennel and juniper berries for pickling cabbage to make sauerkraut. Today it is not much used in England, where the milder flavour of caraway is preferred to it, but Cumin is still very popular in all Oriental cooking.

It is a herb of great antiquity, mentioned several times in the Bible, as well as in the works of Hippocrates, Dioscorides and Theophrastus. Among the ancient Greeks Cumin was the symbol of cupidity and misers were jocularly spoken of as having eaten Cumin. It was a popular spice for fowl in the Middle Ages and the ancient cookery book *Le Ménagier de Paris* (1393) gives a recipe for *Cumminée de Poulaille*.

Oil of Cumin, now largely replaced medicinally by Caraway oil, is sometimes used as an anti-spasmodic and carminative. But what now strikes us as a rather peculiar remedy was proposed by Parkinson, who declares that "Cumin seede bruised and fryed with a hard Egge and bound to the back part of the head easeth an old head-ache".

Further, he states that "Cumin seede is sayd to make any one looke pale that useth it inwardly, or applyeth it outwardly," a statement he probably borrowed from Pliny,* who suggested that the followers of the rhetorician Porcius Latro used it to give themselves a pallor indicative of long hours of study.

The *Speculum Mundi* is more practical. It says: "Chew this seed in your mouth after the eating of onions, garlic or leeks, and it taketh away their smell. The smoke of this herb driveth away gnats."

Although until fairly recently Cumin had some reputation as a drug, its chief medical use nowadays is in veterinary medicine.

* *Natural History*, XX, Cap. 57.

DANDELION   *Taraxacum officinale*   Compositae
(Weber)
FR *Dent-de-lion*; *Pissenlit*
GER *Gemeiner Löwenzahn*; *Pissblume*

Shock-headed Dandelion
That drank the fire of the sun.
ROBERT BRIDGES

This wholesome salading is almost completely neglected in England nowadays, though in France it is still widely used. Although now a troublesome weed in most parts of the world, the Common Dandelion, if looked upon with disfavour by gardeners, nevertheless has its uses. Its name of "Lion-tooth", which may have come to us through the French in Norman times, is most probably derived from its dentate leaves, for the name seems to be the popular one by which it is known in most European tongues.

The brilliant golden yellow flowers, with their strap-shaped florets, enliven the dreariest of waste-lands, and the resemblance of the globular seed-heads, once bereft of their downy seeds, to a shaven skull may have suggested the country folk's name of "Priest's Crown".

Although the leaves, when young and not too tough, may be used for salads or as pot herbs, it is the root of the Dandelion which is the valuable part, and which was at one time cultivated on a commercial scale in Germany. The fresh root, often a foot or more in length, exudes a milky juice containing a crystalline bitter, taraxacin, together with insulin. Extract of taraxacin is expressed from the fresh root and preserved by adding alcohol. It is employed as a diuretic, whence the plant derived its names of "Pissenlit" and "Pissblume", and in cases of atonic dyspepsia. The Dandelion root can be gathered either in the spring, when the yield of taraxacin is highest, or in the autumn, when the yield of insulin is greater.

In some parts of Europe Dandelion coffee is made from

autumn-gathered roots, washed and dried in a slow oven where they are gently roasted until of a golden brown colour. For use the dried roots are ground and infused in the same manner as ordinary coffee, and the resultant brew is reputed as a sedative.

Evelyn, in his *Acetaria*, writes "Macerated in several Waters, to extract the bitterness, Dandelion, tho' somewhat opening, is very wholesome, and little inferior to Succory, Endive, etc. The French Country-People eat the Roots; and 'twas with this homely Sallet the Good-Wife *Hecale* entertained *Theseus*" (an incident celebrated by Callimachus in the poem which bears her name).

The name Taraxacum is derived from two Greek words: *taraxis*, a disease of the eye; and *akeomai*, to cure. For it appears that in ancient times the milky sap of the Dandelion was used for some definite disease of the eye, though later its use for this specific purpose was abandoned – perhaps when some more effective herb was discovered.

As a diuretic the Dandelion was at one time in great demand; so much so that in the 18th century it was termed *Herba Urinaria*. In Holland it is still called *beddepissers* by country folk.

One of the very best poetical descriptions of the Dandelion, its golden flower followed by the grey seed-head, is that of the Oxford don James Hurdis, in his poem *The Village Curate*, 1788.

> Dandelion this,
> A college youth that flashes for a day
> All gold; anon he doffs his gaudy suit,
> Touch'd by the magic hand of some grave Bishop
> And all at once, by commutation strange,
> Becomes a Reverend Divine.

DILL   *Anethum graveolens* L.   Umbelliferae

FR *Aneth*
GER *Dill*

> Here holy vervayne and here dill,
> 'Gainst witchcraft much availing.
> *The Muses' Elysium*

The name "dill" is derived from a Norse word *dilla*, meaning to lull, because a decoction of the seeds was at one time given to babies to make them sleep. Or so say most writers. But the Oxford Dictionary is more cautious, and says "etymology dubious".

Dill, a native of southern Europe, is now found all round the world in temperate or sub-tropical regions. It is an annual, or occasionally biennial, herb, erect in habit, growing to a height of about three feet, with feathery leaves rather suggestive of Fennel, and small umbels of yellow flowers.

Today Dill is cultivated for its use as a condiment, but in earlier times it was treated both as a medicinal and as a magic herb, whence the popular distich:

> Trefoil, Vervain, John's Wort, Dill,
> Hinder witches of their will.

With the sublime superstition which went hand in hand with pharmacy in ancient times, Pythagoras taught that holding Dill in the left hand would prevent epilepsy.

In old folk-lore Dill was considered a plant of lucky omen. In Germany the bride put Dill and salt in her shoes or pocket, and in Flanders the bride pinned a sprig of Dill to her dress. In former times it was also considered a cure for insomnia. We read in *Speculum Mundi*: "Of the green herb it is said that it procureth sleep, sound and secure; according to which we have an old saying that

> Whosoever weareth Vervin or Dill
> May be bold to sleep on every hill."

Dill 153

Nowadays Dill is grown chiefly for its culinary uses, and the seed has an aroma and flavour reminiscent of Caraway. Many food products contain Dill as a flavouring, and one of its best-known uses is for Dill pickles, which were popular in the days of Evelyn, who was very partial to "Gerckens muriated with the seeds of Dill" and gives in his *Acetaria* of 1680 a recipe for "Dill and Collyflower Pickle". Addison, too, was "always pleased with that particular time of the year which is proper for the pickling of Dill and Cucumbers". The leaves of Dill are also used for making Dill Vinegar and can be blended into sauce for fish, in the same way as Fennel.

Dill is used in medicine as a carminative, and all mothers know that Dill Water is a safe remedy for "wind" in infants. As long ago as 1525, the immensely popular *Banckes' Herbal* stated that "it destroyeth the yexing" (i.e. hiccups).

Two types of oil are made from Dill, one from the plant and the other from the seed, which are of different composition and taste, the seed oil being preferred for flavouring. The commercial harvesting of Dill depends on which type of oil is required. If from the herb, harvesting is carried out immediately after flowering; for the extraction of seed oil the crop is gathered as soon as the first seeds are ripe and left to dry under cover.

Dill used to be cultivated in East Anglia, but nowadays most of the Dill used in Britain is imported. In the United States a considerable acreage is devoted to the commercial cultivation of Dill in the North Central States and the Pacific Northwest.

The earliest recorded use of Dill in medicine is in the ancient Egyptian medical papyri. The ancient Egyptian word for Dill, says Warren R. Dawson, is *imse*, from which is derived the Coptic *emise* or *amise* – a word which is wrongly translated in the Authorised Version of the Bible (Matthew XXIII.23) as "anise".

ELECAMPANE   *Inula Helenium* L.   Compositae
Scabwort
FR *Aunée*; *Enule campane*
GER *Alant*; *Helenenkraut*

> Elecampane, the beauteous Helen's flower,
> Mingles among the rest her silver store.
>   RAPIN *Of Gardens*

This stately herb, a beautiful plant resembling a double Sun-flower, was very popular in former times, and almost always to be found in the Elizabethan herb garden. "The flours are in their bravery in June and July," writes Gerard, and he tells us, too, that the plant in his day grew plentifully "in the fields on the left hand as you go from Dunstable to Puddlehill". It is nowadays commercially grown in Holland.

Elecampane enjoyed a great reputation among the ancients for its soothing action in chronic pulmonary affections, or what Blackwell calls "the stuffing of the lungs". It was used for that purpose in Tudor times, and *The Widowes Treasure* (1595) gives a recipe "For the Rewme and Cough of the Lunges" in which the young roots of Elecampane are cut into small slices and boiled in water together with freshly gathered Setrach and Maidenhair. When the liquid has reduced to about a third of the quantity, sugar is added and the concoction boiled again, until the liquid is reduced from its original five pints to three quarters of a pint. "Then", the recipe continues, "take two yolkes of newe laied egs and beat them, and let them boyle together while you may say the Psalme *Miserere*, and take hereof at night a spoonefull, and another in the morning, lying on their backes an houre after they have received it; and in foure dayes, keeping them warme, it will rid the greatest cough that is."

In the MS cookery book known as the *Form of Cury* (B.M. Add. MS 5016), thought to have been written about the beginning of the 15th century by the master cook of Richard II,

ELECAMPANE

there is a recipe for preparing Elecampane, which shows that the root was at one time used as a pot herb. It says: "Take elena campana and seep it in water; take it up and grynde it wel in a mortar. Temper it up with ayren [eggs], safron and salt and do it over the fire and lat it not boile; cast above powder douce and issue it forth."

Elecampane was also used in the form of an ointment – *Unguentum Enulatum*, which was at one time official – for use in cases of scabs and itch, and this usage gave the herb its popular name of Scabwort.

The plant is a perennial, which grows best in moist fields and meadows. Its stout stems, growing to a height of between three and five feet, bear large, ovate leaves, dark green above, hairy underneath, with a fleshy mid-rib, and on account of its broad leaves the plant is sometimes called Elf-dock. The single terminal flowers, which blossom from the end of June until September, are bright yellow.

Elecampane is a corruption of the Latin name *Enula campana*, and the specific name reminds us of the legend that when Paris carried off Helen of Troy she had in her hand a nosegay of this plant, which was thenceforth named Helenium in her honour. Thus runs one story; another says that the plant sprang from Helen's tears.

Inulae Radix, the dried root of Elecampane, contains a volatile oil, and, in addition to a bitter principle, helenin and insulin. Helenin is apparently the substance which has a calming effect on spasms of the respiratory organs, and makes an extract of the root a favourite domestic remedy for bronchitis.

ERINGO   *Eryngium maritimum* L.   Umbelliferae
Sea-Holly
Sea-Hulver
FR *Panicaut maritime*
GER *Stranddistel*

> *Falstaff*: Let the sky rain potatoes; let it thunder to the tune of "Green Sleeves"; hail kissing-comfits and snow eringoes.
>
> *Merry Wives of Windsor*, 5, v

The Eringo is a beautiful perennial plant which grows mainly on sandy soil near the sea throughout Europe. About 2 feet in height, with leaves of pale green, white striped, its blue flowers are protected with spines which give the plant the general appearance of a thistle. Hence the German *Stranddistel* (sea-shore thistle) and the generic name *Eryngium*, which comes via Latin from the Greek word for a thistle.

Formerly the roots of the plant had a commercial value, and when candied formed the Eringo comfits of our ancestors. Colchester, as Evelyn points out in his *Diary*, was famous for candied Eringo-root, which was still sold there as late as the middle of the last century. On the occasion of the visit to Colchester of Queen Charlotte in 1761, she was entertained by a prominent townsman who presented her with a box of candied Eringo-roots. Gerard remarks that "the rootes condited or preserved with sugar are exceeding good to be given unto old and aged people that are consumed and withered with age". He adds: "it is also good for other sorts of people that have no delight or appetite to venery." That it had a reputation as an aphrodisiac is borne out by a passage in *Fuller's Worthies*, which says that "Sea-holly, like potatoes, were formerly supposed to be strong provocatives".*

The plant seems to have had a predilection for the south-eastern coast of England, for Gerard found it growing plenti-

---

* *Cf* Pope: *January and May* – Satyrion near, with hot Eringo's stood, Cantharides, to fire the lazy blood.

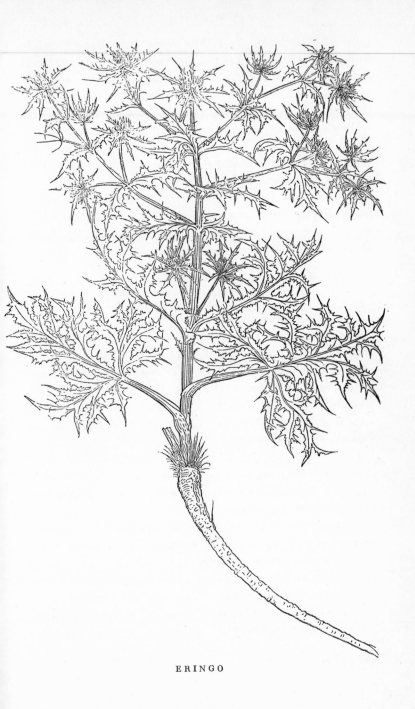

ERINGO

fully at Whitstable, Rye, Winchelsea and Harwich, while Bullein saw much of it growing between Lowestoft and Orford Ness. "This indeed is called Eringium," writes the latter, "but the true name is *centum capita*, because of the number of the heddes." To this day one of the folk-names for the Eringo is Hundred Thistle, though this name is applied more especially to the Field Eringo (*E. campestre*), also known as Dane-weed.

Plutarch records a quaint superstition of the ancient Greeks concerning the Eringo, for he says that if a goat ate the herb "it caused her first to stand still, and afterwards the whole flock, until such time as the shepherd took it from her mouth". It was also supposed to ensure constancy in a lover, for Rapin, in his poem *Of Gardens* describes how

> Grecian Eryngoes now commence their fame,
> Which, worn by brides, will fix their husbands' flame,
> And check the conquests of a rival dame.

From Schroder's *Chymical Dispensatory* (1669) we learn that Sea-Holly "is Hepatick, and Nephritick, and Alexipharmick, temperately hot and dry, opens, discusseth, provokes Terms and Urine, opens Liver, Gall and Spleen, etc., and good in Jaundies and Colick". To which list of virtues Bullein adds that "the juce or oile of this dooe cleane recover any venome of the bodie infected with a Spider".

In more practical vein Lord Bacon suggests as a nourishing drink good for strengthening the back, the yolks of eggs in Malmsey together with "some few slices of Eringium-roots and a little Amber-grice".

Dr John Hill, in his *History of the Materia Medica* (1751), writes: "This root, moderately eaten in the candy'd state, has not the appearance of a medicine, yet will have all the good effects of one; it has also the credit of being a provocative to venery, and many eat it continually under that opinion."

But by far the most beautiful variety of Eringo is its garden relative known as Oliver's Sea-Holly (*E. amethystinum*), the upper leaves of which shade off from a silvery grey into a lustrous sheen of amethyst blue.

EYEBRIGHT   *Euphrasia officinalis* L.   Scrophulariaceae
Euphrasy

FR *Euphraise officinale*; *Brise-lunettes*

GER *Augentrost*; *Zahntrost*

> Yet Euphrasie may not be left unsung,
> That gives dim eyes to waner leagues around.
> SPENSER

A tiny herb this, "not above two handfulls high", and as Gerard observed, abundant on heath and hillside, where its little white flowers, veined with purple and yellow, can be seen through a long season from May to October, especially in chalky districts.

As the name suggests, this herb was held to be a remedy for poor vision and other defects of eyesight. Culpeper tells us that it "helps all infirmities of the eyes that cause dimness of sight. If the herb was but as much used," he writes, "as it is neglected, it would half spoil the spectacle maker's trade." Which seems to indicate that many people were not so credulous as the herbalists. The *London Dispensatory*, too, stated that "a drachm of it taken in the morning is worth a pair of spectacles", and Coles says it obtained the name of Eyebright from being employed by the linnet to clear its sight. But its virtues were not solely ophthalmic; for Dr James says it is useful for "a decayed memory".

Under its more literary name Euphrasy, which was a corruption of Euphrosyne, one of the Graces, the plant seems to have been a favourite with poets, for Milton, Drayton, Shenstone and Spenser are among those who have celebrated the powers of Euphrasy.

For medicinal purposes, Eyebright was used in a variety of ways: the powder of the dried herb was made into an electuary with honey, or mixed with fennel, mace and sugar, was taken in broth; there was a conserve of the whole herb and the flowers, a water of the whole herb, and a wine of the infusion of the tops.

The adjective *officinalis* points to its former use in the Pharmacopoeia, but today Eyebright is used only as a home remedy for its tonic and astringent properties.

FENNEL   *Foeniculum vulgare*   Umbelliferae
                      (Miller)
FR *Fenouil*; *Aneth doux*
GER *Fenchel*

> A ferdynge worth of fenel-seed for fastyng dayes.
> *Piers Plowman*

Fennel is a tall, graceful perennial, of vigorous growth, indigenous to the regions around the Mediterranean, but now cultivated over most of temperate Europe and western Asia. Short-lived as a perennial, it is sometimes cultivated as an annual or biennial, though there may be relatively little seed on the plant the first year. The flowers are in large umbels, of fifteen or more rays, and are bright yellow. The seeds or fruits in an umbel mature at about the same time, but the umbels on a plant do not all mature simultaneously.

At one time Fennel was far more commonly grown in England than it is today, for Gerard says "it is so well knowne amongst us, that it were but lost labour to describe the same". He must have been writing of *F. vulgare*, for Florentine Fennel, *F. dulce*, was not introduced into England until the days of the early Stuarts.

The whole plant is aromatic and has long been held in high repute for both culinary and medical purposes; its importance in olden times led to its inclusion in the old Anglo-Saxon herbals and it is also mentioned as *fenicolum* in the ancient *Capitulare de Villis*. Both Hindus and Chinese held it to be a

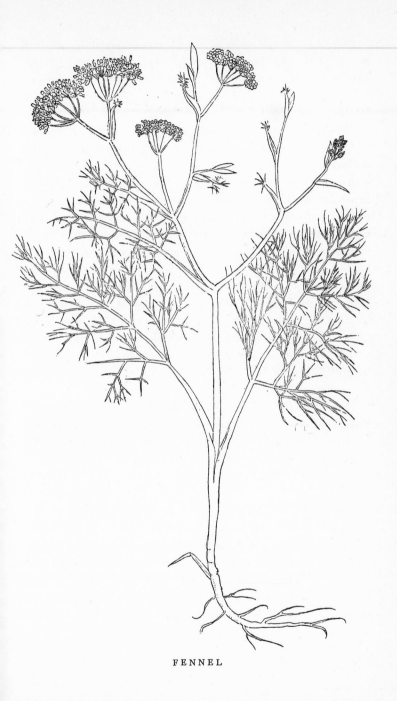

FENNEL

remedy against the bites of scorpions and serpents; a belief which spread to Europe, for Christopher Wirtzung, in his *Praxis Medicinae* says "the confected Fennell seede is good against all poyson, and especially against the venim of Snakes".

Although appreciated by our forefathers as a culinary herb, Fennel is nowadays almost completely ignored by English cooks. An excellent sauce for fish can be made by incorporating into a *sauce mousseline* some finely chopped leaves of Fennel. In Shakespeare's day this herb was a frequent accompaniment to fish, and does not Falstaff say of Poins that he "eats conger with fennel"? Culpeper, who was born in the year in which Shakespeare died, wrote: "One good old fashion is not yet left off, viz. to boil Fennel with fish; for it consumes that phlegmatic humour which fish most plentifully afford and annoy the body with, though few that use it know wherefore they do it. I suppose the reason for its benefit this way" (and here Culpeper inserts some of the astrological observations with which 17th century botany was so strongly impregnated) "is because it is a herb of Mercury, and under Virgo, and therefore bears antipathy to Pisces."

The craze for slimming is evidently no modern fad, for William Coles, in his *Adam in Eden* (1657), tells us that "both the seeds, leaves and roots of our Garden Fennel are much used in drinks and broths for those that are grown fat, to abate their unwieldiness and cause them to grow more gaunt and lank".

There are many varieties of Fennel, and delicious as a vegetable is the *F. azoricum*, or Dwarf Fennel, an annual whose thickened stalks are blanched to be eaten either raw or cooked, especially in Italy. In the south of France it is customary to sprinkle mackerel with chopped Fennel leaves before frying, and a delicious meal can be made of red mullet and fennel, cooked in olive oil or butter, together with white wine and tomatoes, and then baked in the oven.

In days long ago men set much store by the anti-diabolic properties of Fennel. It was hung in the house to ward off evil spirits, and often the keyhole of a room would be stopped up at night with powdered fennel-seed to enable the inhabitants to sleep undisturbed by any nocturnal manifestations. In the stalls of the farm the udders of the cows would be smeared with a decoction of fennel to forestall the bewitching of the milk.

From the dried ripe seeds of Fennel, which are roughly oval in shape, and from one-fifth to two-fifths of an inch long, is obtained the volatile oil which figures as *Oleum Foeniculi* in many Pharmacopoeias, and is used for its stimulant and carminative properties. The Fennel grown in Saxony is said to yield the largest proportion of this oil. Fennel seed is also used as a flavouring agent in the preparation of liqueurs of the anisette type, and the half-ripe seeds are used for flavouring pickled gherkins and cucumbers, herring fillets and sauerkraut. It is said that the Puritans were so addicted to chewing the seed of Fennel in church that in America it was known as "meeting seed".

To conclude, here is Charles Estienne's most original recipe for cultivating sweet Fennel. "To have very sweete fennell," he writes, "put your seede in a Marsellis fig and so sow it, or else mixe honie with the earth wherein you sow it."

FEVERFEW   *Chrysanthemum Parthenium*   Compositae
            (Bernhardi)
Featherfew
FR *Pyrèthre matricaire*; *Espargoutte*
GER *Fieberkraut*; *Mutterkraut*; *Jungfernkraut*

> There's many feet on the moor tonight,
> And they fall so light as they turn and pass,
> So light and true that they shake no dew
> From the Featherfew and the Hungry-Grass.
>> NORA HOPPER *The Fairy Music*

Three only of the Chrysanthemums are natives of England:

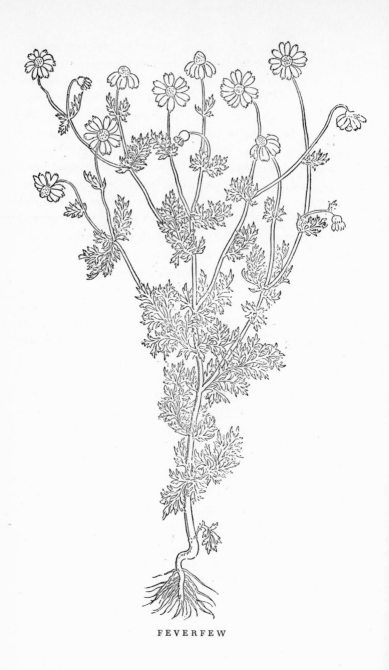

FEVERFEW

the Corn Marigold (*C. segetum*); the Ox-eyed Daisy (*C. leucanthemum*); and Feverfew, or Featherfew as it is sometimes called. Both names are corruptions of "febrifuge", for the herb was once cultivated in monastic gardens and used to allay fevers. According to the old leeches a special ritual had to be employed for the efficacious use of the herb; it had to be pulled from the ground with the left hand, the name of the fevered patient being uttered aloud while so doing, and on no account was the herbalist to look behind him during this operation.

The plant is mentioned in the early herbal known as *Banckes' Herbal* (1525), where we find the entry "Febrifuga. This is named Federfoy. His vertue is to conforte a mannes stomake. It is good to asswage the axes cotydyan, ye crampe, and to tempre it that cometh of colde stomakes. Also it is good to lay to a soore that is byten with venymous beestes, it will hele it shortly an it be layde thereto."

Charles Estienne says: "stampt and applied unto the teeth or eare of the side that aketh, it wholy asswageth the paine of the teeth. And this is the cause why the Parisiens doe call it *Espargoutte*: because the leaves . . . doe cause to distill out of the mouth drop after drop [*a guttis spargendis*] the flegmaticke humour which causeth the said toothache."

The plant, a hardy biennial or perennial, from 2 to 3 feet in height, grows on waste ground and, declares Gerard, "it joyeth to grow among rubbish". It has deeply notched, light green leaves and small white daisy-like flowers with a yellow centre. It has a smell reminiscent of Chamomile, of which it is the progenitor. Some writers refer to it as Wild Chamomile.

Fernie says that "Feverfew is best calculated to pacify those who are liable to suden, spiteful, rude irascibility", but Gerard says it is also good "for such as be melancholike, sad, pensive and without speech".

FOXGLOVE   *Digitalis purpurea* L.   Scrophulariaceae
Bloody Finger
Witches' Thimble
FR *Digitale*; *Gant de Vénus*; *Dé de Notre Dame*
GER *Fingerhut*

> when the foxglove, one by one,
> Upwards through every stage of the tall stem,
> Had shed beside the public way its bells,
> And stood of all dismantled, save the last
> Left at the tapering ladder's top . . .
> WORDSWORTH *The Prelude*

Leonhard Fuchs (1501–66), the physician of Memmingen in Bavaria, was the first author to give an exact description of the Foxglove in his Latin herbal *De Historia Stirpium*, published in 1542. He gave to it the name of *Digitalis*, in allusion to the German name *Fingerhut* (thimble). The fancied resemblance of the flowers to a thimble is apparent in the popular names given to the plant in different European countries: Witches' Thimble, Dé de Notre Dame, Fingerhut, Vingerhoed, etc.

Although Gerard dismisses the Foxglove with the remark that "they are of no use, neither have they any place among medicines, according to the Antients", he was correct only to the extent that neither Dioscorides nor Pliny made any mention of the plant; but its use in medicine, though only as a vulnerary, goes back at least to Anglo-Saxon times, for it is mentioned in 12th-century leechdoms as *foxes glofa*. Etymologists say that our word "Foxglove" is from A-S *foxesglew*, or "fox music", because of the resemblance of the corolla to an ancient musical instrument composed of bells hung on an arched support, such as we find on Plate 21 of the *Oxford Companion to Music*.

Digitalis purpurea is a biennial, and among the handsomest of our wild flowers, though *purpurea* was perhaps not altogether the right adjective to choose, seeing that the flowers, although generally of a crimson-purple, are sometimes a pure white. In the more common variety the interior of the corolla is prettily mottled with crimson spots on whitish background.

In early times the Foxglove was used mainly as an external application for wounds and ulcers on the legs, and later Parkinson advised its use as a specific in cases of epilepsy. But its outstanding virtues as a diuretic and cardiac stimulant were not known until the Warwickshire doctor and botanist William Withering wrote his medical classic *An Account of the Foxglove and some of its Medical Uses*, published at Birmingham in 1785. In his introduction, Withering writes: "The use of the Foxglove is getting abroad, and it is better the world should derive some instruction, however imperfect, from my experience, than that the lives of men should be hazarded by its unguarded exhibition, or that a medicine of so much efficacy should be condemned and rejected as dangerous and unmanageable." For dangerous it is, since all parts of the plant contain poisonous principles.

Withering, who used digitalis in the treatment of dropsy, was apparently the first man to notice its action in slowing down the movements of the heart. At first he used a decoction of Foxglove leaves, but discarded this in favour of an infusion. Later he employed nothing but the powdered leaves, gathered just before the flowering period. George Eliot, herself a native of Warwickshire, may have read Withering's book, for in *Silas Marner* she describes the use of foxglove by Silas to cure a peasant woman of dropsy, and implies that at the time this was very much of a secret remedy.

Withering's observations were soon confirmed by other doctors, and when he died in 1799 a foxglove was carved on the tablet to his memory in Edgbaston Old Church, where he was buried. Since that time digitalis has been official. The leaves contain various glucosides, among them digitoxin (crystallised digitalin) and gitoxin. The leaf of another species, the Eastern European *D. lanata* contains, as well as the two glucosides mentioned, digoxin, which acts more quickly than digitalin, and so is of great value in urgent cases of heart trouble. *D. lanata* is, for this reason, now cultivated both in England and on the Continent. The standard preparation – to meet the present British Pharmacopoeia demands that the drug shall be biologically assayed – is a mixture of powdered digitalis leaves kept in sealed vials at the National Institute of Medical Research, Hampstead, London.

Although *D. purpurea* is native to western Europe it is now widely naturalised. It grows in eastern Canada, especially Newfoundland and Cape Breton; in many States of the U.S.A.; and in S. America in Chile and Brazil. The leaves are gathered from both first- and second-year plants, but those collected the second year are preferred. The leaves are dried in the shade or by artificial means.

FUMITORY   *Fumaria officinalis* L.   Fumariaceae
Earth-smoke
FR *Fumeterre*; *Fiel de terre*
GER *Erdrauch*; *Taubenkerbel*

> Crowned with rank fumiter and furrow weeds
> *King Lear*, 4, iv

Fumitory is a small, grey-green plant with tiny bright pink flowers sometimes tipped with purple. A native of the Mediterranean regions, it is now common in all temperate regions of Europe and Asia. There is some doubt as to the derivation of the generic name of this plant; Pliny says it took its name from causing the eyes to water when applied to them, as smoke does. Prior says it acquired the name of earth-smoke from the belief that it was produced without seed from vapours rising from the earth, and quotes Platearius to that effect. This legend was credited by Peter Treveris in the *Grete Herball*, and also appears in Dodoens-Lyte's *Newe Herball* of 1586. Some writers, however, consider that the name may have been derived from the smoke-like appearance of the greyish foliage on a dewy summer morning. The name was applied to it in very early times, for the Greeks called it *kapnos* (smoke).

The herb was at one time commonly used for making a cosmetic water to purify the skin. Its flowers, we are told, were

> . . . cropped by maids in weeding hours,
> To boil in water, milk, or whey,
> For washes on a holiday;
> To make their beauty fair and sleek,
> And scare the tan from summer's cheek.

Shakespeare twice refers to the plant as the "rank fumitory", evidently using the word in its sense of a luxuriant grower, for it does spread rapidly over the surface of cultivated ground.

Fumitory was believed by the early herbalists to be beneficial as an eye lotion, and Turner claims that "the juice of thys herbe, whiche in dede is sharpe, maketh clere eyes". The famous physician John of Milan praised it as a sovereign remedy against malaria, and Culpeper claimed that the distilled water of the herb was an excellent preventative against the plague. Nor did that exhaust its virtues, for Gerard affirmed that it helped "those that are troubled with scabs".

Today its chief medical use is as an aperient, and for derangements of the stomach.

GARLIC   *Allium sativum* L.   Liliaceae
Poor Man's Treacle
FR *Ail*; *Thériaque des pauvres*
GER *Knoblauch*

> Wel loved he garleek, oynons, and eke lekes.
>   CHAUCER *The Somnour*

Most Englishmen would without doubt heartily commend the decision of the ancient Greeks not to allow those who had been eating garlic to enter the temple of the goddess Cybele. Evelyn, though he lived in an age when taste was more robust, says: "We absolutely forbid it entrance into our Salleting, by reason of its intolerable Rankness. To be sure, 'tis not for Ladies Palats, nor those who court them, farther than to permit a light touch on the Dish with a Clove thereof, much better supply'd by the gentler Roccombo" (i.e. Rocambole or Sand leek, *allium scorodoprasm*, a variety of garlic, milder in flavour, which is a native of Denmark).

Whilst recognising its value, our English palate has never taken kindly to the strong odour of garlic, so that Parkinson writes, in his *Theatrum Botanicum*: "To alter the strong sent thereof and cause it to be lesse offensive, divers have set downe divers things, as some to eat Rue, or herbe Grace, some to eate a raw Beane after it, others to take of a Beete roote roasted under the Embers and others say by eating a few Parsley leaves."

From early times the medicinal value of Garlic has been widely recognised and Galen gave to it the name of *Theriaca rusticorum*, which was anglicised as Poor Man's Treacle. In France, also, it is popularly called *Thériaque des pauvres*, and it formed the principal ingredient of the "Four Thieves' Vinegar" used as a febrifuge in Marseilles during an epidemic of the plague in 1722. The name is said to have originated with four thieves who confessed that they had plundered the dead bodies of victims of the pestilence whilst protected by this concoction.

There are several species of garlic, but that most extensively cultivated both for its medicinal value and for culinary purposes is *allium sativum*,* which is of such antiquity that it figured in the materia medica of the ancient Egyptians and of the Hebrews, though its main use in Egypt seems to have been as a food, for Herodotus tells us that the labourers who worked

* There are two main varieties: White Garlic and Pink Garlic, the latter having more but smaller *gousses*, or "cloves".

on the Pyramid of Cheops were fed largely upon radishes and garlic. In fact it has been cultivated for so long that its country of origin is unknown, but its main habitat seems to be southern Europe and it grows easily in our own gardens. It was probably introduced into Britain during the Roman occupation.

Many old writers have sung the praises of Garlic as a medicine, and Dioscorides recommended it, mixed with sugar, for clearing the voice, a recommendation which, it is said, is followed to this day by operatic tenors in France and Italy, though the practice seems hardly fair to their stage partners. As Bullein remarks in his *Book of Simples*: "it is a grosse kynde of Medycine, very unpleasant for fayre Ladyes . . . whych often tymes preferre sweete breathes before gentle Wordes."

According to Gerard, "being eaten it heateth the body extremely, attenuateth and maketh thin, thicke and grosse humors; cutteth such as are tough and clammie, digesteth and consumeth them, also openeth obstruction, is an enimie to all cold poisons, and to the bitings of venemous beasts".

Garlic belongs to the Lily family, and the extensive genus *allium* includes a number of plants whose rootstocks or bulbs are used for culinary purposes, both as a foodstuff and as a flavouring agent. Onions, leeks and shallots will at once spring to mind. The white or purplish bulbs, the so-called "cloves" of Garlic, contain as their chief constituent a volatile oil, diallyl disulphide, which is responsible for the characteristic smell. Syrup of Garlic, made by the addition of honey or sugar to the expressed juice, is often prescribed for bronchial complaints.

As a condiment Garlic is widely used on the Continent, especially in the regions bordering the Mediterranean, where it is claimed to possess an extraordinary number of virtues. Maybe the eating of garlic is indeed the secret of good health, but alas! it is a secret very difficult to keep. As Shakespeare admonishes his actors in *A Midsummer Night's Dream*: "And, most dear actors, eat no onions nor garlic, for we are to utter sweet breath."

Sir John Harington summed the whole matter up in a quatrain in *The Englishman's Doctor*, 1609:

> Sith Garlicke then hath powre to save from death,
> Beare with it though it make unsavory breath;
> And scorne not Garlicke, like to some that think
> It onely makes men winke, and drinke, and stinke.

And if we are to believe Gervase Markham the animal world is just as fastidious over the smell of garlic, for he informs us that an excellent way to take moles is this: "Put Garlick, Onions, or Leeks, into the mouths of the holes, and they will come out quickly as amazed!"

The Latin races have always been more fond of garlic than have their northern neighbours. Sir William Temple, in his essay *Of Health and Long Life*, says: "In several provinces of France it is usual to fall into a diet of garlic for a fortnight or three weeks, upon the first fresh butter of the spring; and the common people esteem it a preservative against the diseases of the ensuing year; and a broth of garlic and onions is so generally used the next day after a debauch as to be called *soupe à l'yvroigne*."

GENTIAN   *Gentiana campestris* L.   Gentianaceae
Baldmoney
Bitterwort
FR *Gentianelle*; *Gentiane d'Allemagne*
GER *Deutsche Enzian* ; *Feld Enzian*

> The gentian weaves her fringes,
> The maple's loom is red.
> EMILY DICKINSON

The Gentian family occurs mainly in temperate climates, especially in mountainous districts, and some of its members are found at the highest limits of vegetation. *G. lutea*, the large

Alpine variety, is yellow-flowered, but blue is the more usual colour of the genus, which is named after an ancient king of Illyria, Gentius, who dabbled in herbs.

Recognised for its therapeutic properties since the time of the ancient Egyptians, the plant has been employed medicinally throughout the centuries, and according to H. S. Redgrove it was an ingredient of a famous antidote said to have been invented by the philosopher Pythagoras, and was included in the formula for three of the four special concoctions which, on account of their supposed importance, were called Officinal Capitals.

Of the species of Gentiana found in Britain, the commonest is the Meadow Gentian (*G. campestris*), an erect annual some six inches high, with pointed deep green leaves and four-petal flowers of a delicate purplish-blue, usually found on chalk or limestone. Another species, *G. amarella*, resembles the Meadow or Field Gentian fairly closely, but has five-petal blue flowers and is less branched.

Culpeper knew both species and boldly asserted that the virtues of these two native Gentians were "in no whit inferior to that which cometh across the sea" – despite which the *G. lutea* of central Europe has completely displaced all other species in official medicine. One other species which used to be fairly common in these islands, but is now somewhat rare, is the Marsh Gentian (*G. pneumonanthe*), the tallest of the native species, which grows to a height of about 2 feet. The corolla is variegated in colour, tinged with green outside and with lobes of a beautiful shade of blue mottled with green and white spots within the tube. (Lung-flower – *Pulmonaire des Marais* – *Lungen Enzian*.)

Parkinson wrote that "Gentiana is the generall name given to the Gentians. We call them in English Gentian, Fellworte, Bitterwort and Baldmoney. . . . The wonderful wholesomeness of Gentian cannot be easily known to us, by reason our dainty tastes refuse to take thereof, for the bitternesse sake."

It is, of course, for this bitter principle that the plant is valued, and from which tonic drugs and "bitters" are made. It is an ingredient of the well-known French appetiser called *Suze*, and in Switzerland and Germany the fresh root of the Gentian is employed for the production by fermentation of a "gentian brandy" very popular as a pick-me-up. In the U.S.A. gentian root is derived from *G. puberula*, *G. saponaria*, and *G. Andrewsii*, species with almost identical properties.

The Gentian employed in the drug trade consists of the dried rhizome and roots of *G. lutea*, a perennial which grows on the slopes of the Alps, the Vosges and Jura mountains, and also in the Black Forest and the Pyrenees. The sliced root is dried slowly in artificial heat and packed in bales for export; the bitter glycoside gentiopicrin, the essential constituent, can be extracted with alcohol.

In the mountainous parts of France where *G. lutea* is found, the rights of gathering it from the meadows are sold at a frequently high price. Certain families who specialise in the harvesting of this herb make use of a particular kind of tool with which to lever out the plants.

The most important galenical preparation is the official concentrated compound infusion which is prepared by macerating in alcohol a mixture of dried peel of bitter orange and lemon together with thinly sliced Gentian root.

GROUND-IVY   *Glechoma hederacea* L.   Labiatae
Ale-hoof
FR *Lierre terrestre*; *Rondelette*; *Courroie de saint-Jean*
GER *Gundermannkraut*; *Gundelrebe*; *Hederich*

This perennial, despite its name, has no botanical connection with Ivy, but belongs to the Mint family, and is a close relation of *Nepeta cateria*, or Catmint. It is familiar all over the countryside, where it grows profusely in copses and hedgerows, trailing along the ground (whence its name) and sending up erect flowering branches. It has small heart-shaped leaves, with round-toothed edging, and its blue-purple flowers are borne in axillary whorls of three or four blossoms. The whole plant has a rather bitter taste and a peculiar odour. One of its old country names was "Gill-run-by-the-Ground", or, as Langham spells it, with his Tudor orthography, "gilrun-bith' ground".

Formerly it was put into ale, before the introduction of hops, both to preserve and clear it, and for this reason it acquired the name of Ale-hoof. It once had some reputation as a curative, and Sir William Temple writes in his essay *Of Health and Long Life*:

Alehoof, or ground ivy is, in my opinion, of the most excellent and most general use and virtue of plants we have amongst us. It is allowed to be most sovereign for the eyes, admirable in frenzies, either taken inwardly or outwardly applied. Besides, if there be a specific remedy or prevention of the stone, I take it to be the constant use of alehoof-ale. . . . This is the plant with which all our ancestors made their common drink, when the inhabitants of this island were esteemed the longest livers of any in the known world. The chief reason which I believe gave it vogue at first was the preserving beer upon long sea-voyages.

Pitton de Tournefort wrote that "ground ivy is us'd in most Distempers incident to the Lungs, but especially when absterging, or cleansing and clearing is required". But Dr John Hill says that "notwithstanding all this has been said in praise of this plant, we in a great measure leave it to the common people". And in some parts of the country the "common people" still make "Gill Tea", mixed with honey or sugar to take away the bitterness, as a remedy for coughs and colds.

In the days when cock-fighting was a popular sport, Ground-Ivy was used as a remedy if the birds' eyes were hurt, according to Fairfax's *The Complete Sportsman*. "If your cock has received any hurt in his eye, then take a leaf or two of right ground-ivy, that is such as grows in little tufts in the bottom of hedges. Chew it in your mouth very well, sucking out the juice, which squirting into his eye two or three times, will soon cure it provided the sight is not pierced."

HENBANE   *Hyoscyamus niger* L.   Solanaceae
Hog's Bean
Stinking Roger
Belene

FR *Jusquiame noire*; *Mort aux poules*; *Fève à cochons*
GER *Bilsenkraut*; *Hühnertod*; *Schlafkraut*

> On hills of dust the henbane's faded green,
> And pencil'd flower of sickly scent is seen.
> CRABBE *The Borough*

It was Dioscorides who, long before the Christian era, gave the plant its name of *hyoscyamus*, or hog's bean, because although poisonous to man and many animals, pigs could apparently eat it without harm. Not only did men know of it in ages long past as a poisonous plant, but they made use of it for its therapeutic effects. Dioscorides used it as a narcotic, to allay pain and to induce sleep, and even earlier than the Greeks and Romans, who knew it as a pain-killer, the Babylonians and the ancient Egyptians were acquainted with both its good and its bad qualities.

During the Middle Ages the narcotic properties of henbane were fully recognised and physicians would hold a sponge saturated with the juice of the plant under the nose of those about to undergo an operation. In folk-medicine henbane was used for neuralgia and muscular rheumatism, and as a cure for insomnia; in the hands of the unskilled it was probably often used with dire results, for it can easily cause delirium and convulsions. In fact the family *Hyoscyamus* is closely related to such poisonous plants as the thorn-apple and the deadly nightshade.

Nevertheless it would appear that in earlier times brewers employed henbane in brewing beer, probably in order to make it more intoxicating, for there exists a legal ordinance of 1507 promulgated in the small town of Eichstadt forbidding brewers to mix henbane with their beer.

Jacob van Maerlant, a Dutch poet of the Middle Ages, wrote a long didactic poem called *Naturen Bloeme*, in which some forty lines are devoted to this plant under the name *Jusquiami*, an appellation which still survives in the French name for henbane – *jusquiame*. Anthony Askham, too, in his *Litle Herball* of 1550 alludes to the plant by this title, and says: "Jusquiamus is called Henbane . . . the seede thereof and the seede of Hemlock medled together and a candel made thereof or brent upon a tyle stone and let the smoke go up into a mans mouth in especial among the teeth, and it will flee wormes. Also the rootes be good for the tootheache."

Strange, this belief in worms breeding among the teeth. It occurs also in the work of the Salerno School, made into English in the following fashion by Harington:

> If in your teeth you happen to be tormented
> By means some little worms therein do brede,
> Which pain (if need be tane) may be prevented
> By keeping cleane your teeth when as ye fead.
> Burn Frankonsence (a gum not evil scented),
> Put Henbane into this, and onyon seed;
> And with a tunnel to the tooth that's hollow
> Convey the smoke thereof, and ease shall follow.

Gerard, however, was not deluded by this story of worms. "The seed", he writes, "is used of Mountibanck tooth-drawers which run about the country, to cause worms come forth of men's teeth, by burning it [henbane] in a chafing dish with coles, the partie holding his mouth over the fume thereof: but some craftie companions to gain mony convey small lute-strings into the water, persuading the patient that those

HENBANE

small creeping beasts came out of his mouth or other parts which he intended to ease."

In Gerard's day the Black Henbane grew almost everywhere in England, "in the borders of fields about dunghills and untoiled places". Culpeper says, "Henbane delights to grow in saturnine places, and whole cart loads of it may be found near the places where they empty the common Jakes". But the plant is less common in England now, though whether this is on account of the more hygienic disposal of sewage is difficult to say.

The Henbane usually grown for medicinal purposes is a biennial, and it is from the second year growth, which produces clusters of rather dull yellowish flowers veined with purple, that the official Green Extract is prepared. This drug is used as an anodyne, narcotic and mydriatic, and its chief constituents are the alkaloid Hyoscyamine, together with smaller quantities of Atropine and Hyoscine. Hyoscine is thought to be one of the oldest narcotics known to man and in combination with Morphine is given to induce "twilight sleep" at childbirth.

In some rural districts, not long ago, the leaves of the Yellow Henbane (*Hyoscyamus luteus*) were smoked to relieve toothache. This practice was evidently in use by the end of the 16th century, for Gerard says that "it is used of some in stead of Tabaco, but to small purpose or profit, although it doth stupifie or dull the sences and cause that kind of giddines that Tabaco doth".

All parts of henbane are poisonous and neither drying nor boiling destroys the toxic principle.

Although henbane is indigenous to the Mediterranean area, it has become widely naturalised in the temperate regions of the world, and has been harvested from wild plants in the United States, especially in Montana. Most of the cultivated henbane used for medicinal purposes in Britain and America is imported from southern Europe and Egypt.

Of recent years the drug has been used in the treatment of

motion sickness, to which many travellers are liable, and during the Second World War it was tried as a preventive of sea-sickness for invasion troops.

HOREHOUND *Marrubium vulgare* L. Labiatae
FR *Marrube blanc*
GER *Weisser Andorn*

> Pale hore-hound, which he holds of most especiall use
> And for the labouring wretch that's troubled with a cough,
> Or stopping of the breath by phlegm that's hard and tough.
>
> DRAYTON *Polyolbion* xiii

Horehound, according to Folkard, is one of the five plants stated by the Mishna to be the "bitter herbs" which the Jews were ordered to take for the Feast of the Passover – the other four being nettle, lettuce, horse-radish and coriander. Its astringency is due largely to the bitter principle marrubin which forms part of the chemical constitution of the plant, the generic name of which is said to be derived from the Hebrew *Marob*, meaning "bitter juice". A variety, *M. plicatum*, is the herb looked upon by the ancient Egyptians as sacred to Horus.

Since the time of Hippocrates, who included it in his list of simples, Horehound has enjoyed a measure of fame as a medicinal herb. It figures in the leechdoms of the Saxons and in the *Little Garden* of Strabo occurs the startling injunction: "Drink Horehound hot from the fire if you are poisoned by your stepmother!"

The etymology of the word "Horehound" is uncertain, although the first part of the word is probably the same as "hoary", with reference to the hairy, woolly appearance of the leaves. Despite the qualification *vulgare*, Horehound is not common all over England. It is found in certain localities, particularly in East Anglia. Horehound beer was, and probably still is, brewed and drunk by the country folk of Norfolk and Suffolk, where the plant is to be found not only in gardens, but growing in waste places and by the wayside.

Turner recommended Horehound as "good to be geven with hony unto them that syghg much" (Gerard later recommends Sweet Marjoram for the same purpose). Culpeper says "the green leaves bruised and boiled in old hog's grease and used as an ointment heal the bitings of dogs".

However, the main medicinal use of Horehound is as a pectoral and as a bitter tonic. An infusion of Horehound leaves is a popular remedy for coughs and colds, as it was in earlier days, when Gerard wrote: "Syrup made from the greene, fresh leaves, with sugar, is a most singular remedy against the cough and wheezing of the lungs." Candied Horehound, for the same purpose, is made by boiling the fresh leaves, adding sugar to the juice extracted in this way, and then reboiling the syrup until sufficiently thick to set hard on cooling.

Horehound is a perennial growing up to 3 feet tall, with grey-green, thick and woolly ovate leaves, and dense whorls of off-white flowers. The leaves when crushed emit a pleasant, musky smell, and the plant enjoys a long flowering season. For medicinal use the harvesting is done just before the full flowering and the herb should be dried in the shade to preserve the green colour.

Black Horehound, *Ballota nigra*, with dark purple flowers, was often known as Madwort, since it was supposed to be an antidote to the bite of a mad dog. In Beaumont and Fletcher's *Faithful Shepherdess* we read

> Black Horehound, good
> For Sheep or Shepherd bitten by a wood-
> Dog's venomed tooth.

The generic name *Ballota* is from the Greek, and means "rejected", because animals refuse to eat it, probably owing to its strong odour, which has earned for it the name of Stinking

Horehound. Dodoens tells us that the apothecaries of his time called it *Prassium foetidum*. The peculiar odour has some effect on the nervous system of cats, in a manner similar to catmint. In parts of Belgium it is for this reason called *Kattekruid*.

HYSSOP   *Hyssopus officinalis* L.   Labiatae
FR *Hysope*; *Herbe sacrée*
GER *Ysop*

Although Hyssop is mentioned in the Bible, most authorities consider that the hyssop used by the priests in sprinkling the temples was a species of *Origanum*, allied to our Marjoram. Yet the real hyssop may well have been used also, for Dioscorides refers to it in his *Materia Medica* as "a holy herb". Probably introduced into this country by the Romans, it became an inhabitant of every monastic garden on account of its medicinal virtues as a carminative, stimulant, and pectoral.

Hyssop is a handsome bushy plant, with deep blue flowers which form in small clusters and dark evergreen leaves, and is found growing wild in dry and rocky places in many countries of southern Europe. It is also cultivated for its flower tops, which are harvested when in full bloom, and used for infusions for coughs and bronchial ailments, for as Gerard remarks: "a decoction of Hyssope made with figges, water, honey and rue, and drunken, helpeth the old cough." Hyssop tea, brewed from the green tops of the herb, has for ages been an accepted country remedy, all over Europe, for colds and anaemia.

In the Middle Ages, hyssop was also used as a culinary herb, the finely chopped leaves finding their way into soups, meat pies and stuffings. Its flavour is, however, somewhat too strong for the modern palate, though used sparingly it gives zest to a salad of mixed herbs.

Hyssop grows well where there is warmth and plenty of sunshine, so that in parts of Devon and Cornwall it often forms a garden hedge, filling the air with its peculiar aroma which attracts the bees from afar. Although the flowers are usually blue, there are also pink- and white-flowered varieties. On account of its fragrance hyssop was much employed in the Middle Ages as a strewing herb.

LAVENDER   *Lavandula vera* L.   Labiatae
FR *Lavande officinale*; *Lavande vraie*
GER *Wahre Lavendel*

> Long alleys falling down to twilight grots,
> Or opening upon level plots
> Of crowned lilies, standing near
> Purple-spiked lavender.
>
>   TENNYSON *Ode to Memory*

"Lavender is so well known," says Culpeper, "being an inhabitant of almost every garden, that it needeth no description." If asked to name some typically English perfume, most people would probably think immediately of Lavender. As Eleanour Sinclair Rohde has written so delightfully: "I fancy there are few scents that make those living in far-away parts so homesick. Its exquisitely clean aromatic perfume must be almost painfully suggestive of gardens at home, smooth green lawns, spreading, shady trees, colourful borders of flowers that have been associated with our homes and gardens for centuries."

Lavender is native to the shores of the Mediterranean, growing profusely in Southern France and Corsica. *L. vera* is said to have first been introduced into England about the middle of the 16th century, and approved so highly of our soil that the finest Oil of Lavender is that distilled from English-grown plants. But Lavender of some variety would have been grown in these islands long before that, for the Romans, who made great use of Lavender water to scent their baths, must surely have brought it with them. This may have been *L. stoechas*, or French Lavender, mentioned by Dioscorides as growing near the coast of Gaul in the islands called the Stoechades (today the Iles d'Hyères) from which it derives its name. Gerard terms it Sticadove, and says that the herb was also known as Cassidony corrupted by country-folk into "Cast-me-down".

The first mention of *L. vera* seems to have been in a book of materia medica written by the Abbess Hildegard of Bingen (1098–1179), in which there is a chapter entitled *De Lavandula*; but there are several species of Lavender and often the early writers made no distinction between *L. vera* and *L. spica*, or Spike Lavender, a broader-leafed variety from which is distilled Oil of Spike. *L. spica alba* is the beautiful White Lavender beloved of Henrietta Maria, the wife of Charles I, who had large borders of it in the garden of her manor at Wimbledon. It is, unfortunately, less hardy than other varieties. *L. spica nana* is a dwarf variety with dark purple flowers.

The Romans made great use of Lavender to perfume their baths and according to many writers the origin of the name *Lavandula* is to be found in the Latin *lavare*, to wash. The O.E.D., however, seems to favour a possible derivation from the Latin *lividus*, meaning "of a blue colour".

It is not surprising that a herb with so fresh a fragrance should have been used for centuries in the home. Many a housewife would, and still does in some parts of the country, use Lavender to "crown her kerchiefs clean with mickle rare perfume". Small bags of the dried herb were placed under pillows to soothe headaches and to induce refreshing sleep. Stillroom books, such as Sir Hugh Plat's *Delightes for Ladies* (1609), contained directions for distilling Lavender, and Coles, in *Adam and Eve*, describes the many virtues of the distilled water of Lavender, but warns that "it is not safe to use it when the Body is full of humours, mixed with blood, because of the hot and subtill spirits wherewith it is possessed".

That famous Tudor physician Bullein says of Lavender that

"nothynge is better against the diseases of the sinewes, the coldnesse of the braine, palsie, and fallyng evill: either to be dronke, or smel of this herbe; or also to be anointed with the goodly warme oile made thereof. Whiche oile hath vertue againste all the diseases of the sinewes."

At one time Lavender was cultivated commercially on quite a large scale in England, mainly around Hitchin, in Hertfordshire, and near London in the fields around Mitcham and Carshalton until those once rural villages were swallowed up by the bricks and mortar of 20th-century urbanism. Even that dismal thoroughfare Lavender Hill, in Battersea, commemorates the industry once carried on there.

Lavender spikes will retain their fragrance for a considerable time when dry provided that they are gathered fairly early in the day, as soon as any dew has evaporated, and then spread out to dry out of the sun, each spike separately, for preference on some sort of netting which allows the air to circulate freely around them. The whole of the flowers are thickly covered with radiating hairs bearing minute oil glands, and since the oil is largely volatile, if the spikes are cut during the heat of the day, much of it will be lost.

Oil distilled from *L. vera* is faintly yellowish, with a fragrant odour, and contains, among other constituents, an alcohol known as linalool. The oil has stimulant and carminative properties, and was once official. Today, however, it is little used in medicine, being mainly employed in the making of perfumes, soaps and toilet requisites, usually mixed with Oil of Spike. In Spain the peasants used to extract oil from *L. stoechas* by hanging the Lavender, flowers downwards, in a bottle exposed to the sun. Its antiseptic properties made it a valuable household stand-by for cuts and sores. It also acted as an insect repellent.

But nobody today is likely to use Lavender in the manner recommended by the old ecclesiastical botanist William Turner, who wrote in 1551: "I judge that the flowers of Lavender quilted in a cap and worne are good for all diseases of the head that come from a cold cause and that they comfort the braine very well."

LOVAGE   *Levisticum officinale* (Koch)   Umbelliferae
FR *Livèche*; *Ache de montagne*
GER *Liebstöckel*; *Maggikraut*

Known to both Greeks and Romans as a useful medicinal herb, Lovage was much cultivated in England from the 14th century onwards, and was greatly esteemed both in Tudor and Stuart times for use in salads, in broths and for scenting baths, as well as for its curative properties. Tusser includes it in his list of "Necessary Herbs to grow in the Garden of Physic".

Every part of the plant, which is a hardy perennial, is aromatic and the leaves make a very agreeable flavouring for soups and stews. In fact this herb is an ingredient in the popular Maggi products so widely sold on the Continent, for which reason Lovage is often called *Maggikraut* in Germany and *Maggi-plant* in the Netherlands. Seeds, leaves and stems can be used for culinary purposes, and as they retain their fragrance when dried are useful for seasoning. Finely shredded, the leaves form a pleasant addition to salads, and if the leaves are placed in a air-tight tin after gathering they can be enjoyed all through the winter.

Lovage is a handsome plant to have in the garden, with its large, dark-green shiny leaves, usually divided into two or three segments, and large umbels of small yellow florets. It is a native of the Mediterranean shores and its Latin name *Ligusticum levisticum* is said to be derived from the province of Liguria, in Italy, where it is found in abundance. It was probably introduced into Britain by the Romans.

The stems of Lovage are thick and hollow, resembling those of Angelica, and like them they are often candied for use in

confectionery. The fresh root, cooked and sliced, is eaten in
some countries with oil, vinegar and salt, as a salad, having a
taste somewhat akin to that of celeriac.

MALLOW (COMMON)   *Malva silvestris* L.   Malvaceae
FR *Grande Mauve*; *Herbe à fromage*
GER *Waldmalve*

MALLOW (MARSH)   *Althaea officinalis* L.
FR *Guimauve*; *Althée*
GER *Eibisch*; *Weisse Pappel*

MALLOW (DWARF)   *M. rotundifolia* L.
FR *Petite mauve*; *Fromageon*
GER *Käsepappel*

MALLOW (MUSK)   *M. moschata* L.
FR *Mauve musquée*
GER *Moschus-Malve*

> Hardy and high, above the slender sheaf,
> The slimy mallow waves her silky leaf.
>
> CRABBE *The Village*

There are several species of Mallow to be found in this country,
of which the commonest and largest is *M. silvestris*, a roadside
plant with large five- to seven-lobed leaves and satin-like
flowers of pale reddish-purple marked with darker streaks. Its
popular names are Hockherb, Mauve, and Round Dock.

The flattened disk-like fruit of the Mallow are the
"cheeses" of country children, which John Clare, the
Northamptonshire poet, refers to in the couplet

> Picking from Mallows, sport to please,
> The crumpled seed we called a "cheese".

Note, too, that in France the popular name for the Common
Mallow is *Herbe à fromage*, and the Dwarf Mallow is called in
Germany *Käsepappel*.

The Musk Mallow is a perennial with deeply divided leaves

Mallow 189

and flowers of delicate pink. The Dwarf Mallow is a procumbent annual with much smaller flowers of white streaked with lilac. The three mallows mentioned are fairly generally distributed, but the Marsh Mallow is found only in southern Europe, and in England is not nearly so common as the other species.

Althaea officinalis, the Marsh Mallow, differs from the other mallows in having its leaves and stems covered with down, while the flowers, resembling those of the garden Hollyhock, are large and of a pale pink hue. The name Mallow is derived from the Greek word for an emollient – in allusion to its mucilaginous properties; the generic name *Althaea* comes from another Greek root, *althos*, meaning "a remedy", for in olden times this herb was considered a panacea.

William Turner says: "Althea is called also Hibiscus and Eniscus, and of the potecaryes malva bis malva* and malvaviscus, in Englysh marrysh mallow or water mallow . . . Marrysh mallow, soden in wyne or mead, or brused and laid on by it selfe, is good for woundes, for hard kyrnelles, swellynges, and wennes, for the burnyng and swelling behynd the eares, for impostumes, for the brusynge of the fundament, for wyndy swellynges, for the styfnes of the synnowes."

Pliny extolled its virtues saying that "whosoever shall take a spoonful of the Mallows shall that day be free from all diseases that may come to him".

In the *Capitulare de Villis*, of the time of Charlemagne, the Marsh Mallow was recommended as a herb to be planted for its many virtues. In that document the name appears as *misvalvas*, most probably a scribe's error for *bismalvas* (see footnote). And long before that Theophrastus prescribed the grated root of the Marsh Mallow as a remedy for coughs.

Ever since then the plant has been valued for its ability to sooth and heal inflammation of the throat and chest, its emollient properties being derived from the great amount of

* i.e. twice as efficacious as Common Mallow.

mucilage contained in the fleshy roots. It was also used as a laxative, for Sir John Harington in *The Englishman's Doctor* (1609), with a nice turn of phrase, declares that "Mallowes make men soluble that have been bound". A claim endorsed by Martial when he wrote

> Exoneraturas ventrem mihi villica Malvas
> Attulit, et varias quas habet hortus opes.

Parkinson, in his *Paradisi in Sole*, remarked that "Malva Crispa, French Mallows, is much used as a pot-herb, especially when there is cause to move the belly downward, which by his slippery quality it doth help forward."

The root of the Marsh Mallow is branched, from three to six inches long, and about the thickness of the middle finger, and white and fleshy once the light brown outer layer has been removed. Most malvaceous plants are strongly mucilaginous, and *Althaea radix* contains about 25 per cent mucilage, roughly the same amount of starch, and an amino-succinamic acid known as asparagin. The plant is widely cultivated on the Continent both for medicinal purposes and for confectionery, though the well-known *Pâte de Guimauve*, containing mucilage, flour, sugar and white of egg, is usually made from the root of *Althaea cannabina*, known in France as *Guimauve faux-chanvre*.

A syrup of Marsh Mallow is included in many foreign pharmacopoeias and used for sore throats and bronchitis. According to Fernie, a decoction of Marsh Mallow is made by adding five pints of water to $\frac{1}{4}$ lb of the dried root, then boiling down to three pints and straining.

Another use of Mallow is described by Estienne and Liebault (1600), who say that "the roote of mallowes steept in wine a whole day and afterward wrapt in a paper and rosted under the ashes and dried, is a fine medicine to rub the teeth withall, and to clense and scowre off from them the filth gathered thicke about them. . . . It is singular also for manie other things, and therefore it is called of some *Omnimorbia*."

But perhaps one of the strangest uses for Mallow was that ingeniously devised in the days when a man's innocence of crime or the veracity of his statements might be tested by the ordeal of holding in his hand a bar of red-hot iron. It was found that an ointment made from the sap of Marsh Mallow, combined with the seeds of Fleabane and the white of an egg, formed an adhesive paste which when rubbed on the hands mollified the heat and enabled a man subjected to this terrifying ordeal safely to endure the glowing metal for a few moments.

Dr John Hill, speaking of Mallow in his *History of the Materia Medica*, names it as one of the five Emollient Herbs. "There is scarce a Cataplasm", he writes, "designed for maturating but has Mallows for an ingredient. The herb is a proper remedy, first, where acrimony requires demulcents; secondly, where too great a stricture requires relaxation; thirdly, where pains are to be mitigated; and fourthly, under an excessive glutinosity."

The Marsh-Mallow Decoction of Dr James 1752

Take 2 oz roots of Marsh-Mallow and a handful of the herb. Boil in 3 pints of barley-water until reduced to 1½ pints. Strain and add 4 oz compound horse-radish water and a like quantity of brandy; ½ oz berries of juniper and ditto of bays; 2 drams each of seeds of anise, sweet fennel, caraway, and wild daucus.

Make a warm and close Infusion for two hours. Then strain and dissolve in the liquor, over a gentle fire, 1 oz gum arabic and 4 oz syrup of mercury. Very efficacious, according to Dr Fuller, in removing any gritty matter or gravel that may obstruct the kidneys and urinary passages. At the same time it blunts the points of acrimonious salts and eases pain.

MANDRAKE   *Mandragora officinalis* L.   Solanaceae

Alruna

FR *Mandragore*; *Main de gloire*; *Circée*

GER *Alraunwurzel*; *Hexenkraut*

> The phantom shapes – oh, touch not them! –
> That appall the murderer's sight,
> Lurk in the fleshly Mandrake's stem,
> That shrieks when plucked at night.
>
> THOMAS MOORE *Light of the Harem*

Although no longer, or very rarely, found in Britain, the true Mandrake is possibly better known, by name at least, to the majority of people than many far commoner plants, if only on account of the wealth of fantastic legends with which it is surrounded. For many centuries it was grown as an opiate, Shakespeare's "drowsy syrup", in the herb gardens of the old monastic establishments, but with the disappearance of the ancient religious houses the herb ceased to be generally cultivated in England. Gerard writes: "Mandrake groweth in hot Regions, in woods and mountains, as in mount Garganus in Apulia, and such like places; we have them onely planted in gardens, and are not elsewhere to be found in England."

One of the fables beloved of ancient writers was that, ridiculed by Gerard, of the Mandrake uttering a dreadful shriek when plucked from the ground – a shriek which brought madness, or even death, to him who heard it. To collect Mandrake roots, therefore, it was necessary to tie a dog to the plant, the herbalist remaining at a safe distance and stopping his ears with wax. A piece of meat thrown just out of the dog's reach had the desired effect: the dog tugged, the plant left its bed, and "the dog it was that died". In Dr Charles Singer's book *From Magic to Science* is a delightful illustration of the nymph Discovery presenting a Mandrake to Dioscorides, whilst the dog, attached to the root, is expiring in agony.

Matthiolus, in his Commentaries on Dioscorides, exposes this

13   *Mandrake* 193

belief as a vulgar error, and says: "the roots which the charlatans sell, fashioned in the shape of the human body, and which they boldly claim will ensure conception to hitherto sterile women, are artificial and made of the roots of white briony, etc. They cut and shape these roots, when fresh, into the form of men and women, and in those places where there should be hair they insert seeds of barley or millet. Then, having buried them, they cover the roots with sand and leave them until the seed has germinated. Then they dig them up, and with a sharp pen-knife trim the roots where the grain has sprouted to resemble hair and beard and all other hair on the body."

Another fable of the Mandrake, related by Gerard, was that the plant was seldom to be found growing naturally, "but under a gallowes, where the matter that has fallen from a dead body hath given it the shape of a man and the matter of a woman, the substance of a female plant, and many other such doltish dreams".

The Mandrake is a native of Syria; a biennial with glossy green leaves, dark purple flowers, and bearing shiny orange-coloured fruit known, from their poisonous qualities, as "Satan's Apples". The root is long, fleshy and forked, surrounded by short hairlike fibres. Apothecaries made use either of the root-bark or the entire root, though the leaf provided one of the many ingredients of *Unguentum Populeon** which was supposed to cure the ague, and for which the formula can be found in the Dispensatory of Valerius Cordus.

The Latin name for the plant was *Atropa mandragora*, after Atropos, the eldest of the Parcae, or Fates, who "slits the thin-spun life", an allusion to the poisonous powers it shares with others of the Potato Order, notably *Atropa Belladonna*, or Deadly Nightshade. Its narcotic action was well known to the ancients and Dioscorides recommended it to be given in wine to "such as shall be cut or cauterised . . . for they do not

* Often simply called "popilion" in old medical recipes.

MANDRAKE

apprehend the pain, because they are overborne with dead sleep". Both Shakespeare and a lesser poet, William Browne, link it with the Poppy on account of its narcotic potency, and Browne also associates it with Lethe, the river of oblivion.

What the modern herbalist terms mandrake root has, however, nothing to do with the mandragora so frequently mentioned by Shakespeare, but is the root of a North American plant *Podophyllum Peltatum* L. (May-apple), which is official and used as an hepatic and intestinal stimulant. It often forms an ingredient of "liver" pills.

And to make confusion the greater the name mandrake is also a synonym for the root of red-berried and the black-berried Bryony (*Bryonia dioica* and *B. alba*) of the Marrow family.

The old English name for the Mandrake – *Alruna* – and the German *Alraunwurzel* are derived from Alruna, a prophetess of the ancient Germanic people. Alrunes were little wooden figures which the ancient Germans made their *lares* or household divinities, and these little mannikins were for preference carved from the root of the Mandrake. *Die Alraune* in modern German are the equivalent of our "pixies".

MARIGOLD   *Calendula officinalis* L.   Compositae
Golds
Ruddes
FR *Souci; Fleur de tous les mois*
GER *Ringelblume; Goldblume; Morgenröte*

> The Marigold that goes to bed wi' the sun,
> And with him rises weeping.
> > *The Winter's Tale*, 4, iv

The cheerful Pot Marigold, "the Herb Generall in all pottage" as old Fuller called it, has little in common but the name with some of the gaudy plants that have been developed by the horticulturist. Although in origin an exotic it became naturalised in this country many centuries ago and earned its letters of denization by its usefulness both in kitchen and in pharmacy.

"The yellow leaves of the floures are dried and kept throughout Dutchland against Winter," writes Gerard, "to put into broths, in Physicall potions, and for divers other purposes, in such quantity that in some Grocers or Spice-sellers houses are to be found barrels filled with them, and retailed by the penny more or lesse, insomuch that no broths are well made without dried Marigolds."

Not only in "Dutchland" were dried Marigolds an ingredient of the soup, but in England also, for Charles Lamb, who confessed that he was not indifferent to food, could not stomach the "detestable Marigolds floating in the pail", and perhaps their strong flavour was excuse enough. Marigold puddings had as an ingredient the finely chopped petals; the flowers were used to give colouring to cheese; they were candied and preserved; and they were even made into wine, a recipe for which can be found in Carter's *Recipe Book* of 1737.

Dr Fernie says that the flowers of Marigold were much used by American surgeons for the treatment of wounds during the Civil War, and herbalists to this day make use of the Marigold for dressing wounds, burns and ulcerated chilblains.* It is also used as a diaphoretic, sometimes in conjunction with borage.

The Marigold's botanical name of *Calendula* refers to the plant's reputed habit of blooming on the kalends of every month, and indeed, when the winter is mild the Marigold flowers during the greater part of the year. Thus the Italians call it *Fiore di ogni mese*. As for the word "Marigold" itself, Prior suggests that it originated in the Anglo-Saxon *merse-mear-gealla* (marsh-horse-gowl), that is, the Marsh Marigold (*Caltha palustris*), and that the word was transferred to the Calendula and misunderstood as Mary-gold. In the *Grete Herball* it is called "Mary Gowles", but most of the older writers refer to the plant simply as *Gold*. Nevertheless, once the flower had acquired the "Mary" prefix it became quite

* *See* H. Leclerc: *Précis de Phytothérapie.*

naturally assigned to the festivals of the Holy Virgin. But none of the foreign names of the Marigold have any reference to the Virgin Mary.

The manner in which the Marigold opens out with the sun and follows it through its course was quickly noticed by the old herbalists, and in Lyte's Dodoens we read: "It hath pleasant, bright and shining yellow flowers, the which do close at the setting downe of the sunne, and do spread and open againe at the sun rising." Thus the Marigold becomes also the Heliotropum, Solsequium, Tournesol and Solis Sponsa of our forefathers, and was frequently alluded to under those names.

The Marigold is an annual originating in Central Europe and extremely abundant in Morocco. At maturity the flowers give birth to the achenes commonly called the seed. Pharmacists prefer the double-flowered strains of bright orange colour to those with yellow flowers.

MARJORAM (SWEET)   *Origanum majorana* L.   Labiatae
FR *Marjolaine*
GER *Gartenmajoran*

MARJORAM (WILD)   *Origanum vulgare* L.   *Majerpunka*
FR *Marjolaine sauvage*
GER *Dost*; *Wilder Majoran*

> Indeed, Sir, she was the sweet marjoram of the
> Salad, or rather the herb of grace.
> *All's Well that Ends Well*, 4, V

Wild Marjoram is common all over England, growing with great delight on chalk downs, its oval clusters of reddish-purple flowers enlivening the green pastures and its fragrance giving an added zest to the pure upland air.

The generic name *origanum* derives from the Greek and signifies "Joy of the Mountains", for the Greeks were very fond of it and planted it on graves to ensure the peace and happiness of the departed. In England it was for long esteemed as a medicinal herb; as a remedy for coughs and bronchial complaints, for dropsy and for yellow jaundice, and for many other ills. The *London Dispensatory* of 1649 found that it "helps such as are given to much sighing", while Gerard surpassed himself in graphic description when he wrote that it "is very good against the wambling of the stomacke". What reminiscences of cross-Channel discomfort that lively word "wambling" summons up!

If Wild Marjoram was popular as a herb of healing, Sweet Marjoram was no less so in the kitchen – "a delicate and tender hearbe of a sweet savour" as Lyte termed it. This native of warmer climes is a tender plant which in this country must be treated as an annual, for it cannot endure a hard winter. It is sometimes known as Knotted Marjoram from the flowers being set in compact heads or "knots".

This is the "swete margerome" dear to the old herbalists; the plant which Perdita mingles with the hot lavender, mints, savory and marigold in *The Winter's Tale*; Gerard's herb of "marvellous sweet smell". It is a smaller plant than Wild Marjoram, growing about a foot in height, used in former days, as Parkinson tells us, "to please the outward senses in nosegays and in the windows of houses, as also in sweete powders, sweet bags, and sweete washing waters". The flowers, in short ovoid spikes, vary from white to pink.

Some think that Sweet Marjoram was the *amaracon* of Dioscorides; from its Latin equivalent, *amaracus*,* through Mediaeval Latin *majorana*, come the Old French *majoraine* and Middle English *majoram*, which later acquired another interpolated "r". In England Sweet Marjoram was being cultivated as early as the 14th century, and by the next century we find several allusions to "mergeron gentle", which

* Amaracus, a youth in the service of the King of Cyprus. Frightened to death by smashing a vase full of perfume, he was changed into the herb bearing his name.

may have been a variety of *O. majorana*. We may read in Skelton's poem *To Mistress Margery Wentworth*, printed in *The Garland of Laurel*, 1523:

> With Margeraine jentyll
> The floure of goodlyhede
> Embroidered the mantel
> Is, of your maidenhede.

Turner, in his 1562 herbal, says "I never saw the true Origanum in England, saving in master Ryches gardin in London", but what exactly he means by the true Origanum is not certain, for as Matthioli comments: "all the ancient simplers have badly confused the matter and history of Origanum". It is probable that the herb which Turner called "Righte Dittany" is *Origanum dictamnus*, or Dittany of Crete, a curious plant with cottony leaves and small pink flowers, known to country folk in England as "Hop plant". It is a perennial hardy enough in favourable sites, but susceptible to damp and chilly winds.

Mediaeval writers endowed this herb with the property of extracting iron from a man's body, and Swan, paraphrasing Du Bartas, writes:

> But I suppose not that the earth doth yield
> In hill or dale, in forrest or in field,
> A rarer plant than Candian Dittany,
> Which wounded Deere eating, immediately
> Not onely cure their wounds exceeding well,
> But 'gainst the shooter do the shaft repell.

This curious piece of information echoes that given by Pliny, who says "the wilde Goats or Deer in Candy, when they be wounded with arrows or darts, do shake them out by eating this herb". Lyte says that "the juice of the same is of soveraigne and singular force against all kinds of wounds made with Glaive or other kinds of weapons, and against all bitings of venemous beasts, to be dropped or poured in, for it doth both mundifie, cleanse and cure the same".

Pot Marjoram (*O. onites*) is a larger plant than Sweet

Marjoram, and the whole plant is of reddish hue, bearing purplish flowers on terminal spikes, in shape rather like minute pine cones. Winter Marjoram (*O. heraclioticum*) is native to Greece, but is quite hardy in this country if sheltered from keen winds and given well-drained soil. In all there are some thirty species of Marjoram, but those enumerated are the best-known.

Marjoram is used in flavouring meats, sausages, salads and soups. Though formerly official, it is now not greatly used for medicinal purposes, but the volatile oil is said to be excellent for sprains and bruises, applied externally. Red Oil of Thyme, often adulterated with other oils, is frequently sold as *Oleum Origani*. In the Balkans and the Near East marjoram remains a popular remedy for dysentery and other intestinal troubles.

SPEARMINT   *Mentha viridis* L.   Labiatae
Garden Mint
FR *Menthe verte*
GER *Frauenminze*

PEPPERMINT   *Mentha piperata* L.   Labiatae
Brandy Mint
FR *Menthe poivrée*
GER *Pfefferminze*

PENNYROYAL   *Mentha pulegium* L.   Labiatae
Pudding Herb
FR *Menthe pouliot*; *Herbe aux puces*
GER *Poleiminze*

WATERMINT   *Mentha aquatica* L.   Labiatae
FR *Menthe aquatique*
GER *Wasserminze*

The healthful balm and mint from their full laps do fly.
Polyolbion. Song XV

Mint 201

There are numerous varieties of mint, and about fourteen of them are natives of England. The Spearmint (Mackerel Mint: Lamb Mint) is the most used for culinary purposes, in flavouring peas and potatoes, and for the preparation of that peculiarly English condiment known as mint sauce, of which a Frenchman once remarked that "it astonishes the palate and distresses the stomach of the foreigner".

Peppermint is cultivated largely for medicinal purposes, Oil of Peppermint (Oleum Menthae Piperitae) being used as an aromatic, stimulant and carminative.

But as Walahfrid Strabo, Abbot of Reichenau, wrote as long ago as the 9th century: "If one wanted to enumerate completely all the virtues, species and names of Mint, one would have to be able to say how many fishes swim in the Red Sea or the number of sparks Vulcan can count flying from the vast furnaces of Etna."

Mint was well known to the ancients, and the species alluded to in the Bible (Matthew XXIII.23; Luke XI.42) was probably *M. sylvestris* which was common in Palestine. According to the ancient legend recounted by Ovid, Mint derives its name from Minthe, a daughter of Cocytus beloved of Pluto. When Proserpine discovered her husband's amour, she changed the girl into the plant which still bears her name. In remembrance of her, young girls in Greece used to braid their bridal wreaths with sprigs of Mint and of Vitex (an exotic species of Verbena), though later both were superseded by the Myrtle, dedicated to Venus.

Parkinson says that in ancient times the Greek soldiers were forbidden to eat Mint in time of war because their leaders thought "it did so much incite to venery that it took away, or at least abated, their animosity or courage to fight". But Pliny says that Mint impedes generation by preventing the seminal fluids from obtaining the requisite consistency (*Nat. Hist.*, Book XX, Chap. 53).

The smell of Mint was held to stimulate the appetite, and

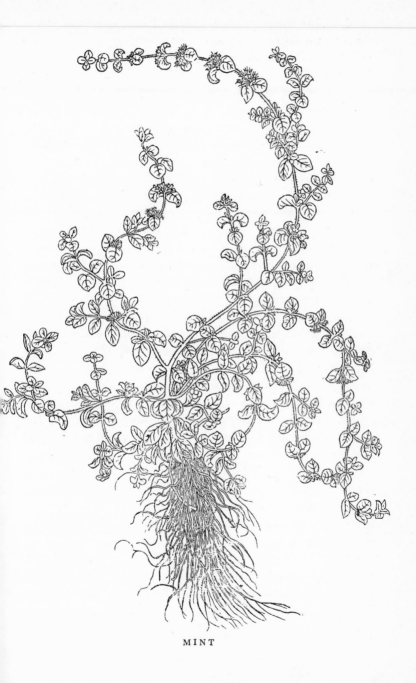

MINT

Ovid depicts the poor but hospitable Baucis and Philemon as scouring the board with green Mint before laying upon it food provided for their divine but unknown guests Jupiter and Mercury. Pliny recommends a Crown of Mint to be worn when studying, since it "exhilarates the mind and is therefore proper for students".

Peppermint, which some botanists consider to be a hybrid between *M. spicata* and *M. aquatica*, is distributed throughout the greater part of the world outside the tropics, and for centuries has been cultivated in England. It is a perennial, with erect, branching stems slightly reddish in hue, dark green ovate leaves, and terminal spikes of purplish flowers. Oil of Peppermint, which contains among other constituents menthol, menthol esters, and menthone, is one of the most commonly used flavourings for confectionery, is used in the perfumery and soap industries, and enters into many pharmaceutical preparations.

There was a time when the trade in Peppermint was largely supplied from the fields around Ewell and Mitcham, in Surrey. But soon after the end of the First World War the extensive peppermint fields gave place to bricks and mortar and genuine Mitcham mint is now no more. But the English essential oil is still the best available and is produced in moderate quantities in Hertfordshire, Lincolnshire and Suffolk. The British Pharmacopoeia formerly admitted as official only oil distilled in Britain, but owing to shortage of local supply this is no longer the case and much is imported. A large amount of the essential oil is now produced in the United States; the amount of menthol present in the American Oil of Peppermint is somewhat smaller than in the English oil, but that of the esters is higher.

One of the commonest uses nowadays for Spearmint is for flavouring chewing-gum. Though once a drug plant it is no longer used in medicine except as a flavouring. Synonyms are *M. spicata* and *M. romana*, for it is extensively cultivated in

Italy, in which country there are many superstitions connected with it. If the women of the Abruzzi come across a plant of mint they will bruise a leaf between their fingers, it is said, to ensure that on the day of their death Jesus will assist them.

Pennyroyal is thought by some to have been the first of the many kinds of Mint to be cultivated, and in appearance and habit it differs considerably from the others. Perhaps this was the Mint which Chaucer had in mind when he wrote

> Then went I forthe on my right honde,
> Down by a little path I fonde
> Of mintes full and fennell greene.

It is a tiny decumbent plant, from six inches to a foot in height, with lilac-coloured flowers in dense whorls. The leaves are short-stalked, and oval, just faintly toothed. Says Lawson: "peny-royall, or Pudding Grasse, creeps along the ground like ground Ivie . . . it hath a pleasant taste and smell, good for the pot, or hackt meat, or Haggas Pudding," which as Gervase Markham tells us were "made of the bloud of Beasts and Oatmeale". Thus the plant acquired its name of Pudding Herb.

But it had another use, just as important, in earlier days, when rush-strewn floors provided a happy breeding ground for vermin, since like Wormwood it was considered highly efficacious in destroying fleas. In fact the name Pennyroyal is derived from the Latin name *puleium regium* (*pulex*=flea). The Dutch name for the herb is *polei*, and in many old English herbals it is called Puliol Royal. Its action as a vermin-chaser is due to a ketone called pulegone, a liquid with a strong and penetrating odour, of which the essential oil contains about 75 per cent. This oil, *oleum pulegii*, was formerly used for female disorders, but nowadays, although country folk still take an infusion of the herb for coughs and colds, its main use is in veterinary medicine.

Menthol is obtained mainly from a variety of *M. arvensis* (Corn mint) cultivated in China and Japan. Although the Oil of Peppermint obtained from this source is inferior in aroma and taste to the English oil, the menthol content is very high. The menthol is separated by fractional distillation, or by cooling the oil to a very low temperature at which the menthol crystallises out.

Water Mint is a perennial, from 2 to 3 feet high, with pale purple flowers, found in wet ditches and marshes in most temperate countries. *M. crispa* is a variety of *M. spicata* with crinkly edges to the leaves. But to enumerate all the Mints would need a book; there are few genera which include more varieties and most of them hybridise.

MOTHERWORT *Leonurus cardiaca* L. Labiatae
FR *Agripaume*; *Cardiaque*; *Queue-de-lion*
GER *Mutterkraut*; *Löwenschwanz*; *Herzgespann*

The Old English termination "wort" shows that this plant was used long ago as a medicinal herb and the prefix indicates that it was used for female ailments. The specific botanical name denotes its employment as a heart tonic. That it was highly valued for these and other ailments is shown by a passage in *The Widowes Treasure* (1595), which reads:

The vertue of Motherworte. It groweth by the high waies and stonie walles, bushing with many stalks, leaved like a nettle, but more ragged: and towards the bottome like Crow foote. It is of wonderfull force against any sicknes of the hart, whereof the cheefe name is derived. It helpeth Crampes and Palsies, it killeth woormes in the bodie, it clenseth the brest from Flegme, it dooth open colde obstructions, it provoketh Urine, moveth Womens flowres the iuce drunk, or the hearbe in decoction, and a spoonfull of the powder of this hearbe given in Wine, helpeth the hard labours of Women.

Culpeper says "There is no better herb to drive melancholy vapours from the heart, to strengthen it and make the mind cheerful, blithe and merry."

Motherwort is not regarded as native to this country, but is indigenous to Europe and parts of Asia. It is a perennial plant, growing up to 4 feet high, with slightly hairy dark green leaves. The flowers (June–September), purplish or red, grow in close axillary whorls. It is not common in this country, but is sometimes to be seen in old cottage gardens, where it has doubt-less been cultivated for generations on account of the virtues formerly associated with it.

MUGWORT   *Artemisia vulgaris* L.   Compositae
Motherwort; Felon Herb
FR *Armoise*; *Ceinture de Saint-Jean*
GER *Gemeiner Beifuss*

> If they'd drink Nettles in March and Mugwort in May
> So many fine maidens would not go to clay.

Mugwort was one of the herbs mentioned in "The lay of the nine healing herbs", written in the Wessex dialect in an early Anglo-Saxon manuscript known as the *Lacnunga*. In the Middle Ages it was known as Herb St John, for a superstition widespread in Europe held that a garland of this plant made on the feast of St John and worn around the waist would confer upon the wearer immunity from all ailments for a year, after which time the garland had to be burned in the fire.

Another virtue attributed to Mugwort was that it cured weariness, for as William Coles expresses it in the *Art of Simpling*, "If a footman take Mugwort and put it into his shoes in the morning he may goe forty miles before noon and not be weary."

Mugwort is a common wayside plant, tall-growing even on poor soil, and was much in evidence on bombed sites in Britain just after the Second World War. It can be distinguished from Wormwood by its leaves, which are green above and whitish on the under side, with sharply pointed segments. Also its scent is less strong. The name Mugwort corresponds in its meaning to Wormwood, from the Old English *mough*, a maggot or moth. The name of Motherwort was applied to it owing to its use at one time for uterine affections.

As the couplet above bears witness, Mugwort is commonly supposed by country folk to be a wholesome spring tonic, and before the introduction of hops into this country from Flanders it was used to flavour beer. It is still employed by herbalists in many countries as an emmenagogue, tonic, and anti-spasmodic. For female disorders it is generally used in combination with Pennyroyal and Southernwood.

From early times the herb was associated with witchcraft and sorcery, and the *Grete Herball* of 1539 says "If this herbe be within a house there shall no wycked spyryte abyde." *Artemisiae radix*, the root of the Mugwort, which contains a volatile oil, acrid resin and tannin, was much used as a remedy for the "falling sickness", as epilepsy was once termed.

> Mugwort! a herb that has gone down to fame
> Despite the hindrance of its horrid name.

MUSTARD　　　*Brassica nigra* (Koch)　　　Cruciferae
　　　　　　　Brassica alba (Boiss)
FR *Moutarde*
GER *Senf*

> *Grumio:* What say you to a piece of beef and mustard?
> *Katherine:* A dish that I do love to feed upon.
> 　　　　　　　*The Taming of the Shrew*, 4, iii

Many species of Mustard are known, but the two of commercial importance are *B. nigra* and *B. alba*, black and white Mustard respectively, though the seed of *B. alba* is usually termed Yellow Mustard. The Cress family, to which Mustard belongs, provides us with a large number of culinary vegetables and saladings. Mustards belong to the section of the genus *Brassica* called *Sinapis* from the Latin (via Greek) word for mustard. (A sinapism means simply a mustard plaster.) Mustard is also used in medicine, and the official Mustard of the Pharmacopoeia is the product of the two species in combination.

Mustard is one of the oldest known culinary and medical herbs. It is frequently mentioned in the Scriptures,* and about Mustard in all its aspects, and of the superstitions and legends woven around it, a book could be written. The Greeks and Romans seem to have employed table mustard in the same manner as we do today, and the oldest known recipe for preparing mustard was written by Columella, a native of Gades, who flourished during the 1st century AD, and wrote – among other things – twelve books on agriculture (*De Re Rustica*), the tenth of which deals with gardens.

Our English word mustard is said to come, via Old French, from the Latin *mustum ardens*, because hot must (new wine or vinegar) was formerly used in preparing this condiment. A legend current in France derives the name from another source. In 1382 Philip the Bold, Duke of Burgundy, granted to the town of Dijon, which has always been renowned for its mustard, armorial bearings with the motto *Moult Me Tarde*. Arms and motto were adopted as a trade mark by the makers of mustard, the motto being shortened to *moult-tarde*.

Parkinson describes the grinding of mustard seed by means of a quern "with some good vinegar added to it to make it liquid and running", and adds that "our ancient forefathers in the more simple and more healthful age of the world were not sparing in the use thereof at their tables". Evelyn, in 1664, wrote that "mustard is incomparable to quicken and revive the spirits, strengthening the memory, and expelling heaviness".

Tewkesbury, in Gloucestershire, was long celebrated for its mustard, and Coles, writing about 1657, tells us that "in Gloucestershire about Teuxbury they grind Mustard and make it up into balls which are brought to London and other remote

* Some authorities think that the "mustard seed" of Matthew XIII was that of *Salvadora persicaria*, a small tree of the Middle East.

places as being the best that the world affords". (*Cf* Falstaff's sarcastic reply to Doll Tearsheet's remark about Poins: "His wit's as thick as Tewkesbury mustard.") Later a Mrs Clements of Durham invented a new method of dressing mustard like wheat flour, and "Durham mustard" became synonymous with quality.

Formerly Mustard was not a cultivated crop to the extent that it is today, and most probably the Tewkesbury mustard was made from the seeds of the Charlock, or Wild Mustard (*Sinapsis arvensis*), which then as now was only too common all over Britain, choking the grain of the laggard farmer who fails to exterminate it.

As a remedy for various ills Mustard was used in many ways; as oil, tincture, poultice and plaster, for headaches, fevers, whooping-cough, asthma, and liver and stomach complaints. The *Speculum Mundi* extols Mustard for clearing the voice: "It is marvellous good against a voice that's hoarse; wherefore, if any be given to musick, and would fain have a clear voice to sing, let him make mustard seeds into powder and work the same with honey into little balls, of which let him swallow one or two down every morning fasting, and in a short time his voice will be clear."

B. alba and *B. nigra* are rather similar in appearance, but whereas the pods of the latter are only about half an inch in length, those of *B. alba* are some two inches long. Both have bright yellow flowers which make a field of mustard in bloom an unforgettable sight. The seeds of black Mustard are much smaller than those of the white variety. As a basis of comparison, whereas it takes about five thousand whole white Mustard seeds to make an ounce, over 12,500 of the black seeds are needed. *

Ground Mustard, or Mustard flour, is made by crushing, grinding and sifting the whole seeds, and for table use as a condiment "double" mustard is employed, a mixture of both

* According to J. W. Parry: *The Spice Handbook.*

kinds of seed, the black for aroma and the white for pungency. Turmeric may be added to heighten the yellow colour and make the mustard more aromatic, and other aromatic bodies, such as extract of tarragon may also be present. But naturally the preparation of mustard in paste form is usually a trade secret and the formulae for some of the famous Dijon mustards have been handed down for generations.

The seeds of *B. nigra* produce a very pungent volatile oil called Allyl isothiocyanate which is known to the Pharmacopoeia as *Oleum Sinapsis volatile*. *B. alba* produces a nonvolatile oil, Acrinyl isothiocyanate, which has a less powerful rubefacient action than the former. Both kinds contain around 25 per cent. of fixed oil having mild rubefacient action. A mixture of equal parts of black and white Mustard is used as a local counter-irritant either in the form of a poultice or as a mustard-paper for the treatment of lumbago and congestion of the lungs. Mustard liniment consists of camphor, castor oil, and volatile oil of Mustard in a solution of alcohol.

A cataplasm of figs and the juice of white mustard is good for the lethargy by laying it upon the shaven head till the skull comes red and the same cataplasm laid on the hip eases the sciatica.

ELIZABETH BLACKWELL *A Curious Herbale*. 1737

PARSLEY   *Petroselinum sativum*   Umbelliferae
                 (Hoffmann)

FR *Persil*
GER *Petersilie*

> Fat colworts and comforting perseline,
> Cold lettuce and refreshing rosmarine.
> SPENSER *Muiopotmos*

In England, if not elsewhere, Parsley must be easily the most popular of culinary herbs. But curiously enough its native habitat is not known for certainty, though modern botanists consider it indigenous to Sardinia. But then again, there are many varieties of Parsley – well over forty according to Eleanour Rhode.

It received its name from the ancient Greeks because it often grew among rocks, but *petroselinon* became corrupted in course of time into "Petrocilium", and this was anglicised into Petersylinge, Perseline, Perseley and, finally, Parsley.

The Greeks held Parsley in high esteem and it was with chaplets of Parsley that they crowned the victors at the Isthmian games. Perhaps it was the fact that this festival had its origin in funeral games in honour of Melicertes, the son of Ino, that the Greeks held Parsley sacred to oblivion and to the dead, and would never use it at table. Or it may have been the belief that the plant sprang from the blood of Archemorus, "the forerunner of doom", in whose honour the Nemean games were instituted. In this festival, also, the victor was crowned with a wreath of Parsley.

Most herbs have various superstitions connected with them, and Parsley is no exception. For instance, the slowness of its germination is due to the fact that it goes to the Devil and back seven times before it will begin to grow, and even then it will thrive only if the seed has been planted by an upright and honest man. Many gardeners refuse to transplant it for that would be inviting disaster. In the days when black magic was taken seriously, if one had a mortal grudge against someone, it was sufficient to pluck up a root of Parsley and utter the person's name; he would surely die in a matter of days. Nor were these superstitions confined to England; they seem to be widespread throughout Europe.

Of the various cultivated varieties of Parsley those with close curled leaves are the most popular, but the Italian plain-leaved Parsley is better suited to withstand the English winter as the leaves do not retain the moisture. The plant is a biennial or short-lived perennial, but is often grown as an annual. It is an excellent source of vitamin C, the more so when fresh.

The Hamburg, or turnip-rooted Parsley (*Carum petroselinum fusiformis*), is hardy, and will survive most winters, but for some reason it is rarely grown in Britain nowadays. It has a large tap-root, rather like a parsnip, and can be cooked and eaten in the same way as that vegetable, the taste resembling that of celeriac.

Turner informs us that "Perseley heleth fyshes that are sycke if it be casten into them in the pondes" and also that "the sede taken before hand, helpeth men that have weyke braynes to bare drynke better". And, since body-odour was probably very common in those early days of the 16th century, he adds "the use of the same maketh a mans body savour well".

Parsley has considerable medicinal value, for the drug apiol, which is one of its constituents, is employed for kidney complaints. Apiol is also considered to be a safe and efficient emmenagogue, and is usually administered in the form of capsules or perles. But it is as a culinary herb that Parsley is known to all, though it is regrettable that it should be only too often used merely as a decorative garnish instead of being eaten, thus wasting its useful iron and vitamin content.

Parsley sauce is, of course, an excellent accompaniment for certain boiled or steamed fish, and for this purpose the leaves should not be chopped, but, deprived of their stalks and blanched for a few moments in boiling water, should then be placed in the melted butter to be used for the sauce. The parsley will soon break up into small shreds, and in this manner imparts the utmost flavouring to the sauce.

Parsley Piert, or Parsley Breakstone, is the name given to *Alchemilla arvensis*, a small herb of the Rose family used as an infusion in cases of gravel, kidney and bladder complaints.

PELLITORY OF THE WALL

Wallwort   *Parietaria officinalis* L.   Urticaceae
FR *Pariétaire*; *Perce-murailles*; *Espargoule*
GER *Glaskraut*; *Mauerkraut*

Often to be seen on old walls in England and southern Scotland, and in waste, stony places throughout Europe, Pellitory-of-the-Wall was once found in every apothecary's shop, and long ago it was used by the monks as a medicinal herb. It is a small, branching perennial, growing to a height of about a foot, with reddish stems spreading out in clumps, narrow, downy leaves and tiny reddish-green flowers in sessile clusters. Although a a member of the nettle family, it has no stinging hairs, and so is often called in France *Ortie douce*.

Its demulcent properties make it a popular remedy for local inflammations, and an ointment is made of the expressed juice of the herb, warmed together with lard, which is used for sore throats and bruises. An infusion of the leaves is drunk in country districts as a blood cleanser. The French make from it a medicinal preparation called "Sirop de Pariétaire".

The plant's botanical name is derived from the Latin *paries*, "a wall", from its habit of growing in the crevices of walls. Of this plant Dr James says "It absterges and is somewhat astringent and cooling. Tragus very much commends the decoction to remove obstructions in the lower belly. Camerarius prescribes it bruised with vinegar and applied hot to the testes in case of ruptures."

Persian Pellitory (Pyrethrum roseum) is a member of the Daisy family and is used as an insecticide.

PLANTAIN (Greater) *Plantago major* L.   Plantaginaceae
Waybread
FR *Grand plantain*
GER *Grosser Wegerich; Wegebreit*

> These poor slight sores
> Need not a plantain.
> *The Two Noble Kinsmen*, 1, ii

Everybody knows the Plantain, many to their exasperation, for it has a way of making an unwelcome appearance on the best kept lawns. The Saxons called it *Waeybraede* because it is commonly found growing by the wayside, and this name has persisted, changed slightly to *Waybread* and *Waybroad* (*cf* German *Wegebreit*). The name Plantain is apparently derived from the Latin *planta*, the sole of the foot, either from the appearance of the leaves or from its habit of growing along paths trodden by the foot of man. According to Grimm, the Plantain or Waybread was once a young girl who, worn out with constantly watching the roadway for the lover who never came, was changed into a plant which still takes up its position by the wayside.

Since the time of Pliny, and maybe earlier, the Plantain has been used as a styptic and vulnerary. Romeo praises the excellence of the plantain leaf as a healer of a broken shin, and Costard, in *Love's Labour's Lost*, requires "no salve, sir, but a plantain".

As late as the 17th century it was considered something of a heal-all, for the *London Dispensatory* of 1649 refers to the plant in this manner: "A herb, though common let none despise it, for it prevails mightily against tormenting pains and excoriations of the guts, bloody fluxes, it stops the terms and spitting of blood, Phtisicks, or Consumptions of the lunges, the running of the reins, the whites in women, pains in the head, and frenzies; outwardly it cleers the sight, takes away inflamations, scabs, itch, the shingles, and all spreading sores, and is as wholsom an herb as can grow about a house."

PLANTAIN

Plantain is said to have been used as a medicine in twenty-two different diseases, among others for the tertian ague. Although no longer considered a panacea, Plantain leaves contain a mucilage which affords rapid relief against the bites of wasps and mosquitoes. As for the seeds which abound on the dense spikes once the lilac-coloured flowers are faded, birds love them, and they form an important part of commercial bird-seed mixtures.

There are many varieties of Plantain, in addition to the Greater Plantain (*P. major*). They include the following:

Plantago coronopus – Hart's Horn, Buckshorn, or Star of the Earth (FR *Plantain corne de cerf*; GER *Salz-Wegerich*)

P. maritima – Sea-plantain (FR *Plantain maritime*; GER *Küsten-Wegerich*)

P. media – Lamb's tongue (FR *Langue d'agneau*; GER *Blüten-Wegerich*)

P. minor (P. lanceolata) – Ribwort (FR *Petit plantain*; Oreille de lièvre; GER *Spitz-Wegerich*)

P. psyllium – Flea-wort (FR *Psyllium*; *Puciaire*; GER *Floh-samenkraut*)

PURSLANE   var. *Portulaca sativa* (Haworth)   Portulaceae
                    Portulaca oleracea L.

FR *Pourpier des potagers*; *Porcellane*
GER *Portulak*; *Burgel*

> Lord, I confess too when I dine
>   The pulse is thine –
> And all those other bits that be
>   There placed by thee,
> The worts, the purselain, and the mess
>   Of Water Cress.
>
> **ROBERT HERRICK**

The original habitat of this herb is not known for certain, but the Purslane family now has a very wide geographical range.

It was commonly grown during the Middle Ages and writers of the 16th century recommend it for a variety of afflictions. It was also a favourite salad herb and many recipes for pickled Purslane may be found in old cookery books.

Culpeper gives the recipe for a *Lohoch de Portulaca** of the College of Physicians with the remark: "the medicine is so binding that it is better let alone than taken." Seeing that one of the ingredients was "the wool of a Hare toasted" probably he was right.

The Dutch Pharmacopoeia of 1747 describes Purslane as a much esteemed remedy in cases of inflammation of the bladder and as affording great relief to sufferers from piles.

Golden Purslane (*P. sativa*) is a tiny plant, about six inches high, not quite so hardy as *P. oleracea*, but for a bed which gets plenty of sun it makes a pretty edging.

"This plant", says the *New English Dispensatory*, "affords an excellent Aliment and Medicine. Its parts are very succulent and the juice astringent, remarkably aperient, expulsive, and cooling in inflammatory diseases, and very good to wash the gums, when affected with a gangrene." Estienne, also, notes that "Purslane eaten doth cure the roughnes and astonishment [*sic*] of the teeth."

ROSEMARY   *Rosmarinus officinalis* L.   Labiatae
Dew of the Sea
FR *Rosmarin*; *Encensier*
GER *Rosmarin*

> There's rosemary, that's for remembrance.
>
> *Hamlet*, 4, v

A sacred herb, Rosemary, and one of the best-loved of all the mediaeval garden herbs. A native of the Mediterranean basin, it was acclimatised in Britain long before the Conquest, and

* *Lohoch*, the English transcription of an Arabic word, is the same as linctus.

since it was a plant held in great esteem and reverence by both Greeks and Romans, it is very probable that it was introduced into this country by the Roman colonisers.

It was certainly known to the Saxons, for it is referred to in the celebrated *Leech Book of Bald*, written about AD 900: "For the sickly take this wort rosemary, wonderfully thou healest him." In a later age Sir Thomas More grew it in his garden at Chelsea, saying: "As for Rosmarine, I lett it run alle over my garden walls, not onlie because my bees love it, but because 'tis the herb sacred to remembrance, and therefore to friendship; whence a sprig of it hath a dumb language that maketh it the chosen emblem at our funeral wakes, and in our buriall grounds."

The plant derives its name from *ros maris* (spray of the sea), and in both English and Dutch it has the alternative name of Sea Dew. But in the popular mind Rosemary inevitably became firmly associated with the Blessed Virgin Mary, and it is small wonder that there grew up around it a host of beautiful legends and picturesque traditions. One of the best known of these legends tells how, during the Flight into Egypt, the Virgin Mary rested for a while by a bush of Rosemary, over which she threw her mantle, whereupon the originally white flowers of the plant turned to a heavenly blue in her honour, and thus have evermore remained.

Rosemary was a herb of significance at both weddings and funerals, and its ceremonial uses have been described at some length in Brand's *Popular Antiquities*. Its twofold employment is exemplified in Dekker's *Wonderfull Yeare* (1603), where, speaking of a young bride who died of the plague on her wedding-day, he writes: "Here is a strange alteration, for the rosemary that was washt in sweet water to set out the bridall, is now wet in teares to furnish her buriall." At weddings the bridesmaids carried bunches of gilded rosemary*

---

* Gilded Rosemary is a variety described by Parkinson as having leaves edged or striped with a fine gold yellow colour.

as a symbol of constancy in love; at funerals sprigs of the herb ("that's for remembrance") were carried in the hands of the mourners and thrown upon the coffin when it was lowered into into the grave. Shakespeare mentions its use in funeral rites in *Romeo and Juliet* when he makes Friar Laurence say "Dry up your tears, and stick your rosemary on this fair corse".

We find many instances of this use of rosemary at funerals in the old writers. Thus Gay:

> To show their love, the neighbours far and near
> Followed, with wistful look, the damsel's bier;
> Sprigg'd rosemary the lads and lasses bore,
> While dismally the parson walked before.

The ancients often used Rosemary instead of incense, as being less costly, in their religious ceremonies. Cf the French name *Encensier*.

In Elizabethan times Rosemary was valued as a cosmetic, for beautifying the hair and for preventing baldness. As Estienne wrote: "The decoction of the leaves in white wine do comfort weake and oppressed sinewes: if you wash your head therewith it will make a hard skin, and comfort the little braine, and keepe the haire from falling so quickly." Even today Rosemary is used as an ingredient of many hair-oils, for the oil distilled from the leaves and flowering tops is considered a stimulant of the capillary glands. It is also employed by herbalists as a cure for nervous headaches. On the other hand, it is rather difficult to take Lyte's *New Herball* seriously when it alleges that "the ashes of Rosemary burnt doth fasten loose teeth".

Rosemary, of which there are several varieties, is best grown from cuttings planted in August in light loam and protected from frost during the winter. These should be ready for planting out in their permanent home by the following autumn, but the plant is very slow of growth.

Oil of Rosemary, which contains pinene, cineol, borneol and camphor, is employed in making perfumes and scented soaps.

The culinary use of the herb is somewhat restricted owing to its rather powerful flavour, but a leaf or two will add a distinctive flavour to soups and stews. It was probably more used in the kitchen by our ancestors, for Lawson says "the use is much in meats, more in Physicke, most for Bees". It is, indeed, an excellent bee flower, and delightful to have in a garden not only for its lovely blue flowers and bluish-grey foliage, but above all for its wonderful fragrance, for as the *Grete Herball* of 1526 expresses it: "Rosemary hath power to comfort by the good odoure."

There is a water made from Rosemary flowers, which disperseth Films in the Eyes after this manner. Take of Rosemary flowers as many as are sufficient to fill a glass which must be well stopt, and set it in the wall against the South Sun, thence will an Oyl come, which with a Feather anoynt the Eyes with.

DR LAZARUS RIVERIUS 1668

The *New English Dispensatory* says: "Distilled simply with a gentle heat it yields a fragrant water called Dew of Rosemary; distilled with water in the usual way in an alembic it affords a water tasting strong of it, but of a less agreeable smell; with rectified spirit it makes the fragrant and cephalic liquor called Hungary Water."

RUE	*Ruta graveolens* L.	Rutaceae

Herb of Grace (sometimes corrupted to Herbygrass)
FR *Rue officinale*; *Péganion*; *Herbe de grâce*
GER *Weinraute*

> There's rue for you; and here's some for me; we may call
> it herb of grace o' Sundays. O! you must wear your rue
> with a difference. *Hamlet*, 4, V.

Here we have a plant belonging to the large family *Rutaceae*, of which it is the sole representative in our islands. A native of southern Europe, Rue has been long established here and is often found in cottage gardens, a striking plant with its handsome grey-green glaucous foliage and bright yellow flowers.

Its scent is strong and its taste bitter – "sour herb of grace", as Shakespeare, who refers to Rue five times, terms it in *Richard III*.

This acridity has made the herb unsuited for culinary purposes, even for our ancestors, accustomed as they were to pungent flavours, for Lawson says: "Rue is too strong for mine Housewife's pot, unlesse she will brue Ale therewith, against the Plague." Indeed, among the many medical purposes for which the herb was employed in past ages, not the least was its use as a plague remedy. Alexis of Piedmont gives the following recipe for this purpose:

"Take the toppe of Rue, a garlicke head and half a quarter of a walnutte and a corne of salt. Eat thys every mornynge, contynuing so a muneth together and be merry and jocunde." Gerard, too, tells us that "the leaves of Rue eaten with the kernels of Walnuts or figs stamped together and made into a masse or paste, is good against all evill aires, the pestilence or plague". At the Assizes plentiful use was made of Rue, which was strewn over the floor of the courtroom and placed upon the judge's bench as a disinfectant against prison pestilence.

Probably no other herb has been endowed with so many therapeutic virtues as Rue, for in Pliny's day it was popularly supposed to be a cure for no fewer than eighty-four maladies! It was thought to make a warrior invulnerable if he heated the point of his sword in the fire and then smeared it with the juice of the herb. It was also held to nullify poisons, and the *Speculum Mundi* has this to say of it: "Excellent is that medicine approved by Mithridates, King of Pontus, in Asia, viz. that if any do eat fasting two drie wall-nuts, as many figs, and twenty leaves of rue, with one grain of salt, nothing which is venimous may that day hurt him." (*Cum grano salis* is an excellent touch, even if not intended by the author.)

But Mithridates thought no more of swallowing poisons than we do of drinking a cup of tea, for he was celebrated for inventing antidotes. "This monarch", writes Edith Wheelwright, "was the most celebrated pioneer of toxicology, experimenting – if we may believe the records – with poison and antidote in his own person with the spectacular result that when he desired to end his life no poison would act on his hardened system." It is said that he had to command his slave to stab him. There are some delightful lines on this eastern monarch by A. E. Housman which are worth re-quoting:

> And easy, smiling, seasoned sound,
> Sate the king when healths went round.
> They put arsenic in his meat
> And stared aghast to watch him eat;
> They poured strychnine in his cup
> And shook to see him drink it up.

This idiosyncrasy gained for Mithridates Eupator an inexpugnable position in the history of pharmacy, for the *Mithridate* was for long one of the four "officinal capitals", or medicines of highest repute, kept regularly in stock by the apothecary, and was sold in the form of an electuary as an antidote to poisons. It usually contained a vast number of ingredients, of which Rue was one.

Because Rue was considered so efficacious against all manner of venomous beasts, Estienne advised that great quantities of Rue should be planted near "sheep coates, and houses for your foule and other cattle . . . for adders, lizards and other venemous beastes will not come neere unto rue by the length of the shadow of it". Moreover he advises, "that it may grow faire and have a more pleasant smell" the planting of Rue "under the shadow of a fig tree or grafted on the rinde of a fig tree: for the warmth and sweetnes of the fig tree doth temper the sharpnes and acrimonie of the rue". This Estienne has taken from Plutarch's *Symposiaca*.

In some parts of Italy to this day leaves of Rue are carried in a satchet worn round the neck as an amulet, preferably leaves on which butterflies have laid their eggs. And in Belgium and

Holland sprigs of Rue are occasionally worn twined about the wrists by country folk as a means of warding off epilepsy.

Another use to which Rue was put in earlier times was for procuring abortions, à propos of which Vindevogel quotes the following lines:

> L'usage en est connu par les faiseuses d'anges.*
> Si la rue établit un effort expulsif,
> Si donc elle possède un pouvoir abortif.

It was commonly believed, also, that an infusion of Rue was beneficial for the eyes, and Swan says "for those who are feeble in their sight, let them distill Rue and white roses together, and putting the water thereof into their eies, it will open their windows and let in more light". Milton mentions how the Angel restored Adam's sight by means of "Euphrasy and Rue".

Although we no longer look upon Rue as a panacea, the oil distilled from the fresh herb has been found useful as a stimulant and antispasmodic, and fairly recently the essential principle of Rue – rutin – has been used with beneficial effect in the treatment of weakened blood-vessels causing high blood pressure.

SAFFRON (CROCUS)   *Crocus sativus* L.   Iridaceae
FR *Safran*
GER *Safran*

> The English are rendered sprightly by a liberal use of
> Saffron in sweetmeats and broth.   LORD BACON

The saffron of commerce consists of the dried stigmas and tops of the styles from the flowers of a member of the Iris family – *Crocus sativus*. The original home of this plant is unknown, for it does not appear to correspond with any known wild type of crocus; but it probably came from Asia Minor, where it has

---

* A venal female abortionist.

grown for centuries though it has for long been cultivated in Spain, and to a lesser extent in France, Italy and Austria. Most of our Saffron comes from Spain, that from Valencia being considered the finest.

Cultivation of *C. sativus* in Asia Minor dates back to remote ages and it is mentioned in the *Song of Solomon*, being the *Karcom* of the Hebrews. Through the Greek κρόκος and Latin form *crocus* we get our name for the plant, but for the drug and condiment we make use of the old Arabic name *Al Zahafaran*.

When Saffron was first introduced into England is not known with any certainty. As it was cultivated extensively around Tripoli, in Syria, for many centuries, it seems probable that returning Crusaders took it back with them to many western European countries. Hakluyt relates the traditional story that it was brought to England by a pilgrim from the Holy Land, who concealed a head of it in his Palmer's staff, which had been hollowed out for the purpose. Others say that it was introduced by Sir Thomas Smith of Saffron Walden about 1530; but there is a strong probability that it was brought to this country by the Roman colonisers, for the Romans made extensive use of it. In the *Satyricon* of Petronius Arbiter we may read how, at Trimalcio's banquet, not only were the cakes and fruit powdered with Saffron, but it was also sprinkled over the floor.

Throughout the Middle Ages Saffron was a commodity of great commercial importance, and severe penalties were imposed upon those who were found to have adulterated it. In 1444 a certain Jobst Findeker of Nuremberg was condemned to be burnt in the same fire as his adulterated Saffron. But the high price which this commodity fetched led, despite all laws, to the invention of many fraudulent admixtures. Often it was dipped in oil or honey to make it heavier. Frequently it was adulterated with the flower-heads of yellow Compositae such as Carthamus or Arnica.

Saffron was certainly used in this country for culinary purposes early in the 15th century, as many Guild Accounts of that period show in their records of banqueting expenses. And it was probably first cultivated on a fairly large scale in the same century, for according to Lady Rosalind Northcote the Charity Commission of 1481 mentions two saffron-gardens. At first it was cultivated mainly in the herbaries of monasteries and manor-houses, but very soon it was grown on a commercial scale in Herefordshire, Lincolnshire and Essex, where the town of Walden became so famous for the quality of its product that the word Saffron became substituted for its original Saxon prefix of Cheping.

By the 16th century English Saffron was being exported to the Continent, and among the various sorts of Saffron sold by the apothecaries of France at that time, "Safren d'Engleterre" was considered the most valuable.* It was used, Tournefort tells us, "in Venice Treacle, in the Cataplasm of Crumbs of Bread, in the *Elixir Proprietatis* of Paracelsus, in the Reform'd Treacle, in Mithridate, in the Confection of Hyacinth, and in the Troches of Camphire, etc."

But it was used just as much for its culinary as for its therapeutic virtues. "I must have saffron, to colour the warden pies," exclaims the Clown in *The Winter's Tale*; whilst Henry Estienne, in his *Apology for Herodotus*, tells us that "Saffron must be put into all Lent soups, sauces and dishes; without saffron we cannot have well-cooked peas". Certainly in England during the Middle Ages Saffron was the most commonly used commodity in the kitchen, for it was the taste of the time to have every dish so flavoured or garnished. In *The Forme of Cury*, that collection of recipes compiled by the master cook of Richard II, as well as in other early cook books, Saffron was used in more than half the recipes.

It was also taken in the form of a cordial, and in the British Museum there is a quaint 17th-century broadside extolling the "Vertues and Uses of the Cordial Spirit of Saffron", which was sold at 2s 6d for a pint bottle. It reads as follows:

* Evelyn writes that it was "esteemed the best of any forraine country".

SAFFRON itself is of such excellent virtue and of so great use among many nations, as Germans, Polanders, Hungarians, Bohemians, Sclavonians, Croats, Turks, and divers others that they commonly boil no Flesh, no Fish, no Milk, no Herb, or anything else fit for Meals, without some Saffron, which they do, both to cause the better Concoction of the Dyet, and to make their own Spirits chearful, and to preserve themselves against the injury of corrupted Air, or against the violence of any Distemper. . . .

It renders the Heart chearful and the Spirits active, and whets an appetite for Dinner. And in these respects it exceeds all Tankards, or any other Cordial Liquor for the like purpose. For Boon Companions, viz. such as have taken too Chearful or too Liberal a Cup over Night, and thence become indisposed the next Morning: let such at their rising take three Spoonfuls thereof, or more, as they think fit, and walk after it.

Sir William Temple wrote: "The spirit of Saffron is of all others the noblest and most innocent, and yet of the greatest virtue. I have known it restore a man out of the very agonies of death, when left by all physicians as wholly desperate."

Coles, also, informs us that there is not a better cordial amongst herbs than Saffron, which "makes them cheerfull that use it, and therefore it is called *Cor hominis*, the Heart of man, and when we see man over merry we have a proverb *Dormivit in sacco Croci*, He hath slept in a bagge of Saffron".

There were various ways in which Saffron was employed as a flavouring, and Evelyn tells us that in Germany in his day it was rolled into little balls with honey. These balls were then dried, reduced to powder, and sprinkled over a salad. Thomas Hill, author of *The Gardeners Labyrinth* (1577)*, assures us that Saffron "taken in meat causeth a long and easie breathing and helpeth the Asthma". Today, however, Saffron is used less as a flavouring than to give colour to dishes of rice and pasta, and it also enters into the composition of certain liqueurs such as Raspail and Yellow Chartreuse.

Another use of Saffron in olden times was as a fabric dye, for which purpose it was much esteemed by the richly apparelled

* Published under the pseudonym of Didymus Mountain.

Saracens. Although still used in India, where it is extensively cultivated, to colour bridal veils and ceremonial garments, Saffron is now no longer in general use as a dye fabric, for it is too costly and fades too easily.

In France Saffron is cultivated commercially in Provence and, above all, in the Gâtinais, where Pithiviers is the centre of cultivation. Women are employed for the harvest in the autumn, and after the flowers have been collected, the orange-red stigmas and the upper parts of the styles are separated and dried, either in the sun or on a horse-hair screen heated by wood embers. Since between 60,000 and 80,000 stigmas are needed to produce a pound of Saffron, and it takes 5 lb of fresh Saffron to make 1 lb of the dried product, it is little wonder that this is an expensive commodity. Fortunately, for colouring dishes, a very little goes a long way. The Saffrons from the Gâtinais and from Valencia are highly esteemed and command the best prices. Other supplies of the product come from the Levant. Inferior varieties not only consist of smaller stigmas but are often adulterated; one such adulterant is the Safflower, *Carthamus tinctorius* L., sometimes called American Saffron although it has no botanical connection with the Crocus Saffron. The so-called Meadow Saffron (q.v.) is *Colchicum autumnale* (Autumn Crocus) used in the preparation of galenicals.

The *Neu-Eingerichtete Material-Kammer* (The newly-stocked Warehouse) of Georg Niclaus Schurtz gives a very detailed account of the many varieties of Saffron available on the market of Nuremberg from the year 1571 onwards – varieties which came from all over Europe and parts of Asia. That which came from Austria, grown near the River Enns, was considered the finest; not only did it surpass all other European varieties, but even the Oriental ones. The poorest was the Turkish, since the Turks refused to sell their best to Christians, but kept it for dyeing silks. "In England", writes Schurtz, "there are four Saffron markets which take place between Michaelmas and All Saints. The fourth is at Newport, a fortnight before All Saints, and there the greatest quantity of Saffron goes. The English Saffron is mixed together and pressed to the size of a large round plate. When it is well dried and red in colour it is very good.''

From Giovanni Porta's *Natural Magick*, 1658:
If you would know a painted face, do thus: Chew Saffron between your teeth, and stand neer to a woman with your mouth; when you talk with her your breath will foul her face, and make it yellowish. But if she be not painted, the natural colour will continue.

SAGE   *Salvia officinalis* L.   Labiatae
FR *Sauge*; *Thé de la Grèce*
GER *Salbei*

> Marbled with Sage the hardening cheese she pressed.
>   GAY

Cur moriatur homo cui salvia crescit in horto?: Why should a man die whilst sage grows in his garden?* This mediaeval aphorism has its counterpart in the rhyming jingle

> He that would live for aye
> Must eat Sage in May.

Both reflect the ancient belief that the healthful Sage conferred longevity; a belief expressed more rhetorically by Swan in his *Speculum Mundi*. "Such is the virtue of Sage," he declares, "that if it were possible it would cause Clotho evermore to hold the distaffe, and Lachesis to spin perpetually; yea, Atropos must forbear to cut in two the thread of life: such a desire hath Sage to make a man immortall." Its very name Salvia, from *salvere*, "to be well, in good health", is an indication of how highly Sage was valued in olden times.

* To which a sceptic replied *Contra vim mortis Non est medicamen in hortis.*

Sage 229

But today it has rather fallen from its high estate, and its medical virtues are less highly regarded than its culinary uses, for it is mainly employed for stuffing, for flavouring stews, and as an ingredient of rissoles. As the line from Gay's poem, above, suggests, Sage was often incorporated in cheeses, and Sage cheeses are still to be found in Derbyshire. But undoubtedly the greatest users of Sage are meat packers and sausage manufacturers. In some cases, where the use of leaves would detract from the appearance of the product, the essential oil is used.

Although Sage is rarely used medicinally nowadays, country folk still appreciate the tonic and stimulating qualities of Sage Tea, made by infusing the leaves in boiling water. Some consider that an infusion made from the flowers is even better. And, says Gerard, "no man needs to doubt of the wholesomness of Sage Ale, being brewed as it should be, with Sage, Scabious, Betony, Spikenard, Squinanth and Fennell seeds". With due respect to Gerard I imagine that frequenters of the four-ale bar would find such a brew singularly repellent – *autre temps, autre mœurs!* But then Gerard, like Culpeper, was "sold", as they say nowadays, on the virtues of Sage, which he found not only "singular good for the head and braine", but for almost everything else.

Garden Sage (*S. officinalis*) is a perennial native to the Mediterranean region, but now firmly established and cultivated in many other lands. In its native habitat it grows luxuriantly and most of the world's commercial supply comes from Yugoslavia and Albania, the district around Fiume being a notable centre of cultivation. Dalmatian Sage is highly reputed for quality; Cyprus Sage is good, but coarser in appearance and very brittle when dried.

There are several varieties of *S. officinalis*, but the most commonly grown is the broad-leaved variety, with leaves about two inches long, greyish-green, soft and downy. The small-leaved variety, which Parkinson considered of more "force and vertue" than the other, is now seldom seen in English gardens; while *S. gregii and S. grahamii*, said to be the most fragrantly scented of all the Sages are native to Mexico. *S. sclaria*, or Clary, is described on page 142.

Red Sage (*S. splendens*) is a highly decorative foliage plant and there is a variegated Sage, its leaves "diversely marked and spotted with white and red among the greene" which Parkinson chose for his *Garden of Pleasure*. This variety reverts to type very quickly and it is advisable to take fresh cuttings every year.

Among the various Sages cultivated as ornamental plants, *S. leucantha* is useful to florists for winter bouquets, as it flowers from October to April in warm surroundings.

When harvesting Sage, it should be dried in the shade, so as to retain as much as possible of the essential oil, and since the herb loses flavour with exposure to air it is best to keep it in an airtight container. An infusion of the dried herb is recommended as a gargle for relaxed throats, and the essential oil, which contains pinene, cineol and thujone, is a notable antiscorbutic and is also an ingredient of embrocations for rheumatism.

Finally, a curious note from Lyte, who writes: "Sage causeth Women to be fertile, wherefore (in times past) the people of Egypt, after a great mortalitie and pestilence, constrayned their Women to drinke the juyce thereof, to cause them the sooner to conceyve and to bring forth store of children."

ST JOHN'S WORT
Hardhay

Hypericum
perforatum L.

Hypericaceae

FR *Millepertuis officinale; Chasse-diable; Herbe de la saint-Jean*

GER *Johanniskraut; Hartheu*

> Trefoil, Vervain, John's Wort, Dill,
> Hinder witches of their will.
>
> *Old Saying*

St John's Wort, or "Herba Jonnies", was one of the blessed herbs which protected poor folk from the horrid charms

> of wizard seer, whose potent spells
> Could hold in dreadful thrall the labouring moon,

since evil spirits would fly away thwarted at a mere whiff of its scent; for, as Anthony Ascham writes: "the virtue of it is thus, if it be put in a man's house, then shal come no wicked spirit therein".

This hanging of herbs in a house for protection was more particularly practised on the eve of the feast of St John the Baptist, a period of the year to which our ancestors paid particular attention, and which gave rise more than any other to a variety of superstitious observances. Stow, in his *Survey of London*, says "that on the vigil of St John Baptist, every man's door being shadowed with green birch, long fennel, St John's wort, orpine, white Lilies and such like, garnished upon with garlands of beautiful flowers, had also lamps of glass, with oil burning in them all the night". And Pennant informs us that in Wales "they have the custom of sticking St John's wort over the doors on the Eve of St John Baptist".

There were many herbs endowed in popular imagination with the power of warding off witches, but most efficaceous of all was St John's wort, which the French call "All-holy" and the Irish "Mary's Glory". It was the *fuga daemonium*, or "flight of the devil".

Apart from its reputation as a protection against sorcery, St John's Wort was a healing herb, used not only by country herbalists but by the great surgeon Ambroise Paré for the dressing of wounds, and Gerard declared it to be "a most pretious remedie for deep wounds and those that are thorow the body", adding that "in time of wars no gentlewoman should be without St John's wort".

The specific name of the plant was given to it because the leaves are marked with numerous pellucid dots which give them the appearance of being perforated with tiny holes. Hypericum comes from the Greek *hupereikon*, meaning "under the hedge", where the plant is often found.

Its many virtues are set out in Konrad von Megenburg's *Buch der Natur*, written in the 14th century, when St John's wort was considered capable of curing a variety of ills. Modern medicine has more efficaceous methods of healing wounds, and as a domestic medicine the herb is today more or less obsolete, though the red oil prepared by macerating the herb in olive oil is still occasionally used for chest complaints.

Other species of the Hypericum family found in this country include the Slender Hypericum (*H. pulchrum*) found in dry woods and on open heaths; the handsome Tutsan Hypericum (*H. androsaemum*); and the creeping St John's Wort (*H. humifusum*).

SANICLE   *Sanicula europaea* L.   Umbelliferae
FR *Sanicle*; *Herbe de saint Laurent*
GER *Sanikel*; *Heilkraut*

> Qui a la Bugle et la Sanicle
> Fait aux chirurgiens la nicle.
> *Old French saying*

"Faire la nique" (to adopt the modern French spelling) means "to thumb one's nose at, or to snap one's fingers at"; thus, he who has in his garden both Bugle and Sanicle can

SANICLE

laugh at surgeons. For Sanicle was one of those "self-heals" of the old leeches. The French popular name for this plant is derived from the martyred Saint Lawrence who was broiled to death upon a gridiron, and whose intercession was therefore invoked in cases of burns and scalds. Like Comfrey, Sanicle was grown in monastery gardens as a healing herb and Bullein says of it "whatsoever Compharie, called Symphiton, can doe in woundes, the same can Sanicle".

Tournefort explains, in the apothecary's jargon of his day, that "the Faculties of this plant depend upon an Earth and Salt Armoniack, embarrass'd with Sulphur: for upon a chymical Analysis it yields a copious quantity of acid Phlegm, urinous Spirit, concreted volatile Salt, Oil, and Earth; by means whereof it is endu'd with a notable vulnerary Faculty". A 15th-century potion for the healing of wounds was made up of Sanicle, Yarrow and Bugle, pounded in a mortar and macerated in wine. The virtue of this mixture was that "bugle holdith the wound open, mylfoyle [yarrow] clensith the wound, sanycle healeth it".

Sanicle is quite a small herb, a perennial hardly more than a foot in height, with a simple stem, reddish and furrowed, with long-stalked leaves deeply divided into five lobes, serrated, in colour a shiny green above and somewhat paler below. The pinkish-white flowers are clustered in small heads grouped in a rather open umbel. It grows in woods and shady places, and, says Gerard, "it joyeth in fat and fruitefull moist soile".

The name Sanicle, probably derived from *sanare*, to heal, is often applied to various plants of other genera, such as the Great Sanicle, or Lady's Mantle (*Alchemilla vulgaris*).

Although modern medicine takes no account of Sanicle as a heal-all it is still used as an astringent, and given, combined with other herbs, in cases of blood disorders.

SAVORY (SUMMER)   *Satureia hortensis* L.   Labiatae
FR *Sariette*; *Herbe de Saint-Julien*
GER *Bohnenkraut*

> Savery seeds and dyes the first yeere, good for my Huswyfe's
> pot and pye.
>
> WILLIAM LAWSON *Country Housewife's Garden*, 1626

This is one of the many Labiates which, though originally
exotic, are now to be numbered among our English culinary
potherbs. A native of Southern Europe, it was introduced into
Britain long ago and quickly became established in the kitchen
garden. The leaves have a distinctive flavour, but one which,
by its pleasant and delicate savour, is more immediately
acceptable to the modern palate than the robuster tang of those
herbs which our ancestors employed to give piquancy to their
often monotonous diet.

Summer Savory is an excellent herb for stuffing, whether
for sausages, meat dishes or turkey, and in France it is a
frequent accompaniment to broad beans, either finely chopped
and strewn over the beans or cooked with them. It is excellent,
too, in lentil soup.

If Estienne's words are to be believed, Savory might make a
useful addition to school dinners, for he writes that "the
leaves and flowers applied unto the head in forme of a cappe
or garland, doth awake the drowsily inclined".

Summer Savory is an annual, raised from seed, which should
be sown in April, for preference in light soil and in a sunny
position.

SAVORY (WINTER)   *Satureia montana*   Labiatae

Winter Savory is woodier and more bushy than Summer
Savory, and if given proper attention will develop into a small
shrub. Its specific name *montana* shows that its native habitat
is on the hills, and it will grow better in a poor but well-

SAVORY

drained soil than in a rich one. It will grow well for several years, but when the plant gets old the shoots grow shorter and do not provide so many leaves, so that it is often advisable to divide the roots in spring.

Parkinson calls Winter Savory one of the "farsing" (i.e. stuffing) herbs, and says that "some do use the powder of the herbe dried to mixe with grated bread, to bread their meat, be it fish or flesh, to give it the quicker relish". In France it is used in preparing trout for the table, and in the Netherlands and Belgium, on account of its agreeable aroma, Savory is used for pickling and marinating. In Cotton's sequel to the *Compleat Angler* we read of a "handful of sliced horse-radish root, with a handsome little faggot of rosemary, thyme and winter savoury".

Although Savory is today regarded purely as a culinary herb, in former times it was extensively used as a remedy for griping pains and as a cure for flatulence, and both species of Savory rubbed on bee or wasp stings give quick relief.

In Tudor days the Winter Savory was frequently included, on account of its decorative leaves, in knot gardens, and in mazes of dwarf shrubs. *The proffitable Arte of Gardening*, by Thomas Hill (1568), says that such a maze "may either be set with Isope and Tyme or with winter Savory and Tyme. For these do well endure all the winter through grene."

SOLOMON'S SEAL   *Polygonatum officinale*   Liliaceae
                        (Allioni)
Lady's Seal; David's Harp
FR *Sceau de Salomon*; *Genouillet*; *Faux muguet*
GER *Salomonsiegel*; *Gelenkwurz*

This perennial woodland plant, now becoming rare in England, is a close relative of Lily-in-the-valley (*cf* the French name "faux muguet"). This plant has a single, erect, arched stem, all along the top part of which are alternate, oval leaves,

SOLOMON'S SEAL

glossy and pale green. The white flowers, tinged with green, hang suspended in drooping racemes beneath the leaves; the fruits which succeed them look like small blue-black cherries. The root is a long rhizome running horizontally just below the surface of the ground. The generic name means "with many knees", possibly from the numerous nodes of the stem (*cf* the popular German name *Gelenkwurz*).

The rhizome, which is white inside, contains much starch, together with tannin and mucilage, and is somewhat astringent. Gerard has a delightful paragraph about it in which he says: "The root of Solomons seale stamped while it is fresh and greene, and applied, taketh away in one night, or two at the most, any bruise, blacke or blew spots gotten by fals or womens wilfulnesse, in stumbling upon their hasty husbands fists, or such like."

As to the origin of the name "Solomon's Seal", opinions are divided. Some say it is because the rhizome is marked at short intervals with circular impressions which bear some resemblance to those made by a seal. Gerard was of this opinion. Another suggested origin is from the legend that Solomon made use of this herb as a magic charm for blasting the boulders used in the construction of the Temple.

In Galen's time the distilled water of the herb was used by ladies for removing freckles and pimples, and the expressed juice of the rhizome is said to be good for the complexion. In parts of Europe it is blended into a pommade for use on boils and abscesses.

John Josselyn, [*] writing about fifty years after the landing of the Pilgrim Fathers, tells us how he found in New England, among such plants as he had already known in his homeland, three kinds of Solomon's Seal – "the first common in England; the second, Virginia Salomon's Seal, and the third, differing from both, is called Treacle Berries, having the perfect taste of Treacle when they are ripe".

[*] *New England's rarities discovered.* 1672.

Old Man

Lad's Love

FR *Aurone mâle*; *Ivrogne*; *Garde-robes*

GER *Eberraute*; *Eberreis*

> There the large branches of the long-lived hart,
> With Southernwood their odours strong impart;
> The monsters of the land, the serpents fell,
> Fly far away, and shun the hostile smell.
>
> LUCAN *Pharsalia*, Book IX

This is one of the most delightfully scented of the Artemisias, and is still a feature of many cottage gardens. A native of southern Europe, it likes a sunny situation; even so, it rarely flowers in England, but can be enjoyed for its feathery grey-green leaves and its fragrance. The name is a contraction of Southern Wormwood. The Rev William Hanbury informs us that it "is usually planted by the outside of flower-gardens, for the improvement of nosegays, it being possessed of a strong odour, which to many is very agreeable".

Southernwood is one of the twenty-three plants described in the *Hortulus* or "Little Garden" of Wahlafrid Strabo, written in the 9th century, and of it he writes that "it has well-nigh as many virtues as leaves". William Turner, in his herbal of 1551, says that this herb "is good for them that shake or shudder with colde, sodden in oyle and layde upon the bodye". Gerard writes that "being strewed upon the bed, or a fume made of it upon hot embers, it driveth away serpents". This he merely copies from the ancient herbals.

It is said to have been introduced into England in Tudor times, and was certainly well established by the 17th century, for Culpeper said it was so well known that he had no need to describe the herb, which he found "a gallant mercurial plant, worthy of more esteem than it hath". Furthermore, he says: "It takes away inflammations of the eyes, if it be put with some part of a roasted quince, and boiled with a few crumbs of bread and applied." But Thornton is more sceptical of its many virtues and says its beneficent results are brought about because it "operates on the mind of the patient", and as a fomentation he considers it scarcely more useful than "cloths wrung out of hot water".

Its reputation as a deterrent of fleas and clothes moths is probably more justifiable, for the leaves contain an essential oil which does seem to keep away these obnoxious insects. For this reason one of the French names for the plant is *Garde-robes*. How it acquired its English folk-name of Lad's Love it is difficult now to say. Folkard says it got the name from an ointment made with its ashes and used by young men to promote growth of hair on the face. Others say – and this seems a more likely explanation – that it was because a few branches of Southernwood were generally added to the nosegays with which country youths regaled the maids of the village.

The French name of *Ivrogne* (literally "drunkard") needs explanation. It is really a corruption of *Avrone*, or *Aurone*, itself a contraction of the old French name for the plant, which was *Armoise du Rhône*, the word *Armoise* being the French term for the genus *Artemisia*.

STAVESACRE   *Delphinium staphisagria* L. Ranunculaceae
Licebane
FR *Staphisaigre*; *Herbe aux poux*
GER *Stephanskraut*; *Lausekraut*

> Looke how much Tobacco wee carry with us to expell
> cold, the like quantitie of Staves-aker wee must provide
> us of to kill lice in that rugged country of rebels.
> THOS NASH *Lenten Stuffe. 1599*

This plant, a relative of the Larkspur, was extensively used in the Middle Ages to get rid of head lice, for which reason it was given the popular names of "lousewort" and "licebane". It has since become scarce as a garden plant, probably as a result of the growth of more cleanly habits and living conditions. It is a stout, erect herb, growing to a height of about 4 feet, indigenous to southern Europe and Asia Minor. Its specific name of *staphisagria*, meaning "wild grape", was given to it because of the similarity of its leaf to that of the vine.

Says Tournefort: "Staves-acre or Louse-wort seeds are used in Masticatories or Apophlegmatisms; they do likewise not a little contribute to the killing or destroying of Lice or Vermin by strewing the powder of the seeds upon the head or clothes; upon which account they are frequently used by the monks and friars living in monasteries." Dr James said that Staves-acre was also used for toothache and as an abstergent in ulcers and pustules.

The seed, which is about a quarter inch long and with an extremely disagreeable flavour, was largely imported from Holland in the 18th century to supply the shops of the apothecaries, by whom it was prepared as a vermifuge, powdered and mixed with Cocculus Indicus.

SWEET CICELY *Myrrhis odorata* (*Scopoli*) Umbelliferae
Giant Sweet Chervil
FR *Cerfeuil musqué*; *Persil d'anis*
GER *Süssdolde*; *Aniskerbel*

This herb with the lovely name is a tall, beautiful plant, growing to a height of 5 feet or more, and having, as Parkinson phrases it, "divers great and faire winged leaves, very like and resembling the leaves of Hemlocks". Culpeper, too, says "it groweth like the Hemlock, but of a fresher green colour, tasting as sweet as the Aniseed" (*cf* Fr. and Ger. names).

Some plants are merely beautiful. Sweet Cicely is both ornamental and useful, and so is entitled to a place both in the herbaceous border and the kitchen garden, though as a culinary herb it is seldom used nowadays. In former days, however, its aromatic foliage found its way into salads, "being exceedingly wholsome and chearing the spirits", according to Evelyn. The thick root, which has a marked taste of aniseed, used to be boiled and eaten with oil and vinegar. Apparently the seeds were also used, for Gerard writes: "The seeds eaten as a sallad whiles they are yet green with oile, vinegar and pepper, exceed all other sallads by many degrees, both in pleasantness of taste, sweetnesse of smell, and wholesomenesse for the cold and feeble stomacke."

Sweet Cicely is a native of central and southern Europe, and may, indeed, be indigenous in certain regions of Great Britain. It is, at all events, perfectly naturalised in this country, though the depredations of the thoughtless have now made the wild plant somewhat rare.

Both root and herb are used in popular medicine for flatulence and digestive ailments, and, according to the Abbé Cariot, *Myrrhis odorata* is one of the main ingredients of *Chartreuse*.

TANSY   *Tanacetum vulgare* L.   Compositae
FR *Tanaisie*; *Barbotine indigène*; *Ganelle*; *Herbe de saint Marc*
GER *Gemeiner Rainfarn*; *Wurmfarn*

> Some camomile doth not amiss
> With savory and some tansy.
> *The Muses' Elysium*

The name *Tanacetum* seems to occur for the first time in the *Capitulare de Villis*, regulations drawn up about AD 795 by Louis the Pious, son of Charlemagne, for the governance of his estates in Aquitaine. This document contains a list of plants to be grown in the gardens, among them *Tanaritam*, as it is written.

According to Wootton the name *Tansy* was abbreviated by the old herbalists from Athanasia. In Lucian's *Dialogues of the Gods* Jupiter tells Hercules to take with him the beautiful

Ganymede, whom he has stolen from earth, "and when he has drunk of Athanasia [Greek *athanatos*=immortal] bring him back and he shall be our cup-bearer". As a consequence the ancients sought for that herb, Athanasia, which would confer upon them immortality. Dodoens states that the Tansy acquired its name because it lasts so long in flower.

This pretty plant with its yellow button flowers and its fragrant scent was at one time grown in every cottage garden, but nowadays it is seldom cultivated, though it grows wild in most parts of Great Britain, showing a marked preference for regions of chalk and limestone.

For many centuries it was grown both as a medicinal and a culinary herb, and Tansy puddings were eaten on Easter Sunday to celebrate the end of Lent. But our forefathers were accustomed to rather more pungent flavourings than we could stomach today, and we would probably find the rather acrid taste unpalatable, though the old custom is said to persist in Lincolnshire. In Ireland, too, according to J. T. Burgess* "the flavour of the Tansy is much liked and is used especially in the flavouring of the Cork luxury *drisheens*, immortalized by Lady Morgan".

Evelyn himself, although living in the 17th century, found the flavour rather strong, for he writes: "Tansy is hot and cleansing but in regard of its domineering relish sparingly mixt with our cold Sallet and much fitter (tho' in very small quantity) for the Pan, being qualified with the Juices of other fresh Herbs."

Leaves and tops of the Tansy are nowadays used as a stimulant and an anthelmintic, or worm-dispelling, drug, a use to which it has been put for centuries, for *Bullein's Bulwarke* (1579) remarks that "Tansye doeth kyll and caste Wormes from Chyldren". The plants are cut when in full flower, the leaves and tops being stripped from the stalks and dried in the shade.

* *English Wild Flowers.*

COSTMARY (*Tanacetum balsamita*) is allied to Tansy, but has a pleasanter taste. Spenser, in his *Muiopotmos: or the Fate of the Butterfly*, alludes to "Fresh Costmarie and breathfull Camomill". In cottage gardens it was grown under various country names, such as "Mace", "Allspice" or "Alecost". The last name is a reminder of the days when home-brewed ale was apt to be a somewhat insipid drink, to which Costmary would be frequently added to give it more flavour, "and thereupon I thinke it tooke the name of Alecoast", says Parkinson (FR. *Costus des jardins*).

Costmary was apparently introduced into this country by the Romans and the fact that it is seldom seen today, though in Culpeper's day it was "an inhabitant in every garden", may be due to the fact that its propagation is not by seed, but by division of the roots. Costmary was to be found in the Pharmacopoeia up till the end of the 18th century, but is no longer used for medicinal purposes. Its fragrance, however, makes it a useful ingredient of pot-pourri.

If you would know how a Lenten-Tansie was prepared in the 17th century, here is a recipe from William Salmon's *Family Dictionary or Household Companion* (2nd edn., 1696):

Take Tansie, Fetherfew, Parsley, Violet-leaves; bruise them and strain out the Juice into 8 or 10 eggs well beaten; then stamp Almonds with the Spawn of a Pike or Carp and strain them with the Crumbs of fine Manchet, Sugar and Rose-water, and fry it thin in sweet Butter, or put the Juice of the Herbs only strained with 8 or 10 Eggs; fry them in sweet Butter and dish them up with Sugar; or you may put a little Flour and Rose-water to them.

TARRAGON   *Artemisia dracunculus* L.   Compositae

FR *Estragon*; *Herbe dragonne*
GER *Esdragon*

> *Tragonia*, an herbe nowe callid Taragon, late sene
> in this realme, which hath a tast like gynger.
>
> Sir Thomas Elyot's *Dictionary*, 1538

Tarragon is a many-branched perennial herb with greenish-white flower heads in spreading panicles. The cultivated plant seldom produces seed in Britain, but is easily propagated by root division or cuttings. Two varieties are commonly cultivated in Europe, known respectively as French Tarragon (*A. dracunculus*) and Russian Tarragon (*A. redowskii*); the former a smallish plant with deep green leaves, the latter with rather lighter leaves and a stronger flavour.

The herb, which is closely allied to Wormwood, is one of the ingredients of "fine herbes". It is the only correct flavouring for Sauce Tartare, is excellent for fish sauces, and is used as a flavouring for vinegar and gherkins. Tarragon vinegar is made by steeping the leaves in the best wine vinegar in the ratio of eight ounces of leaves to two quarts of vinegar. French cooks usually mix their mustard with Tarragon vinegar.

Gerard says, with reason, "Tarragon is not to be eaten alone in sallades, but joyned with other herbs, as Lettuce, Purslain and the like, that it may also temper the coldnesse of them". And Evelyn commends it as "highly cordial and friendly to the Head, Heart, Liver, correcting the weakness of the Ventricle".

"There are some Authors", says Parkinson, "that have held Tarragon not to be an herb of its own kind, but that it was first produced by putting the seed of lin or flax into the root of an onion, being opened and so set into the ground, which whence it hath sprung hath brought forth this herb Tarragon; which absurd and idle opinion Matthiolus by certain experience saith, hath been found false."

THISTLE (BLESSED)   *Cnicus benedictus* L.   Compositae
Carduus Benedictus

FR *Chardon bénit*; *Centaurée sudorifique*
GER *Kardobenediktenkraut*; *Heildistel*

> Get you some of this distilled Carduus Benedictus, and lay it
> to your heart: it is the only thing for a qualm.
>
> *Much Ado About Nothing*, 3, iv

This handsome annual from southern Europe has for centuries
had a high reputation as a heal-all and was regarded as a
specific remedy in cases of the plague. Thomas Brasbridge
extolled its virtues in *The Poore Mans Jewell* (1578), to which
was annexed a *Treatise of the Pestilence* containing "a de-
claration of the vertues of the hearbes Carduus Benedictus and
Angelica". Of the former he wrote: "I may say it is a preservative against all diseases. . . therefore I councell all them
that have gardens to nourish it, that they may have it alwaies
for their owne use, and the use of their neighbors that lacke it."

William Turner, also, looked upon the Blessed Thistle as a
remedy for most ills – "very good for the headache and the
megram . . . good for any ache of the body . . . fasteneth
loose sinews . . . also good for the dropsy. It helpeth the
memory and amendeth thick hearing . . . there is nothing
better for the canker and old rotten and festering sores than
the leaves, juice, broth, powder and water of Carduus Benedictus."

The astrologer *cum* botanist Culpeper wrote: "It is an herb
of Mars, and under the sign Aries . . . By antipathy to other
planets it cures the venereal disease; this by antipathy to
Venus, who governs it." Culpeper, too, looked upon the Blessed
Thistle as a veritable panacea.

But Parkinson is rather more meagre in his praise, and
contents himself with saying "the distilled water hereof is
much used to be drunk against agues of all sorts, either pesti-
lential or humoral . . . but the decoction of the herb given in
due time hath the more forcible operation".

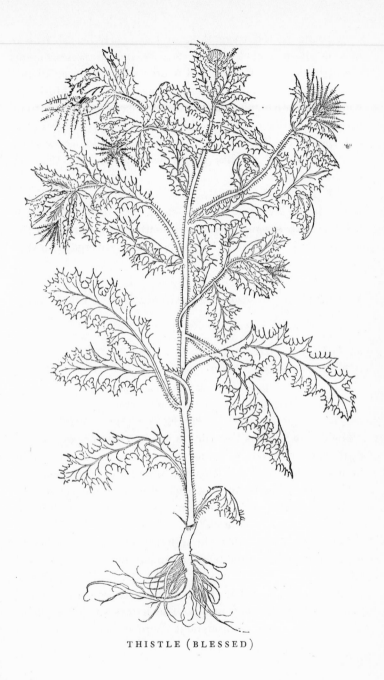

THISTLE (BLESSED)

Allowing for the exaggeration of these early herbalists, it is well established that this herb does indeed possess many useful therapeutic virtues, and is used medicinally as a stimulant, diaphoretic and emmenagogue. The warm infusion is widely used as a diaphoretic in cases of bad colds or intermittent fever. In addition to tannin, which is largely responsible for the bitterness of the infusion, the plant contains cnicin, a crystalline neutral body which has properties analagous to those of salicin.

The Blessed Thistle grows to a height of about 2 feet and has a much-branched reddish stem. The leaves are long, narrow, with irregular teeth terminating in a spine, and the flowers are pale yellow. The whole plant is covered with thin down.

VALERIAN *Valeriana officinalis* L. Valerianaceae
All-heal
Setwall
FR *Valériane*; *Herbe aux chats*
GER *Baldrian*; *Katzenkraut*

> They that will have their heale
> Must put Setwall in their keale
> *North Country saying quoted by Gerard*

"The dry root", says Gerard, "is put into counterpoysons and medicines preservative against the pestilence: whereupon it hath been had (and is to this day among the poore people of our Northerne parts) in such veneration amongst them, that no broths, pottage or physicall meats are worth any thing, if Setwall were not at an end."

Certainly if one looks through the old herbals Valerian seems to have been credited as a remedy for a whole series of ailments. In England it was called "All-heal"; in France "guérit-tout"; whilst its Latin name derives from *valere* – to be well, or in good health. The names speak for themselves. Even today, throughout Europe one can find in almost every country cottage a small bottle of Valerian; an old and tried household remedy for those suffering from functional disturbances of the nervous system.

In fact Valerian has been used for its therapeutic properties for many centuries and has its place in every pharmacopoeia for its action in nervous complaints. Dr Manson, in an article in the *British Medical Journal* in 1928, wrote that Valerian "was perhaps the earliest method of treating the neuroses". The drug is now mostly given in the form of ammoniated tincture of Valerian.

The medicinal Valerian is a perennial herb, growing to a height of as much as 5 feet, with flowers varying from white to pink in broad terminal corymbs. Native to Europe and Asia, it grows best in moist, rich loams and is often found in England in damp hedgerows and woodlands. It is cultivated extensively as a drug plant in Holland and Germany, and is still cultivated in England, more especially in Derbyshire, and parts of Oxfordshire and Suffolk. In Derbyshire, says Florence Ranson, " 'Valerie growers' have handed down the art of cultivation through many generations".

The rhizome and roots of *Valeriana officinalis* are collected in the autumn, sliced longitudinally when large, and dried in kilns or ovens, during which process they give off a characteristic and rather disagreeable odour. The volatile oil which is the most valuable constituent of the drug contains, among other things, bornyl isovalerianate and various esters, free isovalerianic acid being formed during the drying process by enzyme action, the amount of acid varying according to the age of the rhizome. Although Valerian has long been included in the British Pharmacopoeia, it is not now an official drug in the United States.

This herb should not be confused with the very decorative Red, or Spur, Valerian (*Centranthus ruber*), with its mass of ruby flowers, often found in this country growing wild on walls and the sides of chalk pits. This plant is not used medicinally.

VERVAIN   *Verbena officinalis* L.   Verbenaceae

FR *Verveine sauvage*; *Herbe sacrée*; *Herbe aux sorciers*
GER *Eisenkraut*

> Bring your garlands, and with reverence place
> The vervain on the altar.   BEN JONSON

Strange that a herb of such insignificant appearance should
have held so important a place in mankind's estimation
through long centuries; but it was a sacred and magic herb in
Persia, in ancient Greece and Rome, and in ancient Britain,
where the Druids had a special reverence for it, ordering it to
be gathered about the rising of the great dog star, but only
when neither sun nor moon were above ground at the time
to see it. Moreover, those who uprooted it were expected to
place upon the spot where it had grown honey in the comb to
make amends for having deprived the earth of so holy a herb.

The Greeks called it *hiera botane*, or Holy Herb, and in
France to this day Vervain is popularly called *Herbe sacrée*.
From time immemorial it was the symbol of enchantment, for
white and against black magic. In philtres it engendered love,
and was one of the plants dedicated to Venus, for did not
Venus Victrix wear a crown of Myrtle interwoven with
Vervain? The Romans purified their houses with it to ward off
evil spirits, and with it they swept the altars of their gods.

Like Dill, it possessed the power of overcoming the spells
of the sorcerer, being "'gainst witchcraft much avayling".
Edith Wheelwright tells us that the Welsh in the Middle
Ages called it "Devil's Bane", and after cutting it in the dark,
brought it into the churches to use as a sprinkler of holy
water.

The Romans were great observers of the custom of New
Year's gifts, and those royal colleagues Romulus and Tatius
ordained that every year Vervain should be offered to them
with other gifts as an augury of good fortune for the coming
year.

252 *Vervain*

Vervain has always taken an important place in herbal medicine since the days of Dioscorides. It was considered efficacious in cases of scrofula, and Lupton, in his *Book of Notable Things* (1660), says "the root of Vervain hanged at the neck of such as have the king's evil, it brings a marvellous and unhoped help". It was also held to be a cure for the ague and in that curious book of Dr John Schroder, the *Chymical Dispensatory* (1669), we read that "some cure Tertians and Quartans peculiarly therewith: in the Tertian they take the third joynt from the Earth and gather it by pulling it upwards and give it to be drunk; and in a Quartan the fourth joint". This I fancy the good doctor cribbed from Dioscorides. But, as Gerard says: "many odde old wives fables are written of Vervaine."

A plant so popular was bound to have many names, and among them we find Holy Herb, the Simplers' Joy, Tears of Juno, Blood of Mercury and Pigeon's Grass or Columbine. This last reminds us that Vervain was called *Peristereon* by the Greeks, from a word meaning "doves", because those birds were said to be fond of hovering around the plant.

As a herb of good omen Vervain was one of those associated with the Eve of St John, and in an old book called *Ye Popish Kingdome* appears the following couplet:

And young men round about with maides doe dance in every streete,
With garlands wrought of Mother-wort, or else with Vervaine sweete.

The common Vervain is an erect perennial, growing from 1 to 2 feet in height, with notched lime-green leaves and lilac-coloured flowers in slender spikes. It is slightly aromatic when bruised, but otherwise has no scent. In taste it is bitter and contains a glucoside, verbenalin, which is employed in herbal medicine as a febrifuge and in nervous complaints. Some say that as an anti-thermic it compares favourably with quinine. This plant should not be confused with *V. odorata*, the garden Verbena, which the French call *Citronelle*, and which is used in scents and cosmetics.

WOODRUFF   *Asperula odorata* L.   Rubiaceae
Woodrowel

FR *Aspérule odorante*; *Reine des bois*; *Belle étoile*
GER *Waldmeister*; *Herzfreude*; *Sternleberkraut*

> The crosswise flowers were white and pure,
> And started from a ruff demure,
> And every tiny cluster lent
> A fresh and most entrancing scent.
> This pretty Puritan I claim,
> And Woodruff is its charming name.
>
> JOHN WYNN

A dainty little plant is the sweet Woodruff, with its thick clusters of tiny white flowers in terminal corymbs and numerous coronals of bright green leaves, about eight in a whorl. With the exception of lavender there is probably no herb with such fragrance when dried, for which reason it was in olden times used as a strewing herb and also laid in chests among the linen. Fernie puts it rather delightfully when he writes that Woodruff "like the good deeds of the worthiest persons, delights by its fragrance most after death". Gerard says that the plant was "made up into garlands or bundles and hanged up in houses in the heate of summer, and doth very wel attemper the aire, coole and make fresh the place, to the delight and confort of such as are therin". The delightful smell given off by Woodruff is due to the presence in the plant of coumarin, found also in the tonka bean, and now synthesised from coal-tar constituents.

Hieronymus Tragus, otherwise Jerome Bock, in his *Neuw Kreutterbuch* (1539), says "we use this herb Herzfreude in the month of May. Laid in wine and afterwards drunk it will refresh the heart and restore an injured liver". He is alluding, of course, to the hock cup known as *Maibowle* or *Maitrank*, which owes its fragrance to the Woodruff and was the drink to which the Polish king, Stanislas, attributed his robust health.

The name *asperula*, meaning "rough", is given to this herb on account of the rough feel of the leaves. In Holland it acquired the popular name of *bedstro* (bed-straw) because at one time it was used for stuffing beds.

Of the same family as the Woodruff is the Squinancywort (*A. cynanchica*), a small perennial growing on chalky soil which gets its common name from the fact that it is considered an excellent gargle in cases of quinsy. It is, however, devoid of perfume.

The Field Woodruff or Blue Woodruff (*A. arvensis*) is an annual now confined to a few districts in England. Its blossoms are bright blue.

The following verses in praise of Woodruff admirably sum up its virtues and its former uses:

> The Woodruff is a bonny flower, her leaves are set like spurs
> About her stem, and honeysweet is every flower of hers.
> Yet sweetest dried and laid aside in kist with linen white,
> Or hung in bunches from the roof for winterly delight.
>
> The Woodruff is a bonny flower; we press her into wine,
> To make a cordial comfort for sickly folk that pine.
> We plant our graves with Woodruff, and still on holy days
> Woodruff on country altars gives out her scent for praise.

WORMWOOD   *Artemisia absinthium* L.   Compositae
Old Woman
Absinth
FR *Absinthe*; *Aluine*
GER *Wermut*; *Wiegenkraut*; *Grabkraut*

> Where chamber is sweeped and wormewood is strowne
> No flea for his life dare abide to be knowne.
> TUSSER'S *Husbandry*

Wormwood is a well-known plant, common on roadsides and waste places over most of Europe, though sometimes confused with Mugwort (*Artemisia vulgaris*) (q.v.) .Employed as a medi-cinal herb from the earliest times, Wormwood was one of the drug plants used by Hippocrates. The plant, according to legend, was christened with her own name by the goddess Artemis in gratitude for the benefits it conferred. Its specific name comes from two Greek words meaning "devoid of delight", probably on account of its rank smell and extremely bitter taste.

Seeing that the herb has always been valued as an anthel-mintic, or expeller of worms, the origin of the common English name of the plant seems obvious, but according to Dorothea Eastwood (*Mirror of Flowers*) " 'Ware-wood' – 'that which preserves the mind' – is the source of its name in English. Certainly it was an antidote against madness, yet now the name appears more as a joining of the two words which tell of its twin virtues: 'worm' because it is a powerful vermi-fuge, and 'wood' because that was the old English word for the madness which it cured." Dr Fernie, however, in his *Herbal Simples*, tells us that the name is derived from *wehren*, "to keep off", and *mought*, "a maggot or moth". In this he might have support from the shade of the worthy Dr William Bullein, whose *Bulwarke of Defence against all Sicknes* (1562) says "it keepeth clothes from moths and wormes". Prior, in his *Popular Names of British Plants*, also opts for an Anglo-Saxon derivation from *wer-mod*, a compounded word meaning to keep off maggots, "which by an accidental coin-cidence of sound has been understood as though the first syllable were 'worm'".

That Wormwood was once considered a panacea is evident from an entry in the *London Dispensatory*: "Wormwood its several sorts . . . all help weakness of the stomach, cleanse choller, kil worms, opens stoppings, helps surfets, cleers the sight, resists poyson, cleanseth the blood and secures cloathes fro moths." Estienne says that "Wormwood amongst other his vertues almost infinite and admirable doth especially comfort the stomacke laden with cholericke humours, but not the stomacke oppressed with flegmaticke humours, and for that cause there is a wine made of wormwood and called by the same name". In Sir Hugh Plat's *Delightes for Ladies* (1609) is given a recipe "How to make wormewood wine verie speedily and in great quantitie".

For making this wormwood wine the variety known as Roman Wormwood was used (*Artemisia ponticum*, or *romanum*), which seems to have been introduced into England in the latter half of the 16th century, for William Turner, in his *New Herball* (1551), writes that "Wormwood pontyke groweth in no place of Englande that ever I coulde se, saving only in my lordes garden at Syon, and that I brought out of Germany . . . about Colen it is called grave crowt [Grabkraut] because they set it upon their frendes graves. The Freses call it wyld Rosmary, the Pothecaryes of Antwerpe Absinthium Romanum. Howbeit there is some difference betwene it that groweth in Rome and it that groweth in Germanye."

Strangely enough, although one of Wormwood's supposed virtues was to "help surfets", or, as we might say, to cure a hangover, in later times it was extensively used, its bitterness modified by admixture with anisette, in the manufacture of that once popular French apéritif Absinthe, which was banned by the government of that country in 1915 owing to its pernicious effects, due to the narcotic poison contained in the essential oil which formed the active ingredient of the liqueur.

The herb is official in the pharmacopoeias of many countries, as a tonic and febrifuge, though it is of minor importance today. The flowering stems of the *A. absinthium* grow from 1 to 2 feet high, and can be distinguished from Mugwort by the silky down of the leaves on both upper and under surfaces and the fact that its yellowish flowers are larger. The variety known as Sea Wormwood (*A. maritima*), known in France as *Absinthe maritime*, and in Germany as *Meer-Wermut* or *Küstenbeifuss*, grows in salt marshes along the coast throughout most of southern Europe and as far east as the Caspian and Black Seas. Not so tall as *A. absinthium*, it is less bitter and without fragrance.

Since Biblical times Wormwood has been a symbol of bitterness but the wormwood of the Bible was most probably *A. cina* (Bergius), sometimes called *A. judaïca*, and in French *sementine* or *semence sainte*.

The dead roots of Wormwood, being black and rather hard, used to be known as "wormwood coal"; and it was a popular belief that a piece of this dead root, if placed under a lover's pillow, would induce a dream of the beloved one.

YARROW   *Achillea millefolium* L.   Compositae
Milfoil
Thousand weed
Nose Bleed
FR *Millefeuille*; *Herbe aux charpentiers*; *Sourcil de Vénus*
GER *Gemeine Schafgarbe*

> The Yarrow, wherewithal he stops the wound-made gore.
>   DRAYTON *Polyolbion*

The Yarrow is one of the commonest of British plants, which grows everywhere and can soon develop into a troublesome weed. But although today this rather unattractive plant is considered more of a nuisance than it is worth, it figured as late as 1820 in the Edinburgh Pharmacopoeia, and for centuries was highly regarded as a vulnerary, one of its many popular names being "Staunch Weed". For the same reason it was once known as "Soldiers' Woundwort", and "Knighten milfoil". Linnaeus extolled it for rheumatism.

The generic name *Achillea* comes from the Greek legend which tells how Achilles, who had learned the use of healing herbs from his preceptor Cheiron, cured the wound of Telephus, King of the Mysians, with the juice of yarrow and the rust of his spear. The specific name is derived from the numerous deeply pinnatifid segments of the leaves. The English name is a corruption of the Anglo-Saxon name of the plant, which was *gearwe*, also alluding to the many indentations of the leaf, and obviously closely allied to the many Dutch names for the plant, such as Gerwe, Hazegerwe, Schapegerwe.

Parkinson says of Yarrow, "if it be put into the nose assuredly it will stay the bleeding of it", and this use of the herb as a styptic is said to go back to the time of the ancient Greeks, who made use of it in cases of internal haemorrhage. This reputation for staunching bleeding was the origin of the popular designation "Nose Bleed" for this plant. (*Saigne-nez* in France.)

Among other folk-names given to Yarrow are "Sneezewort" and "Old Man's Pepper", since on account of the pungency of the foliage, it used to be dried, ground, and used as snuff.

For Culpeper the plant had many virtues. "It stops the bloody flux" he writes; "the ointment of it is not only good for green wounds, but also for ulcers and fistulas, especially such as abound with moisture. It stayeth the shedding of hair, the head being bathed with a decoction of it. . . . There is an ancient charm for curing tertian argues with Yarrow. A leaf of it is to be pulled off with the left hand, pronouncing at the same time the sick man's name; and this leaf is to be taken." Yarrow was, indeed, at one time considered a magic herb, used for divination and the casting of spells, for which reason it acquired the name of "Devil's Nettle".

In Iceland and in Scandinavia Yarrow is, or was, used as a substitute for hops in the brewing of beer. The herbalist, Jacob Theodor of Bergzabern, who called himself Tabernaemontanus (1520–90), wrote in his *Neuw Kreuterbuch* that to prevent wine from deteriorating and becoming unpalatable, one should, when the wine is a year old, take a fair quantity of Yarrow seed and hang it, in a little sack, in the cask.

In parts of Germany Yarrow was considered a sovereign remedy for the gout, for which reason the herb was called by the Mecklenburgers "Stand up and go away". In cases of dermatitis and eczema the eruptions were washed with an infusion of Yarrow. As a febrifuge Yarrow was also used, and in France it still bears the popular name of "herbe à la fièvre". Yet strangely enough, despite the numerous healing virtues attributed to it through the centuries, this plant is not mentioned in the *Capitulare de Villis*.

The word Yarrow, with defining adjectives, is often given to plants of other genera, e.g. *Stratiotes aloïdes* (Soldier Yarrow), *Batrachium aquatile* (Water Yarrow), and *Artemisia rupestris* (Alpine Yarrow).

APPENDIX

The *Capitulare de Villis*

Often in botanical works we come across the remark that such and such a plant is mentioned in the *Capitulare de Villis*. This was an ordinance of about AD 795, drafted by Louis the Pious, son of Charlemagne, for his estates in Aquitaine. Formerly it was thought that these ordinances were drawn up in AD 812 by Charlemagne for his domains, and this view was held until fairly recently. But during the last decade the former theory has prevailed.

It is section 70 of this ordinance which interests us especially for this gives a list of plants and trees to be planted and maintained in the royal domains. The section begins *Volumus quod in horto omnes herbas habeant, id est . . .* and below is given the list of plants as printed in Baluze: *Capitularia Regum Francorum*, Paris, 1780. In the first column are the names as given in the *Capitulare*, in the second column the Latin botanical name, and in the third column the common English name.

Lilium	Lilium candidum	White Lily
Rosas	Rosa gallica	Common rose
Foenigraecum	Trigonella foenum graecum	Fenugreek
Costum	Chrysanthemum balsamita	Costmary
Salviam	Salvia officinalis	Sage

Rutam	Ruta graveolens	Rue
Abrotanum	Artemesia abrotanum	Southernwood
Cucumeres	Cucumis sativas	Cucumber
Pepones	Cucumis melo	Melon
Cucurbitas	Lagenaria vulgaris	Squash
Faseolum	Phaseolus vulgaris or var.	Kidney Bean
Cuminum	Cuminum cyminum	Cumin
Rosmarinum	Rosmarinus officinalis	Rosemary
Carvum	Carum carvi	Caraway
Cicerum Italicum	Cicer arietinum	Chick pea
Squillam	Scilla maritima	Squill
Gladiolum	Iris germanica	Iris
	or Iris florentina	Orrice
Dragontea	Artemisia dracunculus	Tarragon
Anisum	Pimpinella anisum	Anise
Coloquintidas	Citrullus colocynthis	Bitter apple
Solsequium	Cichorium intybus	Chicory
Ameum	Ammi majus	Ammey
Silum	Laserpitum siler	Mountain caraway
Lactucas	Lactuca scariola	Lettuce
	or Lactuca sativa	
Git	Nigella sativa	Nigella
Erucam albam	Eruca sativa	Garden rocket
Nasturtium	Lepidium sativum	Garden cress
Bardanam	Lappa major	Common burdock
Pulegium	Mentha pulegium	Penny Royal
Olisatum	Smyrnium Olusatrum	Alexanders; Horse Parsley
Petroselinum	Petroselinum crispum	Parsley
Apium	Apium graveolens	Celery
Levisticum	Levisticum officinale	Lovage

Sabinam	Juniperus sabina	Juniper (Savin, Sabine)
Anetum	Anethum graveolens	Dill
Fanicalum	Foeniculum vulgare or var.	Fennel
Intubas	Cichorium endivia	Endive
Diptamnum	Origanum dictamnus	Dittany of Crete
Synapi	Brassica nigra	Mustard
Satureiam	Satureia hortensia	Savory (Summer)
	or Satureia montana	Savory (Winter)
Sisimbrium	Mentha crispata	Curled mint
Mentam	Mentha piperata	Peppermint
Mentastrum	Mentha longifolia?	Horsemint
Tanaritam	Tanacetum vulgare	Tansy
Nepetam	Nepeta cataria	Catmint
Febrifugiam	Chrysanthemum parthenium	Feverfew
Papaver	Papaver somniferum	Poppy
Betas	Beta vulgaris	Beet
Vulgigina	Asarum europaeum	Hazelwort
Bismalvas alteas	Althaea officinalis	Marshmallow
Malvas	Malva sylvestris	Common mallow
	or Malva rotundifolia	Dwarf mallow
Carrucas	Daucus carota	Carrot
Pastinacas	Pastinaca sativa	Parsnip
Adripias	Atriplex hortensis	Garden orache
	or Atriplex patula	Common orache
Blitum	Spinacia oleracea	Spinach
Ravacaulos	Brassica	Kohlrabi
Caulos	,,	Cabbage
Uniones	Allium (species)	Onion var.
Britlas	Allium schoenoprasum	Chives
Porros	Allium porrum	Leek
Radices	Raphanus sativus	Radish

Ascalonicas	Allium ascalonicum	Shallots
Cepas	Allium (species)	Onion var.
Allia	Allium sativum	Garlic
Wacentiam	Rubia tinctorum	Dyer's madder
Cardones	Cynara cardunculus	Cardoon
	or Cynara scolymus	Artichoke
Fabas majores	Vicia faba	Bean
Pisa maurisica	Pisum arvense	Marrowfat pea
Coriandrum	Coriandrum sativum	Coriander
Cerefolium	Anthriscus cerefolium	Garden chervil
Lacteridas	Euphorbia var.	Spurge
Sclareiam	Salvia sclarea	Clary

BIBLIOGRAPHY

Allport, N. L., *The Chemistry of Vegetable Drugs*, 1943
Arber, Agnes, *Herbals: Their Origin & Evolution*, 1912
Bombast von Hohenheim (Paracelsus), *Paracelsus his Dispensatory*, 1656
Bullein, W., *Bullein's Bulwarke*, 1562
Cary, W., *A boke of the propertyes of herbes*, 1530
Coles, W., *The Art of Simpling*, 1656
  Adam in Eden, 1657
Culpeper, N., *The English Physitian enlarged*, 1653
Dioscorides, *The Greek Herbal*, 1934
Dodoens, R., *A Niewe Herball* (trans. Henry Lyte), 1578
Ellacombe, H. N., *Plant lore of Shakespeare*, 1896
Evelyn, J., *Acetaria*, 1699
Folkard, R., *Plant Lore*, 1884
Gerard, J., *The Herball, or Generall Historie of Plantes*, 1579
  ditto, (enlarged and amended by Thomas Johnson), 1633
Hill, Thomas, *The Gardeners Labyrinth*, 1656
  The Proffitable Arte of Gardening, 1658
Howe, Sonia, *In Quest of Spices*, n.d.
James, R., *Pharmacopoeia Universalis*, 1752
Johnson, Thomas, *Mercurius Botanicus*, 1634
La Wall, C. H., *4,000 Years of Pharmacy*, 1927
Leyel, C. F., *The Magic of Herbs*, 1926

MacKenzie, D., *The Infancy of Medicine*, 1927

Northcote, Lady R., *A Book of Herbs*, 1901

Parkinson, J., *Paradisi in Sole Paradisus Terrestris*, 1629
  Theatrum Botanicum, 1640

Pechey, J., *Compleat Herbal*, 1694

Pitton de Tournefort, J., *Materia Medica*, 1716

Prior, R. C. A., *Popular Names of British Plants*, 1879

Redgrove, H. S., *Spices and Condiments*, 1933

Ridley, H. N., *Spices*, 1912

Rohde, E. S., *Old English Herbals*, 1922

Salmon, W., *Family Dictionary*, 1696

Schroeder, J., *The Chymical Dispensatory*, 1669

Singer, C., *From Magic to Science*, 1928

Swan, J., *Speculum Mundi*, 1665

Theodor, J. (Tabernaemontanus), *Neuw Kreuterbuch*, 1588

Thompson, C. J. S., *The Art of the Apothecary*, 1929
  Magic and Healing, 1947

Turner, W., *The Names of Herbes*, 1548
  A New Herball, 1551
  The seconde parte of William Turner's herball, 1562

Walsh, J. J., *Mediaeval Medicine*, 1920

Wootton, A. C., *Chronicles of Pharmacy*, 1910

INDEX

Made and printed by William Clowes & Sons, Limited, London and Beccles